THE HISTORY OF
THE WORLD

First published in 2017 by Worth Press Ltd.,
Bath, England
worthpress@btconnect.com

British Library Cataloging in Publication Data
A catalog record for this book is available from the British
Library.

ISBN: 978-1-84931-139-7

1 2 3 4 5 6 7 8 9 10

Publisher's Note Every effort has been made to
ensure the accuracy of the information presented in
this book. The publisher will not assume liability for
damages caused by inaccuracies in the data and makes
no warranty whatsoever expressed or implied. The
publisher welcomes comments and corrections from
readers, emailed to worthpress@btconnect.com, which will
be considered for incorporation in future editions. Every
effort has been made to trace copyright holders and seek
permission to use illustrative and other material. The
publisher wishes to apologize for any inadvertent errors
or omissions and would be glad to rectify these in future.

Consultant Editor: Meredith MacArdle

Editor: Chandra Creative & Content Services
Design and layout: Chandra Creative & Content Services
DTP: Chandra Creative & Content Services
Picture research: Chandra Creative & Content Services
Editorial concept and design: Chandra Creative & Content
Services

Printed and bound in China.

Features section: Provides information on various aspects of history.

Timeline section: Entries on significant events flow in chronological order.

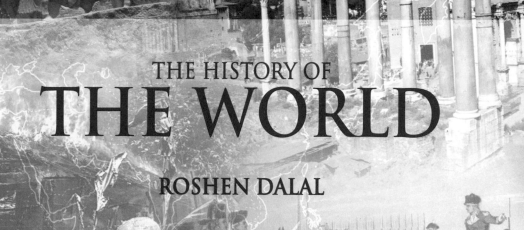

THE HISTORY OF
THE WORLD

ROSHEN DALAL

WORTH
PRESS

CONTENTS

TIMELINE HISTORY OF THE WORLD

Up to 60,000 BCE

Human evolution took place over several million years against the backdrop of the changing earth, climate, and vegetation. According to present knowledge, human and chimpanzee ancestor lineages split between 8 and 7 mya (million years ago), and hominids, walking on two legs, began to develop. By 2.5 mya, *Homo habilis* (Handy man), the first tool-making hominid, had developed in Africa, and by 1 mya, the more advanced *Homo erectus* was in many parts of Asia and Europe.

Theories of human evolution

Charles Darwin's (1809–82) theory of evolution through natural selection forms the basis for today's studies on evolution, though there have been many advances on his theory. Theodosius Dobzhansky (1900–75), in 1937, showed how new species could emerge through mutation, genetic variability, and isolation. In 1981, Lynn Margolis (b. 1938) elaborated on the theory of endosymbiosis, indicating that organisms from different lineages could join together to create new ones. Stephen Jay Gould (1941–2002) referred to changes in regulatory genes affecting development, which could explain variation in evolution. In 1972, Gould and Niles Eldredge put forward the theory of episodic rather than gradual change. Random mutations, the study of DNA, genetic similarities, and the theory of genetic drift and genetic bottlenecks are also incorporated into theories of evolution. Generally, though all scientists agree that evolution took place, refining and explaining theories of evolution is an ongoing process.

A caricature of Darwin from the 1870s, lampooning evolutionary theory.

Up to 1 MYA

4600 MYA Earth is formed.
3500 MYA Life starts: Bacteria and algae.
145–65 MYA Present-day continents begin to form.
8–7 MYA Hominids evolve.
7.2–6.9 MYA *Sahelanthropus tchadensis* (discovered in Chad, 2001).

6.5–5.9 MYA *Orrorin tugenensis* (Kenya, 2000).
5.8–5.2 MYA *Ardipithecus kadabba* (Ethiopia, 1992).
5.3 MYA TO 11,700 YEARS AGO Australopithecus species appears.

Homo sapiens

The ancestors of modern humans, *Homo sapiens*, perhaps originated in Africa and then spread to Europe and Asia. Another theory is that parallel evolution occurred in various parts of the world. The first evidence of *Homo sapiens sapiens*, modern humans, is from Africa (Ethiopia), and is dated to about 190,000 years ago. By around 40,000 BCE, they had spread all over Eurasia, and were present even in Australia.

Neanderthals

Homo neanderthalensis (Neanderthal), sometimes called *Homo sapiens neanderthalensis*, was named after the Neander valley in Germany, where their remains were first found. They lived in Europe and West Asia between about 250,000 and 28,000 years ago. Neanderthals, with brains larger than present day humans, walked upright, and used tools. Evidence of skin scrapers from southern Russia, dated to about 33,000 BCE, suggests they wore clothes made from animal skins. Neanderthal burials have also been found. One such, in Samarkand, Uzbekistan, is the grave of a child buried in a ring of horns, possibly indicating some sort of a belief in an afterlife. There may have

USE OF FIRE

Fire was a major aspect of human development. There were three early stages: Use of natural or accidental fire; lighting fires from naturally caused ones (controlled or deliberate use); and learning to make fire at will. It is impossible to say when fire was first deliberately used, but there is evidence that dates as far back as 1 mya (ashes and bone fragments from a recent discovery at Wonderwerk Caves in South Africa) and 1–1.5 mya (burnt animal bones from Swartkrans Cave in Transvaal, Africa). Effective means of making fire were probably acquired only after 10,000 BCE.

As discovered by an international team of archaeologists in 2012, human ancestors have lived for 2 million years in Wonderwerk Cave, a massive cave in the Kuruman Hills of the Northern Cape Province of South Africa. The team uncovered ashes that appeared to be the remains of a million-year-old campfire. This discovery is claimed to be the oldest evidence of a human-controlled fire to date. The excavations and the objects unearthed in them point out that the human ancestor *Homo erectus* was the first species who used fire, probably to cook.

3.9–2.9 MYA *Australopithecus afarensis* (nicknamed "Lucy," Ethiopia, 1974).

3–2 MYA Early homo species.

2.6–2.2 MYA *Paranthropus aethiopicus* (Kenya, 1985).

2.5 MYA *Homo habilis* (Tanzania, 1962).

- Pebble chopper tools found at Koobi Fora, Kenya; earliest type of stone tool.

2.4–1.5 MYA *Homo habilis* inhabits parts of sub-Saharan Africa.

2–1.5 MYA *Homo erectus* evolves.

1 MYA Fire arguably used by Early Man.

been a social support system, as the finding of a Neanderthal skeleton without a right arm—lost long before his death—suggests that he must have survived with help from others. Though caves and natural shelters were the norm, in some areas simple shelters were built. Neanderthals died out about 30,000 years ago.

Hominids to Humans

1 Australopithecus africanus   2 Homo habilis   3 Homo erectus   4 Homo sapiens neanderthalensis   5 Homo sapiens sapiens

Homo erectus

Homo erectus, an ancestor of modern humans (*Homo sapiens*), most likely had its origins in Africa but possibly in Eurasia as well. The dispersion of the species probably started around 1.9 mya, moving through the African tropics, Europe, South Asia, and Southeast Asia, the evidence for which are the many sites with the preserved fossils of *Homo erectus*.

As the name indicates, *Homo erectus* walked upright. He had a low brain case, a receded forehead, and wide nose, jaws, and palate. His brain was smaller and teeth were larger as compared to the modern humans. Interestingly, it was *Homo erectus* who tamed the flames first, in order to cook his food. The species seems to have flourished until approximately 200,000 years ago, before *Homo sapiens* came into the picture.

Homo habilis

The discovery of the most ancient representative of the human genus, *Homo habilis*, was a breakthrough in the science of paleoanthropology, as the oldest previously known human fossils were that of *Homo erectus*. *Homo habilis* inhabited parts of sub-Saharan Africa from approximately 2.4 mya to 1.5 mya. The first fossils of *Homo habilis* were discovered at Olduvai Gorge in Northern Tanzania. With the excavations of more specimens at locations such as Koobi Fora, it was understood that these fossils were different from that of *Australopithecus* and the more advanced *Homo* species.

The species was given a special name on the basis of the increased cranial capacity, comparatively smaller molar and premolar teeth, and a human-like foot of the fossils.

Up to 70,000 BCE

1.9 MYA First evidence of building; a wall of piled stones at Olduvai Gorge, Tanzania.

1.9–1 MYA *Homo erectus* moves out of Africa; spreads to Asia and Europe.

1.5 MYA–200,000 YEARS AGO Acheulian industry, standardized method of making stone tools, particularly hand axes, found at several sites in Africa, Europe, and Asia.

The species had hand bones that allowed them to manipulate objects effectively—hence they came to be known as *Homo habilis* or "handy man."

Australopithecus

Australopithecines were a group of hominids that evolved earlier than the *Homo* genus. They are thought to be the direct ancestor of the genus *Homo* or a close relative of such an ancestor.

This species lived approximately 5.3 million to 11,700 years ago, and the specimens were found in eastern, central, and southern Africa. Having both human- and ape-like features, various species of *Australopithecus* such as *Australopithecus afarensis*, *Australopithecus africanus*, *Australopithecus anamensis*, *Australopithecus garhi*, and *Australopithecus sediba* were bipedal, but had smaller brains like those of apes.

One of the most famous discoveries of the genus *Australopithecus* was a specimen of a human skull at a limestone quarry in Taung, South Africa in 1925. Anthropologist Raymond Dart named it as *Australopithecus africanus*—meaning "southern ape of Africa." Since then, there were many excavations that led to discoveries of more specimens of *Australopithecus africanus*.

Arguably, the most famous specimen of *Australopithecus* is "Lucy," a fossilized skeleton from Ethiopia, which is dated to 3.2 mya.

Evolution of the human brain

Owing to the different environmental challenges, the increase in body size, and various other reasons, the human brain has seen an increase in size—from *Australopithecus afarensis*, having an average brain mass of 435 grams (*Australopithecus garhi*, 445 grams; *Australopithecus africanus*, 450 grams), to *Homo habilis* (600 grams) and

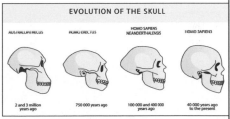

EVOLUTION OF THE SKULL

AUSTRALOPITHECUS — 2 and 3 million years ago
HOMO ERECTUS — 750 000 years ago
HOMO SAPIENS NEANDERTHALENSIS — 100 000 and 400 000 years ago
HOMO SAPIENS — 40 000 years ago to the present

Increasing size of the skulls during different phases of human evolution.

Homo sapiens (1,350 grams). A large and a complex brain meant it was capable of processing more information, which was an advantage during times of dramatic climate change.

500,000 YEARS AGO Archaic *Homo sapiens*, ancestors of *Homo sapiens sapiens*, modern humans, develop.
500,000–200,000 YEARS AGO A range of hominids species co-exist such as "Peking Man," Neanderthals, and Swanscombe man.

190,000 YEARS AGO–40,000 BCE *Homo sapiens sapiens*, modern humans, develop.
100,000–50,000 YEARS AGO Caves in Dordogne, France, occupied.
70,000 YEARS AGO Neanderthal man uses fire.

HUNTERS AND GATHERERS

Neolithic stone tool.

Homo sapiens began to spread across the world, walking long distances or traveling by sea until much of the world as we know it today was occupied. Neanderthal man died out around 30,000 BCE, and soon only *Homo sapiens sapiens* or modern humans existed in the last—and coldest—stages of the Ice Ages. Perhaps 10 million people populated the whole world by 20,000 BCE.

The human brain gradually began to develop its capacity to reason and think. Humans began to understand and adapt themselves to their surroundings. Important changes were acquiring the ability to walk upright, to carry things, make tools, and wield weapons for protection.

The Paleolithic Age or Prehistoric Age

The Paleolithic Age is also referred to as the Prehistoric Age, as there is no written record of it. Humans originated on the earth in the Paleolithic Age. Since humans during this period used stones for almost everything they did, it is also called the *Stone Age*. The life of Paleolithic people was tough and exhausting. They were hunters and gatherers, eating fruits, roots, nuts, the flesh of animals, and even insects.

In 2015, primitive stone tools, dating as far back as 3.3 million years, were found embedded in the rocks by a dry riverbed near a lake in Kenya. The oldest specimens of

THE STONE AGE

Referring to the period when all tools were made of stone, this term is convenient although controversial, as a culture cannot be characterized only by its tools. The dates are only indicative, as they vary across different areas of the world. For example, in areas such as New Guinea, the Paleolithic Age lasted into historic times.

STONE AGE DIVISIONS

Paleolithic Age (Old Stone Age)
Lower 2.5 mya–120,000 years ago
Middle 120,000 years ago–35,000 BCE
Upper 35,000–8000 BCE

Mesolithic Age (Intermediate Stone Age)
12,000–4000 BCE

Neolithic Age (New Stone Age)
10,000–c. 2000 BCE

Chalcolithic Age
1800–1000 BCE
[Humans used both stone and copper tools during this period.]

60,000 YEARS AGO–40,000 BCE Aboriginal ancestors reach Australia by sea.
50,000 YEARS AGO Humans begin to create art and construct burials; Shanidar cave, northern Iraq, is an important burial site.
40,000 Modern humans evolved.

40,000–6000 Rock art at Ubirr, Australia.
35,000 Counting device made from baboon bone in South Africa.
35,000 First early modern humans in Europe (Cro-Magnon man).

Homo are known to be 2.2 million years old, which would dictate that the origins of these tools dated back to the same era as the Australopithecines. The very earliest tools, known as the Olduwan industry, were mainly hammerstones and choppers, but later on, large flake tools such as hand axes were made. More refined axes and other cutting edge tools were found in the Acheulean industry in Africa, Middle East, and Asia.

Living in groups

Human beings in the Paleolithic Age realized the necessity of living in groups, which made hunting much easier. They did not have a permanent place to live and wandered like nomads. They used animal skins or the leaves and bark of trees to cover their body.

Living in groups.

Lifestyle

Humans increasingly started building their own shelters, and living more settled lives. Though food still included what was obtained by hunting and gathering, life began to grow more complex. Recent evidence suggests that wild cereal grains were processed and eaten as far back as 26,000 BCE.

Stone tools became more complex, and along with common stones such as flint and obsidian, a wider range of materials came into use, such as wood, bone, antler, and ivory. Small flint points were probably attached to weapons like spears, arrows, and harpoons. Some groups buried or cremated their dead with reverence. Beautiful paintings were made in dark caves.

LANGUAGE

An important part of human evolution, simple forms of language must have developed by 1 mya, although some scientists propose that early spoken language developed much later, perhaps around 30,000 BCE.

34,000 Lesotho and Zambia in Africa occupied.

34,000–32,000 Horse figurine carved from mammoth ivory discovered at Vogelherd, Germany.

33,000 Appearance of other types of art such as decorated and colored objects, small figurines of stone, bone, terracotta, or clay.

30,000 Female figurine carved from serpentine found at Galgenberg, Austria.

30,000–17,000 BCE

Art

New research suggests that the first paintings ever made by human hands were outlines of human hands; and they were created not in Spain or France, but in Indonesia. Sixty years ago, a group of archaeologists discovered a series of paintings spread across the Indonesian island of **Sulawesi**. The images featured stencil-like outlines of human hands and stick-legged animals in motion; they were quite similar to the cave paintings that had already been discovered, and, made famous, in Spain and France.

Stencilled outline of hands in yellow and ochre, executed between 13,000–9500 BCE, Cueva de las Manos, Rio Pinturas, Patagonia, Argentina.

Paleolithic art covered a wide range of forms and materials. In dark caves, paintings of animals, human figures, and hunting scenes were made with natural materials, perhaps as a type of "sympathetic magic," a visualization of a successful hunt. Another theory suggests links to shamanism. As artifical light was needed in the caves, some kind of a fire torch must have been used. Cave paintings dating back to 28,000 BCE have been found in France, Spain, Africa, India, and other places.

From about 33,000 BCE, other types of art included decorated and colored objects, even weapons, fashioned out of bone and ivory, as well as small figurines of stone, bone, terracotta, or clay.

CHAUVET CAVE

The earliest cave paintings found in Europe, the pictures in the 1,300-feet-long Chauvet cave in southern France, depict an unusually large variety of animals: Lions, mammoths, rhinoceros, cave bears, horses, bison,  ibex, reindeer, red deer, aurochs, megaceros deer, musk oxen, panthers, and owls. Radiocarbon dating reveals two periods of occupation: 30,000–28,000 BCE and 25,000–23,000 BCE. In addition, the cave contained fossilized remains of animals, while on the floor, footprints of both humans and animals are preserved.

Early hunters used arrows with flight feathers and flint arrowheads.

30,000–17,000 BCE

30,000–15,000 Bow and arrow invented.
30,000–13,000 Human migration into America across Bering Strait, or by sea.
28,000 Cro-Magnon carvings on bone, possibly representing phases of moon, found at Blanchard, France.

- Presumably the first cave paintings, images of human hands, in countries such as France, Spain, Africa, India, and other places.
26,000 Wild cereal grains are processed and eaten.
20,000 Bow and arrow are created.

Mesolithic Age

The Mesolithic Age or Intermediate Stone Age is the transitional period between the Paleolithic Age and Neolithic Age, or from the Old Stone Age to the New Stone Age. During the Mesolithic Age, early humans' most important concerns were hunting, fishing, and food gathering.

Tools

During this period, man gradually learned to make sophisticated weapons. Mesolithic tools were smaller and more refined in their finish. Better weapons were eventually developed. People also used cliffs and **tar pits** as ways of killing animals. Around 20,000 BCE, the invention of the bow and arrow made hunting comparatively easier and safer. Some of the other common weapons were:

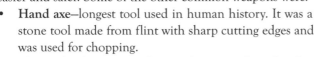

Hand axe.   Flint.

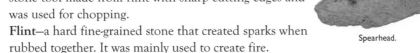

Spearhead.

- **Hand axe**—longest tool used in human history. It was a stone tool made from flint with sharp cutting edges and was used for chopping.
- **Flint**—a hard fine-grained stone that created sparks when rubbed together. It was mainly used to create fire.
- **Spear**—a pole usually made of wood, with a sharp, pointed head. A spear was usually longer and lighter than an axe.

A few of the first tools ever created are shown above. Today, these designs might seem crude, but they were the first of their kind and have substantially influenced and revolutionized our current weaponry.

Domestication of plants and animals

During the Mesolithic Age, the primary sources of food were hunting, fishing, and food gathering. It was not until much later that it was discovered that seeds can grow into plants, if watered and nourished properly. Domesticated animals such

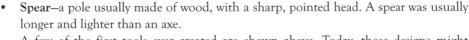

25,000–24,000 Cave paintings at Apollo site, Namibia, Africa.
24,000 Cremations in Australia.
- Houses with clay roofs in Europe.

24,000–22,000 Female figurine known as "Venus of Willendorf" found at Willendorf village, Austria.
21,000 Ivory boomerang used for hunting in Poland.
18,000–11,000 Kutikina cave, southern Tasmania, occupied by users of stone tools.

as cattle, sheep, and goats proved to be useful not only for meat but also for milk, hides, agricultural operations, and transport. The first animal to be domesticated was the dog, which may have helped with hunting.

Burials

The first undisputed **human burial** took place some 100,000 years ago at Qafzeh in Israel, although some archaeologists believe that Neanderthals may also have buried people in shallow graves accompanied by grave goods. By the late Stone Age, it was common to bury or cremate the dead with respect. In some cases, two individuals were buried in a single grave. The dead were occasionally provided with grave offerings, which included chunks of meat, grinding stones, and ornaments made of stones, bones, and antlers.

The Neolithic Age

The Mesolithic Age was followed by the Neolithic Age or the New Stone Age, a period that saw a transition from hunting-gathering to food production known as the Neolithic Revolution. The word *neolithic* in Greek means "new stone." Although new stone tools were made, the real change in the Neolithic Age was the shift from hunting and gathering to **systematic agriculture**. Historians sometimes call this settled farming during the Neolithic Age the first **agricultural revolution**.

Farming and herding

Agriculture brought a great change in human society. This shift from hunting and gathering to food production, however, did not happen quickly. Humans gradually began to control their environment. They changed from being food gatherers to food producers. They started growing wheat, barley, and rice. They gave up the nomadic life and began to live a settled life to produce crops. They began to settle where water was available, mainly on the banks of rivers and lakes. Dogs helped them to hunt, goats gave them milk, and sheep gave them meat and wool.

17,000–10,000 BCE

17,000–15,000 Wadi Kubbaniya, Late Paleolithic site in Upper Egypt.

16,000–10,000 Dwellings in Europe made of mammoth bones.

15,000–10,000 Cave paintings at Lascaux, France.

14,000–12,000 Cave paintings at Altamira, Spain.

13,000 Cave paintings at Bhimbetka, India.

• Terracotta figurines in Algeria.

12,000 Dog domesticated.

Polished tools

The Neolithic people, when they took to cultivation, began to use tools made of basalt, which is particularly hard and strong, and could be shaped and polished with the help of a grindstone. The Neolithic saw a much wider variety of stone tools than before, often with handles fixed to them. Bones were also used to make needles, blades, and other tools.

Pottery

The oldest known pottery jars, found in China, date to about 20,000 BCE, and even before then, Paleolithic Europeans were making small ceramic figures between 29,000 to 25,000 BCE. But Neolithic farmers had a great need for containers, for example to store grain and milk. At first, baskets were woven from wild grass and plastered with wet clay. But these could not store liquids. Later, people learned to bake clay pots over fire to make them waterproof. Neolithic pottery was often well made and decorative.

Invention of the wheel

One of the greatest inventions of the Neolithic period was the wheel, possibly as a result of observing the way that logs roll easily. Fitting wheels to **sledges** and **carts** made traveling quicker and more comfortable. Apart from this, the wheel was used for making pottery, spinning, and weaving.

The Chalcolithic Age or Copper Age

Metal was accidentally discovered in the Chalcolithic or Copper Age. In order to bake clay pottery, people used furnaces. The strong heat of the furnaces melted the metal present in the earth near the furnaces. Possibly this is how copper was discovered, although we do not know exactly where and when. But copper was the first metal that was hammered into various tools, weapons, and ornaments. The discovery of copper was followed by the discovery of zinc and tin, which made way for new tools and weapons.

12,000–4000 Humans gradually learn to make sophisticated weapons.
- Primary sources of food were hunting, fishing, and food gathering.
- First **human colonization** takes place.

11,000 Chile, South America occupied.
- Cave dwellings in Fukui, Japan.
- Wheat cultivated in northern Mesopotamia.

EARLY SETTLEMENTS

Although geological changes were still taking place, the topography of the earth was relatively stable by 9000 BCE. As the last Ice Age receded between 13,000 and 10,000 BCE, large amounts of water were released. The surface of the earth transformed, and the climate grew warmer. In some areas, regular rainfall made the land more fertile, and, although hunter-gatherer communities continued to exist, all over the world more communities began to grow crops and keep domestic animals, with the first major developments seen in West Asia around 9000 BCE. With crop cultivation, food storage began and settled villages emerged; by 6000 BCE, villages were widespread in the region and a few of these had developed into towns. Among these were Jericho and Çatal Hüyük, both located near water sources.

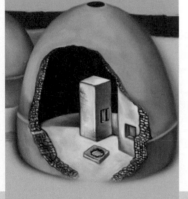

An artist's rendering of a Neolithic hut at Khirokitia, Cyprus.

Small farming communities in other parts of Asia, as well as in Europe, Africa, and the Americas developed distinctive styles of house-building and craft production. Crops grown and animals domesticated varied according to the climate and region. Canal irrigation began in Mesopotamia. Painted pottery, along with other artifacts such as terracotta figurines, have been unearthed from several areas. Implements were made from bone and ivory, as well as stone, and toward the end of this period, copper began to be used. There was no writing at this time, but petroglyphs, signs that were possibly the precursor of writing, have been found at several sites.

KHIROKITIA

Village settlements began around 7000 BCE on the island of Cyprus, one of the earliest of which was Khirokitia, near the southern coast. Surrounded by a defensive wall, it had circular houses, usually with domed roofs. Dwelling walls were often of stone, and within were shelves, benches, and windows. Khirokitia's dead were buried beneath the floor of the house, and its people cultivated cereal crops, picked wild fruits, and domesticated sheep, goats, and pigs. Deer bones found here indicate hunting. At least 20 similar sites have been discovered across Cyprus, but Khirokitia was deserted by around 6000 BCE.

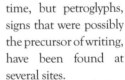

The ancient city of Jericho.

10,000–8000 BCE

10,000 Semi-permanent agricultural settlements begin in many parts of the world.
10,000–8200 Natufian people establish settlements in eastern Mediterranean; build houses, bury dead, and domesticate dogs.
10,000–6000 Cave art continues in Australia.

10,000–2000 Neolithic settlements in China.
10,000–300 Jomon culture flourishes in Japan.
9500–3000 Clovis culture at Blackwater Draw, North America.

Above: A reconstructed Jomon village (10,000–300 BCE) in Japan.
Left: Neolithic carving of the Seated Goddess of Çatal Hüyük, Turkey.

ÇATAL HÜYÜK

Çatal Hüyük in Turkey, dated between 8000 and 6000 BCE, is estimated to have been inhabited by about 5,000–10,000 people, living in mud-brick and plaster houses. The houses had no doors, and entrances were through the roofs. People grew cereals, kept herds of cattle, and made stone weapons and pottery. They also traded goods and performed rituals for the dead. Numerous figurines of females have been found, as well as shrines dedicated to a so-called Mother Goddess. Other finds include animal figurines, bone tools, wooden bowls, woven baskets, and pottery.

JIAHU CULTURE

Jiahu, located on the Huang (Yellow) river in China, was a complex Neolithic culture around 7000–5700 BCE. The whole site covered 592,000 sq. ft (55,000 sq. m), surrounded by a moat. Remains of houses, pottery, turquoise carvings, and tools from bone and stone have been discovered here. From the middle phase, there are markings carved on tortoise shells and bone, some of which are similar to characters in later Chinese writing. Some bone flutes found at the site are playable even today. Rice and millet were cultivated, and alcohol was brewed from fermented rice mixed with honey and hawthorn.

9000 Cow's milk becomes part of human diet.

9000–3000 Rock paintings in caves, central India.

9000–2000 Cochise culture in North America.

8200 Stone engravings, Wonderwerk cave, South Africa.

8000 Clay tokens used in Mesopotamia.
- Sheep, goats domesticated at Ali Kosh, Iran.
- Shellfish eaten in European coastal areas.

THE FIRST CIVILIZATIONS

Farming and the domestication of animals (such as cattle, pigs, camels, and dogs) became widespread. Advanced stone tools were used, along with copper and bronze tools and the potter's wheel. Art and building construction developed further, and urban centers continued to emerge. City civilizations dawned in Mesopotamia, Egypt, India and Pakistan, and the Mediterranean.

Mesopotamia

Upper part of the stele of Hammurabi's code of laws.

Broadly the region of modern Iraq, Mesopotamia lies between the valleys of the Tigris and Euphrates rivers. Its first cities were founded by c. 5000 BCE in Sumer, the name given to southern Mesopotamia, and developed into city states controlling the regions around them. Around 2500 BCE Sumerian culture was at its height, extending from the Zagros to the Taurus mountains, and from the Persian Gulf to the Mediterranean Sea. Crafts flourished; irrigation canals from rivers to villages and cities enabled crops of barley, wheat, millet, and sesame; and a system of writing was developed, first pictographic, and later stylized (cuneiform). These can be seen on the numerous stone seals and clay tablets that have been found in the region. The Sumerians worshipped a number of deities, and from 2200 to 500 BCE, great temples on stepped towers known as ziggurats were built. The legendary Tower of Babel was probably the ziggurat of the temple of Marduk in Babylon.

Around 2334 BCE, Sargon I of Akkad, a so-far unidentified city in central Mesopotamia to the north of Sumer, conquered the Sumer region. The joint culture came to be known as Akkadian. Later, King Hammurabi of Babylon (1792–1750 BCE) conquered Sumer and Akkad, and created a strong empire. He is remembered for his code of law, engraved on stone pillars and clay tablets, the oldest such code known today. The Hittites, a people who spoke an Indo-European language, and had settled in Asia Minor around 1900 BCE, conquered Babylon in 1590 BCE.

THE EPIC OF GILGAMESH

Perhaps the oldest text in the world (the earliest version was written soon after 2100 BCE), the Epic describes a king who is said to have ruled at Uruk in Mesopotamia c. 2700–2650 BCE. Late versions include the story of a great flood and the building of an ark, which enabled one family to survive.

8000–5900 BCE

8000–6000 Textiles woven, clay and plaster statues made at Jericho.

7000 Neolithic period begins in Europe; first farming communities.

- Fishing communities in the Sahara region.

7000–5700 Jiahu culture, Huang (Yellow) river, China.

7000–4500 Neolithic cultures in Egypt.

7000–4000 Cave painting depicting marching warriors at Cingle de la Molla, Spain.

6750 Pigs domesticated in Jarmo, Iraq.

Hammurabi

On an eight-foot-high stone column, all the existing earlier laws were carved and codified by **Hammurabi**, the greatest ruler of the **Babylonian Empire**, who also guided his subjects to record their laws and customs. At the very beginning of the code, it was mentioned that Hammurabi had been given royal powers by God to protect the weak from the oppression of the strong. It contained 282 articles of law pertaining to all aspects of life. His code epitomized the **Law of Retribution**, which is more commonly known as "an eye for an eye and a tooth for a tooth." These laws also ensured fair treatment for women.

Assyria

Assyrians had built their capital at **Assur** and settled in the valley of the River Tigris by 2000 BCE. The aggressive Assyrians, who were at the peak of their power between 1000 BCE and 612 BCE, conquered the Mesopotamians. However, in 612 BCE, neighboring people joined forces to crush the once-dreaded Assyrian armies, and a ruthless king, Nebuchadnezzar, revived the power of Babylon. His empire eventually stretched from the Persian Gulf to the Mediterranean Sea.

The achievements of ancient Mesopotamia

The Babylonians were firm believers in astrology. Astrologers were especially interested in studying the stars and planets which they felt had a great influence on all events on earth. Thus, the Babylonians learned to recognize planets and foretell eclipses, thereby recording data that later on proved to be essential for astronomy.

The Great Ziggurat at Ur
(in present-day Iraq),
built of mud bricks.

6500 Copper objects made in Anatolia.
6000 Crops cultivated in several parts of the world.
- Canal irrigation in Mesopotamia.
- Drum used in Moravia.
- Cattle domesticated in Greece and Crete.

6000–5500 Halaf farming culture with polychrome pottery in north Mesopotamia, Syria.
6000–3000 Khartoum Mesolithic and Neolithic cultures in southern Nubia, Africa.
5900 Beer brewed in Sumer and Babylon.

THE FIRST CIVILIZATIONS

The Babylonians were the first who counted by sixties, and divided an hour into sixty minutes and a minute into sixty seconds. This division of sixties is still used in clocks today. A circle was divided into 360 degrees. They studied the positions of stars and planets, divided the sky into twelve zodiacs and used the **ziggurats** as observatories.

Indus Valley civilization

Right: Steatite seal, Indus valley culture.
Below: Brick structures at Lothal, India.

Another great civilization rose on the fertile plains of the Indus river on the Indian subcontinent. At its height during 2600–1800 BCE, the culture was dominated by large cities such as Harappa and Mohenjodaro in the Indus valley, Lothal and Dholavira in Gujarat, and Kalibangan in Rajasthan. The cities contained baked brick structures and an elaborate drainage system, and numerous objects have been found made of a range of materials—stone, metals, ivory, terracotta—as well as red pottery and stone seals that feature an undeciphered script.

Researchers from the Indian Institute of Technology (IIT), Kharagpur, India, and the Archaeological Survey of India (ASI) have recently claimed to have discovered evidence that suggests that the Indus valley civilization is

LOTHAL: A TRADING PORT

A major center of the Indus Valley civilization, Lothal was located on the coast of Gujarat in India, and was probably involved in external trade. As well as the usual houses, streets, and drains, Lothal had a large warehouse, and a baked-brick structure that was possibly a dock for ships. This measures approximately 700 x 118 feet, and at high tide, ships could sail into it through a 40-foot gap. The whole city was enclosed by a massive defensive wall to resist floods.

5500–4500 BCE

5500–3500 Vinca copper culture in Balkans: Serbia, Romania, Bulgaria, Macedonia.
5200–4000 Several Neolithic farming cultures in Africa.
5000 First copper and gold metalwork in Europe.

• Cochise culture continues, in North America.
• First cities in Sumer, West Asia.
• Farming and domestication of animals in Egypt.
• Copper used in Mesopotamia.

at least 8,000 years old and not 5,500 years old as earlier believed. This discovery dates back to a time earlier than that of the Egyptian and Mesopotamian civilizations, thus making it the oldest in the world.

Dholavira

Dholavira in Gujarat, India, was a city of exquisite planning, aesthetic architecture, monumental structures, and an amazing water management system. Sixteen reservoirs of various sizes have been discovered, of which five have been excavated extensively. There is evidence of water harvesting throughout the site, and it is possible that water was stored for irrigation.

The Great Bath

The most remarkable feature at **Mohenjodaro** was the **Great Bath**, built with burnt bricks which were coated with natural tar. The structure was basically like a swimming pool at the center with steps from two sides leading to it. The size of the pool was 39 feet long, 23 feet wide, and 8 feet deep. There was provision for water to be drained out through one channel and for the Bath to be cleaned and then refilled through another duct. The Great Bath was surrounded by beautiful changing rooms, and the pool also had galleries and rooms all around indicative of **ritual bathing**. It is the finest specimen of the engineering skills of the people of that era.

The Great Granary

At Mohenjodaro, a large building that was originally labeled as a **granary** was possibly just a public building. There were other large granaries for storing grains such as wheat, barley, and sesame, and to the south of the granaries there were rows of circular brick platforms According to archaeologists, it is possible that these were working floors used for threshing grains.

The Great Granary at Mohenjodaro.

- Settled village culture in China and India.
- **5000–4000** Gumelnitsa-Karanova culture in Romania, Bulgaria, and Thrace.
- **5000–3500** Corn cultivated in Mesoamerica.
- **5000–3000** Neolithic cultures in several parts of Europe.
- **5000–2800** Megaliths in various parts of Europe; earliest at Evora in Portugal.
- **4500–2000** Megaliths and menhirs constructed at Carnac, France.

Presumably, the grains were collected from the peasants as tax and stored in the granaries. For convenient transportation, the granaries were built on the banks of the river.

Town planning

The Indus valley civilization had occupants who were skilled urban planners. This is evident from the elaborate drainage system, well-planned street grid, and efficient management of water. Almost every house within the city had a clearly demarcated bathing area and proper drainage system. The ruins also indicate that the streets had lighting arrangements and even dustbins, which were placed to keep the roads clean.

Town planning of the Indus Valley civilization.

Occupation of the people

The Indus valley had people with diversified occupation. Agriculture was the main occupation. Ploughs and sickles were commonly used agricultural tools. The chief crops were wheat, barley, cotton, maize, and millet. A large number of spindles were found indicating that cotton was extensively grown. Another major occupation was weaving and spinning. Discovery of needles and buttons at various sites suggests that people stitched clothes.

Many tools have been found, suggesting that there were artisans skilled in the use of metals. Copper and bronze were widely used to produce tools and weapons, and the art of bronze-casting was known, as indicated by the discovery of the statuette of a dancing girl. The right arm resting on the hip and the heavily bangled left hand indicate that the women of that age were fond of ornaments and elaborate hairstyles.

A dancing girl in bronze.

4000–3100 BCE

4000 Farming in Sahara region, Africa.
- Crops cultivated in the British Isles.
- Grape cultivation in the Middle East.
- Horse domesticated.

4000–3200 Cernavoda culture succeeds Gumelnitsa in southeast Europe.
4000–3000 Funnelbeaker culture in Europe.
c. 3600 Chinese raise silkworms and weave silk.

THE FIRST CIVILIZATIONS

Pottery

In addition to agriculture and metal casting, **pottery** making was the most popular occupation of the people. They were not only familiar with but also skilled in the use of the potter's wheel. **Clay**, mostly of reddish-brown color, was extensively used. It was baked, glazed, and decorated with various designs. These are evident from the excavation of vessels with **motifs** of animals and geometric designs.

Harappan pottery.

Seal-making

More than 2,000 seals made of terracotta and **steatite**, a soft stone, have been discovered at various sites in the Indus Valley. Most of these seals are rectangular but some are circular in shape. Some of the seals have a knob at the back, which contains a hole. It is presumed that merchants and traders used these seals for stamping their consignments. These seals also have a carved picture on one side and some inscriptions on the other, which indicated the religion, customs, and economic activities of the society.

A seal showing a male god seated in a yogic posture, surrounded by a rhino and a buffalo on the right, and an elephant and a tiger on the left, is known as the **Pashupati seal**. Animals were common subjects for the seals, including a single-horned "unicorn," as well as geometric designs.

Apart from the above occupations, jewelry making was also practiced. Archaeological findings show that the Harappans were aware of and loved ornaments and used various metals and animal bones for making them.

Indus seals.

The Indus script

The people of the Indus valley used a script containing picture-like signs called **pictographs**. However, the Indus script has not yet been deciphered.

Egyptian civilization

Some time after 4000 BCE, villages along the Nile river grouped into two kingdoms: Upper and Lower Egypt, which were united by King Menes around 3100 BCE. Thirty dynasties are said to have ruled between Menes's time and Alexander's conquest of Egypt in 332 BCE, mainly grouped together into the Old Kingdom, Middle Kingdom and New Kingdom, with some intermediate periods. Egyptian civilization included: An advanced system of government; irrigation works; magnificent buildings; the sciences of astronomy, mathematics, and medicine; a 365-day calendar; a hieroglyphic script used on monuments and a simpler hieratic script; and the invention of papyrus sheets for writing.

During the Old Kingdom, great pyramids, which were actually elaborate tombs, were developed. The dead were embalmed as mummies and buried inside, and large temple complexes were attached to the pyramids.

Osiris was the king of the dead, and he, Isis, Nephthys, and Seth were part of a group of nine gods worshipped at Heliopolis, Egypt.

The Nile's fertile plains allowed fruits, vegetables, and pulses to be grown, and the ancient Egyptians also indulged in wine and beer.

EGYPTIAN PYRAMIDS

About 80 pyramids have been found at various sites. Three of the greatest were built at Giza: Those of kings Khufu (2547–2524 BCE), Khafre (2516–2493 BCE), and Menkaure (2493–2475 BCE). The pyramid of Khufu (Cheops) is the largest in Egypt, with each of its base sides measuring 761 feet. It took 20 years and supposedly 100,000 men to build.

The Great Pyramid of Cheops, Giza, Egypt.

3000–2400 BCE

3000 Wheel used in Mesopotamia.
- Arched harp used in Egypt and Sumeria.

3000–2000 Beaker culture in Europe.
3000–1450 Minoan civilization.

2925–2575 Early dynastic period (1st–3rd dynasties), Egypt.
2700 Tea known in China.
2600–1800 Indus Valley civilization in northwest India and Pakistan at its peak.

Religion

The Sun god Ra.

The Egyptians worshipped many deities, including the important Sun god Ra, known as **Amun-Ra**. Both tombs and temple walls featured the deities, in Egypt's naturalistic art. Some of the major deities were.

Ra: In Egypt, Ra was the Sun god and was their chief deity, as he was the giver of life. Ra is usually depicted as a man with the head of a hawk and a headdress of a Sun disk. Later on he was also referred to as Amun-Ra.

Isis: For protection, the Egyptian had a mother goddess called **Isis**, who would help people in need.

Osiris: Osiris was the god of the dead, and was the husband of Isis and father of Horus. Osiris was perceived as a mummified man with a feathered headdress.

Horus: He was the god of the sky, and was the son of Isis and Osiris. The image of **Horus** was a man with the head of a hawk. The pharaohs, that is, the rulers of Egypt, were seen as the living images of Horus.

Thoth: Thoth was the god of knowledge. He enlightened the Egyptians with the wisdom and knowledge of medicine and mathematics. His image was drawn with the head of an ibis bird.

Architecture

The Sphinx.

The Egyptians were great builders. They built pyramids and temples. A four-sided stone structure that symbolizes the sacred mountain is called a pyramid. These marvelous pyramids have made Egypt famous as they are considered one of the world's greatest architectural wonders. To date, no authentic evidence has been found to show how pyramids were built.

One extraordinary feature of Egyptian architecture is the use of huge columns with horizontal **lintels** instead of arches.

A splendid work of sculpture, which has been carved out of a single rock, is known as the **Sphinx**. It is a unique figure which has the body of a lion and a human head. It is believed that the face of the Sphinx at Giza resembles Pharaoh Khafre.

2575–2130 Old Kingdom (4th–8th dynasties), Egypt.
2547–2475 Great Pyramids built at Giza, Egypt.
c. 2543 Ur-Nanshe, 1st king of Lagash dynasty, begins rule in Mesopotamia.

2500 Potato grown in Peru.
c. 2400 Egyptians use papyrus to make writing material.
• City of Kerma, capital of kingdom later known as Kush, established in northeast Africa.

THE FIRST CIVILIZATIONS

Mummification

As the Egyptians believed that there was life after death, they evolved a process of embalming the dead bodies and wrapping them in thin linen strips. The bodies, or "**mummies**" were thus preserved for years. These mummies were put in a coffin and placed inside tombs that were filled with not only treasures but also items which the dead person would require to sustain life into eternity. The Egyptian mummies remain well-preserved to this day, which testifies to their knowledge of the human body, blood circulation, and surgery.

Embalming the dead bodies.

Script

Papyrus sheets were used in ancient Egypt as a writing material, along with a pointed reed for a **stylus** and ink prepared by mixing gum with soot. The script used various pictures to represent words and was called **hieroglyphs**, meaning "sacred writing." It was used primarily for inscriptions on temple walls and tombs. People who did the writing were called scribes.

Hieroglyphs.

Women

The quality of life of women in Egyptian society depended on the wealth of the families they belonged to. In other words, women of rich families led a better life. They were also very conscious of their looks and beauty. Enhancing looks with cosmetics were prevalent.

2334–1900 BCE

2334 Sargon I of Akkad conquers the Sumer region.

c. 2200–1700 Bactria-Margiana Archaeological Complex (culture), Central Asia.

c. 2200–1600 Kurgan grave culture, East Europe.

2130–1938 1st Intermediate period (9th–11th dynasties), Egypt.

c. 2112 3rd dynasty of Ur begins in Mesopotamia.

2100 Ziggurat built at Ur.

Minoan Civilization

This culture existed on the island of Crete, in Europe, during 3000–1450 BCE. Rich from sea trade, the Minoans built grand palaces such as Knossos. They created pottery, gold and bronze artifacts, and developed several types of writing.

The palace of Minos, Knossos, Crete.

Farming communities in Europe

In western Europe, bronze technology was introduced and massive stone tombs were built, along with megalithic standing stones such as the Stonehenge, in England. Several Neolithic cultures in southeast Europe show evidence of houses, cemeteries, cult objects, and the use of copper.

GUMELNITSA–KARANOVO CULTURE

Gumelnitsa in Romania and Karanovo in Bulgaria are sites typical of a copper-using, farming culture, dating to 4500–4000 BCE and extending from the Black Sea in the east to central Bulgaria in the west, and from the Danube river in the north to Thrace in the south. Amongt the many objects found in the region are female figurines.

SKARA BRAE

This well-preserved Neolithic village on Mainland, Orkney, Scotland dates to 3100–2500 BCE. With few trees on the island, houses and furniture were made of stone, including beds, shelves, tables and hearths, and an indoor toilet linked to a stream.

Neolithic settlement of Skara Brae, Orkney Islands, Scotland.

2000 Assyrians have built their capital at Assur.

c. 2000 Migrations of people speaking Indo-European languages across Europe and Asia.

• Inuits settle in the Arctic.

c. 2000–1900 Palace at Knossos, Crete built.

1938–1630 Middle Kingdom (12th and 13th dynasties), Egypt.

c. 1900–1350 Erlitou culture flourishes in China; known for its bronze work.

EXTENSION OF CIVILIZATION

Aspects of civilization such as urban centers, writing, the use of metals, and large monuments began to extend into new areas. Money began to be used and coins were made. Societies became more complex, with new philosophies and religions, monetary systems, and elaborate artifacts. At the same time there were wars and conquests as empires rose, and fell.

Egypt: The New Kingdom

Tutankhamun's solid gold mask, found placed over the mummy's head and shoulders, was evidently molded to mirror the pharaoh's facial characteristics. The vulture and cobra heads over the brow symbolize sovereignty over Upper and Lower Egypt.

One of Egypt's most prosperous periods, the New Kingdom, was known for its monumental architecture and great art. Ahmose I began the period with the foundation of the 18th dynasty in 1540–1539 BCE, and another notable king, Amenhotep IV (Akhenaten), founded a new cult of the sun god Aten and the new city of Akhetaten (Amarna) near Thebes. Probably the most famous pharaoh of all was Akhenaten's son, Tutankhamun, who died at the age of 19 in 1323 BCE. In the New Kingdom, great buildings were constructed at Karnak and Luxor (Thebes), and at the Valley of the Kings near Luxor, many pharaohs, including Tutankhamun, were entombed in deep graves. Prosperity declined after the time of Rameses III (r. 1187–1156 BCE), with repeated invasions by the Libyans and sea-faring tribes.

THE PHOENICIANS

The sea-trading Phoenicians flourished between 1200–800 BCE along the coastal regions of the eastern Mediterranean. Their port cities included Tyre and Sidon, as well as Berot (modern Beirut), Byblos, and Carthage.

A Phoenician coin.

TROY

Once thought to be a legend telling of the Greeks' rescue of Helen of Sparta, who had eloped with the Trojan warrior Paris, archaeologists now believe Troy is the mound of Hissarlik (Place of Fortresses) in Turkey, a site occupied from c. 3000–1260 BCE when it burnt down, the traditional date of its destruction by the Greeks.

Ruins at Hissarlik, Turkey.

1766–1500 BCE

- **c. 1766–1520** Shang dynasty founded in China.
- **c. 1750** Hierarchical village society develops in Soconusco region, Mexico.
- **1700** Hittite empire extends between Syria and Black Sea.
- **1700–1500** Kush kingdom on lower Nile becomes powerful.
- **1630–1540** 2nd Intermediate period in Egypt.
- **1590 BCE** The Hittites conquer Babylon.

The Shang dynasty

Oracle bones from the Shang dynasty.

In China, the Shang dynasty—known for its advanced bronze work—flourished in the valley of the Huang Ho (Yellow) river. Shang rulers practiced ancestor worship and divination, and were buried in massive grave chambers.

The first ruler of the Shang dynasty, King Tang, focused on working for the betterment of his people rather than seeking pleasure and luxury for himself. He was a role model for his successors, and the Shang dynasty laid the foundations of Chinese culture and civilization. King Tang and his successors were conscious of their social responsibilities and initiated various social programs for the poor. They also started giving special gold coins to the poor during famines when the poor were reduced to selling off their children to survive. The king offered the gold coins to enable them to bring back their children.

In 1046 BCE, the Shang dynasty was overthrown by King Wu of Zhou, who founded the **Zhou Dynasty** (1046–226 BCE).

China went through a long feudal period, from 475 BCE to the end of the 19th century. During this period, Chinese rule and culture spread over a huge territory, which included areas from Inner Mongolia to Vietnam and from Tibet to Japan.

Society

Chinese society had distinct levels, with the king at the top and slaves at the bottom. The joint family system was very prevalent and several generations lived in the same household. The eldest male member was considered to be the head of the family.

Religion

The Chinese worshipped forces of nature, believed in an afterlife, and also practiced **ancestor worship**; the early Shang kings and nobles were particularly

---

1540 Hyksos invaders evicted from Egypt by Ahmose I.
1540–1075 New Kingdom (18–20th dynasties), Egypt.
1500 Civilization in China flourishes under the Shang dynasty.

- Cuneiform script introduced in Asia Minor.
- Maya civilization founded in Mesoamerica.
1500–1200 Probable period within which the Prophet Zarathushtra (Zoroaster), founder of Zoroastrianism, lives in Iran.

EXTENSION OF CIVILIZATION

firm believers in worshipping ancestors. It was thought that ancestors were endowed with supernatural powers that could punish or reward people, so gifts of food and wine were offered to keep the ancestors happy.

Oracle bones

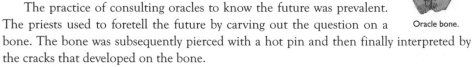

The earliest recognizable examples of written Chinese, dated from 1500 BCE to 950 BCE, were inscribed on ox scapulae and turtle shells called "**oracle bones.**" The Chinese script is **ideographic**, with each picture representing a word or an idea.

Oracle bone.

The practice of consulting oracles to know the future was prevalent. The priests used to foretell the future by carving out the question on a bone. The bone was subsequently pierced with a hot pin and then finally interpreted by the cracks that developed on the bone.

A daily routine for the rulers of the Shang dynasty was divination, as they were extremely superstitious about almost everything, including health, weather, farming, and fortune.

Architecture

The most remarkable example of Chinese architecture is the Great Wall of China. The construction was started by Emperor Qin Shi Huangdi in the third century BCE. It was built in different areas by various dynasties, each adding to the existing portion, to protect territorial borders of their states. It is at least 5,500 miles long, 22 feet high, and 20 feet wide. Watchtowers at intervals of 100 feet were built to enable the soldiers to keep watch and organize movement of troops to tackle enemy forces. Chinese rulers also constructed a network of roads and canals to facilitate trade.

The Great Wall of China.

1500–1250 BCE

1500–1000 Early Vedic Age.
1500 –950 Earliest recognizable examples of written Chinese, inscribed on ox scapulae and turtle shells called "oracle bones."

1500–300 Olmec settlements in Mexico.
1493–c. 1482 Tuthmosis I is pharaoh of Egypt; makes the first underground tombs.

Economy

Fishing grew as an industry in China as people increasingly fished in the freshwaters. The Chinese were the first to grow tea. Tea leaves were initially used for medicinal purposes but eventually became a popular drink.

A vessel from ancient China.

Apart from growing tea, the discovery of silk by raising **silkworms** is also attributed to the Chinese. Silk gradually led people to discard animal skins and tree leaves as garment material. Silk and other woven materials were of a very high quality, which is evident from the clothing on the carefully preserved bodies in Shang dynasty tombs.

The bronze culture flourished during the rule of Shang dynasty. The metal workers produced magnificent bronze cups and vases. The expertise of the craftsmen in stonework, especially jade, was no less.

The availability of wood led to extensive use of timber in building palaces. The Chinese were good at carpentry and used ivory in inlay work. They were also the first to produce paper.

The Chinese were the first to make exquisite pottery known as porcelain or **chinaware**. The pottery was glazed to have a glossy surface with designs painted on the surface.

A porcelain vessel.

Trade

China had trade relations with Egypt, Mesopotamia, Iran, and India. The chief items of export were silk, chinaware, tea, and paper.

In ancient China, agriculture was well-developed and there was also a very efficient irrigation system in place.

China also laid claim to four great inventions which not only changed the world but also accelerated the evolution of world history. These were the **compass**, **gunpowder**, **movable type printing**, and **papermaking**.

The Vedic people

An early text in Sanskrit, the *Rig Veda*, provides some information on life in northwest India between 1500 and 1000 BCE. The text is said to be composed by those who called themselves *Arya* or "noble," which gave rise to the name "**Aryans.**" The origin of these people remains controversial: Some scholars think they originated in India; others believe they were Indo-European speakers who migrated from the Caspian Sea region.

A later manuscript of the *Rig Veda*.

The other Vedas were composed subsequently, along with auxiliary texts including the *Upanishads*, containing deep philosophical thoughts.

During their migration to India, the Aryans had violent clashes with other people who already inhabited these territories. The Aryans subjugated them and occupied their territories. They were known as *dasas* or *dasyus*. The first settlement of Aryans was in the area around rivers, the Indus and her tributaries known as *the* **Sapta Sindhu**—Indus, Jhelum, Chenab, Ravi, Beas, Sutlej, and Saraswati. Gradually, they occupied the whole northern and western India up to the **Vindhya Mountains**. Some scholars are of the opinion that possibly Bharata was the name of the first king of the Aryan tribe after whom India was named "Bharat" (its official Sanskrit name).

Life in the Vedic Period

The Vedic Period has been divided into two: Early Vedic Period (1500–1000 BCE) and Later Vedic Period (1000–600 BCE).

The Early Vedic Period is also referred to as the Rig Vedic Period since it was at this time that the *Rig Veda* was first composed. The word "*veda*" means knowledge. It is the oldest Veda, with a collection of 1,028 hymns, which are divided into ten books. For hundreds of years the Vedic songs and epic poems were told, chanted, and sung orally and were known as "**shruti**," meaning something which was heard. Later on, after a few centuries, these were recorded in written forms.

1225–1050 BCE

c. 1225 Assyrians capture southern Mesopotamia and Babylon.

c. 1200 Exodus: Hebrews leave Egypt for Canaan.

1200 Mayas establish settlement of Chau Hiix in Belize.

1200–800 Phoenicians flourish.

1200–300 Chavin culture in Peru.

Around 1000 BC, during the Later Vedic Period, the three Vedas, namely the *Sama Veda*, *Yajur Veda*, and *Atharva Veda*, were composed or completed. During this time, the epics **Ramayana** and **Mahabharata** were also composed. The Sanskrit language also owes its origin to the Vedic Aryans. It is from these literary sources and archaeological findings at various sites that historians have been able to tell us about the political, social, economic, and religious life of the people.

Different tribal settlements known as **janas** were basically various divisions of Aryan tribes and the small kingdoms that they formed were known as the *janapadas*. In the Later Vedic Period, a number of **janapadas** combined to form large independent kingdoms called **mahajanapadas**. By the sixth century BCE, sixteen *mahajanapadas* were established.

During the Later Vedic Period, the king became the absolute ruler and his power was determined by the size of his kingdom. The more he conquered, the more powerful he became. The king was then bestowed with the title of *Samrat* or **Maharajadhiraja**.

One of the most important *yajnas* was called the **"Ashwamedha"** or horse sacrifice. In this ritual, a horse guarded by some soldiers was let loose for a specific period by a ruler to move around at will. All the territories that the horse covered were claimed by the king and later the horse was sacrificed. If the horse was captured, war followed.

A chariot in the Vedic age.

The main occupations of the early Aryans were agriculture and cattle rearing. The main agricultural products were barley, wheat, rice, fruits, and vegetables. Wooden ploughs and oxen were used to till the land. The Aryans also domesticated several animals like cows, horses, dogs, sheep, goats and oxen.

During the Later Vedic Period, agriculture became the principal occupation and the main source of income. People became cattle breeders.

Other occupations such as hunting, pottery making, spinning and weaving, carpentry, metallurgy (copper and bronze), and leatherwork were prevalent and important. With the discovery of iron, agricultural tools and weapons were made. Trade flourished and village settlements developed into towns.

c. 1120 Mycenaean civilization ends after invasion of Dorian Greeks.

1100–1000 Iron weapons in Cyprus; soon spread across Aegean.

1075 New Kingdom in Egypt ends; period of turmoil follows.

c. 1050–479 *Wu Ching*, or five classics of Chinese literature, composed; includes *I-Ching*.

In the Later Vedic Period, the economic condition of the Aryans changed significantly. Goods were sent as far as Taxila, Central Asia, and European countries. Though the trade was mostly done through a **barter system**, money in the form of gold and silver coins known as "*nishka*" was used as the medium of exchange.

Copper *nishka*

Joint families were known as *kula* and they were patriarchal in nature, that is, the oldest male member (generally a grandfather or father) was the head of the family. All important decisions were made by him.

Women were respected and participation was common in *yajnas* along with their husbands. Women also enjoyed the right to choose their husbands in a special ceremony called *swayamwara*. There was no child marriage and widows were allowed to remarry.

However, in the Later Vedic Period, women lost their high position and were not allowed to read Vedic literature. Their main duty was to look after the husband and children. *Polygamy* was prevalent among princes, the upper class, and the rich. The birth of a son was preferred to that of a daughter.

The Vedic people were very fond of dance and music, and the people played musical instruments such as the flute, the harp, cymbals, and drums. Dancing, dramas, chariot racing, and gambling were their favorite pastimes. Women, however, were not allowed to gamble.

The Aryans wore clothes made of cotton, wool, and animal skin. The noble people wore garments embroidered with gold. Both men and women were fond of wearing jewelry made of gold and other precious stones.

Varna or the caste system and religion

The Aryan society was divided into four groups based on occupation. These groups were called *varnas*, later known as castes. However, during the Later Vedic Period, the caste system became very rigid.

- The **brahmins** occupied the highest rank. They were priests and teachers who performed religious ceremonies. The brahmins occupied a very high position in society

1046–1000 BCE

1046 The Shang dynasty is overthrown by King Wu of Zhou.

c. 1027 (traditional date **1122**) Zhou dynasty founded in China.

c. 1000 King David captures Jerusalem and unites Israel.

• Iron used in Europe and Asia.

1000 Pen used by Chinese calligraphers.

because they were learned and had remarkable knowledge of herbs and medicinal plants for various illnesses.

- The *kshatriyas* were warriors known for their nobility, strength, and valor. They looked after the administration of the country and became kings and rulers.
- The *vaishyas*, who were originally farmers, shifted their occupation to trade, commerce, cattle rearing, and agriculture, and also looked after the financial and material needs of the people.
- The *shudras* belonged to the lowest class and were engaged in manual labor.

There were no temples and the Aryans did not worship images. They worshipped in the open, offering prayers, singing hymns in praise of the elements—earth, fire, water, air, and sky.

The early Vedic people worshipped nature. They feared natural forces and prayed to rain, wind, or earth in the form of **Indra**, the god of thunder; **Varuna**, the god of water; **Prithvi**, the mother of the gods; **Usha**, the goddess of dawn; **Ratri**, the spirit of night; and **Aranyani**, the Lady of the Forest.

Brahmins performing *yajnas*

During the latter part of the Vedic Period, people started building temples. Instead of worshipping nature, they started worshipping idols like **Brahma**, the creator, **Vishnu**, the preserver, and **Maheshwara**, the destroyer.

The concept of *karma* evolved during Later Vedic Period, and it was believed that a person's status, position, and comfort in present life were determined by his actions in the previous. Whatever wrongs one committed would have to be "paid for" by being born to live another life. Humans would continue to be reborn until they lived a life in which they did nothing wrong. Then they would be freed from the cycle of rebirth and attain *moksha* or freedom.

The trinity of Lords Brahma, Vishnu, and Maheshwara.

EXTENSION OF CIVILIZATION

Education and literature

The Aryans followed the **gurukul** system of education. A student or **brahmachari** lived in the household of the *guru* in the *ashrama* and served him by doing various household tasks. *Guru–shishya* or the pupil-teacher relationship was considered very sacred. Education consisted of Vedic literature, both religious and secular, which was imparted orally by teacher to pupil.

During the Later Vedic Period, the three Vedas, **Sama Veda**, **Yajur Veda**, and **Atharva Veda**, were composed. The *Sama Veda* is the "Veda of chants" or "knowledge of melodies."

The *Yajur Veda* consists of rituals to be performed during sacrificial ceremonies. The *Atharva Veda* has about 760 hymns, divided into 20 books. These hymns deal with methods to ward off evil spirits and to control diseases. The *Upanishad* is the last section of the Vedas and is known as *Vedanta*.

Other contributions

Right from the Early Vedic Age, the Aryans had a deep knowledge of architecture. Keeping the oral tradition, the Sanskrit mantras carried the essence of architectural wisdom. It was later recorded and compiled under the title **Vastu Shastra**—possibly the oldest known architectural treatise in the world today. **Maya Danava** was the earliest known master of the *Vastu Shastra*, credited with being the founder of it. These days, *Vastu Shastra* is increasingly being referred to by new-age designers and architects for a healthy and prosperous life. It combines the five different elements such as air, water, fire, earth, and space to send out positive energies and bring about a harmonious and balanced growth between the human and natural environment.

The Early Vedic Period was a Bronze Age culture, whereas the Late Vedic Period was an Iron Age culture, as the **Aryans** had learnt the use of iron by then. This was the beginning of the Iron Age in India. The use of iron sickles, plow heads, and hoes helped the Aryans to clear dense forests of the Gangetic Valley and make the land suitable for cultivation. Swords and shields made of iron were used in warfare. Blacksmiths produced tools, which led to the development of other crafts that needed strong specialized tools such as carpentry and leather tannery.

1000–800 BCE

- **c. 1000–450** City states develop in southern Arabia; Saba is the most powerful.
- **c. 1000–400 CE** Paracas culture flourishes in Peru, South America.

- **c. 970–935** Solomon is king of Israel.
- **c. 950** Battle of Kurukshetra in India.
- **c. 928** Israel splits into Kingdoms of Israel and Judah.

The Celts

The term "Celtic" loosely refers to people speaking a certain branch of Indo-European languages or to people of the Urnfield culture (1200–800 BCE) of north Germany and the Netherlands, and their descendents, the rich Hallstatt culture of 800–500 BCE, which was known for its use of iron, including plough shares and chariot wheels. By 500 BCE, Celtic culture had spread to Iberia, Ireland, and Britain. The mystical druids, priests proficient in magic and ritual, had an important role in Celtic society.

In central and northern Europe the Celts were the most powerful people. The Celts belonged to many tribal groups and spoke dialects which were very similar. The origin of the word Celt is from the Greek word, **Keltoi**. The connotation being barbarians and is pronounced as "Kelt".

The Celts wore bronze helmets with horns which had figures picked out on them. This made them look even taller

The Celts with their traditional horns and weapons.

than they already were. Some others covered themselves with breast-armour made out of chains. They would use weird, discordant sounding horns in chorus with their deep and harsh voices, beating their swords rhythmically against their shields.

Northwest Europe was dominated by three main Celtic groups: the Gauls, the Britons and the Gaels. With the passage of time these groups began to drift apart, each group speaking the tongue a little differently. Broadly, one of the groups chose north-eastern Italy in the region of Venice to settle down. Another group proceeded towards south into the Italian peninsula and the remaining group headed west into France, Spain and Portugal.

900 Napata established as capital of Kush kingdom in Sudan.
c. 850–480 Greeks develop alphabet.
814 Carthage founded. by Phoenicians.

c. 800 Olmecs construct pyramid at La Venta.
• Etruscans found city-states in Italy.
• Hallstatt culture in Austria.

EXTENSION OF CIVILIZATION

Weapons and Warriors

It is believed that a substantial number of Celts went into battle without the protection of any armour or helmets and even fought naked. It is also believed that women warriors fought alongside men. Oval shaped shields, daggers, spears and swords made of iron were the usual weapons used by Celtic warriors.

Celtic weapons and warriors.

The Celtic warriors were most adept at skilfully using the long sword which they used to bring crashing down on the enemy with deadly accuracy. There shields were also a very useful protective gear made of oak with a stripe of iron in the middle.

Houses

Round houses with thatched roofs of straw in well spread out villages were used by the Celtic tribes as their dwelling place. Another feature of these houses were absence of windows.

They used to light a fire for cooking and heating in the middle of the house and had a hole in the roof for the smoke to escape.

Celtic round house.

The farmers used to grow wheat and barley and also reared goats, pigs and cattle. These farming communities lived in scattered farm houses which usually had a ditch **around the houses for protection against wild animals and intruders.**

800–563 BCE

c. 800–700 Homer, Greek poet, is believed to have composed *Iliad* and *Odyssey*.
776 First Olympic Games, Greece.
c. 700 Greek poet Hesiod's books include *Theogony* and *Works and Days*.

668–627 Ashurbanipal is Assyrian king; founds library in Nineveh.
c. 650 Beginning of Archaic period in Greek art; attention to human anatomy, depiction of scenes from epics.

Religion

The Celts were a very superstitious people and had priests formerly called Druids, believed to be linking the supernatural world with the human beings. The priests were supposed to know the future and had the extraordinary power to predict the future through interpretation of nature.

It is also believed that they knew how to read and write, and had knowledge of mathematics, medicine and the position of stars and the planets.

As regards gods, the Celtic people believed in and worshipped **Sucellos**, the sky god and **Nodens** the rain god apart from more than 400 other Gods and Goddesses.

Celtik Cross.

Festivals of the Celts

Based on lunar months, festivities and feasts were organised four times in a year Imbolc, Beltain, Lughnasa and Samhain. Unlike us the day of the Celtic people did not begin at midnight but only at sunset and their feasts also began at sunset.

After Life

Since the Celts firmly believed in an afterlife, they buried their dead with many things that they considered essential requirements for the afterlife. Based on this believe helmet, sword and shield were also buried along with the warriors.

Celtic Princess tomb yields gold and amber riches.

EXTENSION OF CIVILIZATION

The Hebrews

The most prominent people in West Asia were the Hittites and Assyrians, but another important group was the Hebrews. As narrated in the Bible, they settled in Canaan (Palestine) under their leader Abraham.

David being anointed king by Samuel (from a wood panel in the Dura Synagogue, Syria).

Around 1500 BCE, famine forced one group to leave Canaan for Egypt, where they later became enslaved, escaping from Egypt at the time of Rameses II and returning to Canaan. They were also known as Israelites, and later as Jews. Around the 11th century BCE, the dynasty of David was founded. His son, Solomon, built the first Temple at Jerusalem in c. 950 BCE, but after his death the kingdom divided into two: Israel in the north, and Judah in the south. The northern kingdom was destroyed by the Assyrians in 721 BCE, after which several Hebrew tribes migrated away and became the "Lost Tribes of Israel." The southern kingdom lasted until Nebuchadnezzar II of Babylon destroyed the Temple and deported most of the inhabitants to Babylon in 587–586 BCE.

Kush

Part of Nubia in Africa, the kingdom of Kush was influenced by Egypt, but from c. 770–671 BCE actually ruled Egypt until it was overthrown by the Assyrians.

Mycenaeans and the Greek states

The Mycenaeans from mainland Greece began to influence Crete's Minoan culture from around 1500 BCE. Greek city states began to emerge from around 800 BCE, each with its own governing body, military forces, and deities.

JUDAISM

Judaism, the Jewish religion, developed with the Hebrews or Israelites. Its main tenets were belief in one supreme God, Yahweh, and the Ten Commandments, which were revealed in about the 13th century BCE to Moses, who led the Exodus from Egypt to Canaan.

559–492 BCE

559 Cyrus II (the Great) founds the Achaemenid (Persian) empire;

c. 540 Birth of Mahavira, 24th tirthankara (Great Guide) of Jainism and last of the present era.

539 Cyrus II captures Babylon, allows Judeans to return to Jerusalem and rebuild temple.

521–486 Darius I rules Persia.

c. 500 Zapotec culture at Mt Alban, in Oaxaca, Mexico; has a system of writing and calendar.

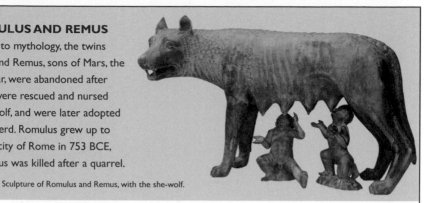

ROMULUS AND REMUS

According to mythology, the twins Romulus and Remus, sons of Mars, the God of War, were abandoned after birth but were rescued and nursed by a she-wolf, and were later adopted by a shepherd. Romulus grew up to found the city of Rome in 753 BCE, while Remus was killed after a quarrel.

Sculpture of Romulus and Remus, with the she-wolf.

Etruscans

The Etruscans, whose origin is unclear, probably settled in parts of Italy between 1200–700 BCE, and maintained close relationships with the people who already occupied the site of Rome, though the Roman Republic was founded only in 509 BCE.

Olmecs

Known for its massive basalt heads and delicate jade figurines, the later Olmec civilization of Mexico and Central America was centered at La Venta, an urban site with several houses and a complex of temples around a tall pyramid.

A stone Olmec head.

Chavin culture

South America's Chavin culture centered around Chavin de Huantar in the Peruvian Andes. Remains include a stone temple complex and bas-reliefs depicting gods, humans, and animals.

- Adena culture in Ohio, North America reaches its height.
- Nok culture in Nigeria.
- **500–300** Magadha establishes its hold over the entire Gangetic plain.

500–200 Hindu scripture, the *Bhagavad Gita* composed.
496–406 Life of Greek playwright Sophocles.
492–449 Greco-Persian Wars.

CONQUESTS AND EMPIRES

This was an age of great battles and conquests, when vast empires were founded. At the same time, there were peaceful periods, and art, culture, and philosophy flourished.

The Empire of Darius I

Darius I (521–486 BCE) of Persia extended his empire to northwest India, Thrace, and Macedonia. The vast empire was reorganized into 20 satrapies or provinces, each under a governor. Darius lost the Battle of Marathon against the Greeks (490 BCE), and the Persian empire was brought to an end, finally, with Darius III's defeat by Alexander the Great at the Battle of Gaugamela (331 BCE).

Mosaic of Darius III in battle against Alexander, Pompeii, Italy.

ZOROASTRIANISM

Established by the Prophet Zarathushtra (Zoroaster in Greek) of what is now Iran, this religion holds that there is only one god, known as Ahura Mazda. The state religion of the Sasanian Persians, Zoroastrianism was thus the earliest monotheistic religion, influencing Judaism, Christianity, and Islam. In its later form, it saw the world in dualistic terms of opposing forces of good and evil.

Judah

Judah was ruled by Persians, Alexander the Great, Seleucid Greeks of Syria, and Jewish Hasmoneans, before it was taken over by Rome. In 37 BCE, Herod was made king of Judah, then known as Judea. Around 5 BCE Jesus Christ, the founder of Christianity, was born.

485–384 BCE

- **c. 485–221** Zhou kingdom in China breaks up into smaller states (Period of Warring States).
- **484–430** Life of Greek historian Herodotus.
- **c. 480** Admiral Hanno of Carthage voyages along the West African coast.
- **c. 478** Athens becomes powerful; forms the Delian League of Greek states.
- **460** Temple of Hera II (or Neptune) built at Paestum, Italy.
- **c. 451–450** Twelve Tables of Roman Law formulated.

The Parthenon temple, Athens, Greece, c. fifth century BCE.

Greek city-states

S ome of the main Greek city states were Athens (leader of the Delian League), Sparta (head of the Peloponnesian League), Olympia, Corinth, and Argos. After the Greco-Persian Wars, Athens emerged as preeminent, and Greek culture reached its height there, with the introduction of democracy, monumental buildings including the temple to the goddess Athena at the Parthenon, and flourishing arts, science, and philosophy. Aeschylus, Sophocles, and Euripides were among the classical Athenian playwrights, while great sculptors included Phidias, Praxiteles, and Scopas. The Greek civilization declined following wars between Sparta and Athens, and in 338 BCE it was taken over by Philip II of Macedonia. His son Alexander became the king in 336 BCE.

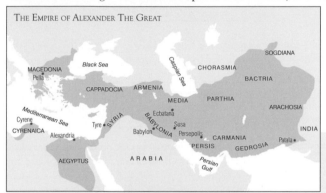

THE EMPIRE OF ALEXANDER THE GREAT

ALEXANDER THE GREAT

Extending control over Greece, Alexander defeated the Persians, then conquered Syria, Tyre, Gaza, and Egypt. Next, he took Babylon, Susa, and Persepolis, and invaded northwest India. His troops refused to proceed further from here, forcing him to turn back. A great general, Alexander also valued learning, and had been a pupil of Aristotle.

431–421 Peloponnesian Wars start between Athens and Sparta; end in Peace of Nicias.

430 Greek sculptor Phidias carves statue of Zeus at Olympia.

415–405 Peloponnesian Wars resume; Athens surrenders to Sparta.

405 Erecthium, temple of Goddess Athena, built on Acropolis in Athens, Greece.

c. 400 Farming settlements at Tiahuanaco, near Lake Titicaca, Bolivia.

• Olmec city of La Venta, Mexico declines.

384–322 Life of Greek sage Aristotle.

CONQUESTS AND EMPIRES

Chandragupta Maurya

The founder of the Mauryan Empire was Chandragupta Maurya. After establishing himself firmly on the throne of **Magadha,** he decided to expand the territories of his empire by conquering the entire northern India. By virtue of his substantial resources, he was able to maintain a formidable army.

In 305 BCE, he defeated **Seleucus Nicator** who had emerged as the most powerful Greek general after the death of Alexander the Great. The defeat of Seleucus resulted in the liberation of northwestern India from Greek control. Seleucus surrendered Afghanistan and Baluchistan, and also arranged for his daughter to marry Chandragupta who, in turn, presented Seleucus with 500 war elephants. Seleucus sent **Megasthenes** as an ambassador to the court of Chandragupta. During his stay as an ambassador, which lasted over five years, Megasthenes traveled through the Mauryan Empire and wrote a travelogue named *Indica.* Chandragupta was the first Indian **imperial** power and his capital was **Pataliputra,** the modern day Patna, in Bihar. He ruled for 24 years and then abdicated his throne to his son, Bindusara, and became a Jain ascetic. According to a Jain text, Chandragupta starved himself to death in order to attain *nirvana.* Bindusara expanded his empire by capturing central India and a part of south India. Only the kingdom of Kalinga was unconquered at the time of his death. His son, Ashoka, succeeded him in 273 BCE.

Ashoka

Ashoka (r. 269–232 BCE), an emperor of India, belonged to the Mauryan dynasty whose capital was at Pataliputra (modern Patna). After seeing the suffering caused by his own wars of conquest, he turned to Buddhism and developed a philosophy

371–300 BCE

371 Sparta defeated by Thebes.
350 Sculpture of Hermes carrying infant Dionysus carved by Greek sculptor Praxiteles **(370–330)**.
337 Philip II of Macedonia defeats Athens and forms League of Corinth.

336 Alexander the Great becomes the king of Macedonia; **332** conquers Egypt; **331** defeats Persia; **327–326** invades India; **323** dies at Babylon.
326 Circus Maximus, a large stadium, constructed in Rome; later rebuilt and enlarged.

of dhamma (Sanskrit *dharma* or "right living") that included a model code of behavior such as respect for people of all classes and religions. He engraved his ideas on pillars and rocks across India.

Mauryan silver punch-marked coin.

Ashoka is known as the greatest king of India. A British scholar named James Prinsep deciphered the inscriptions on the pillars and rocks found in many parts of India. The inscriptions were identified as written in Brahmi Script and gave historians valuable information about Ashoka's rule and his empire. India has adopted the Ashoka Chakra as her national symbol, which can be seen on the national flag. His huge empire stretched from Nepal and Kashmir in the north to Mysore in the south and Afghanistan in the northwest to the river Brahmaputra in the east. The western territory of his empire covered Junagar and Saurashtra.

Ashoka's reign is marked by several battles with the Battle of Kalinga being a turning point. Kalinga was an independent realm, which had remained unconquered despite the Mauryan Empire expanding in all directions.

This kingdom was a fertile land between two rivers, Godavari and Mahanadi. Ashoka desperately wanted to capture this fertile land. A fierce battle followed in which a huge number of people were killed and an enormous amount of property was lost.

Kalinga lost the battle and surrendered, and first time in Indian history, almost the whole subcontinent, except the extreme south, was under a single ruler. Despite winning the battle, death and destruction all around deeply affected Ashoka. The terrible carnage and the tragic sight of the wounded and the dead filled Ashoka with deep remorse. He embraced Buddhism and vowed never to go on war again. The battle of Kalinga (present day Odisha) changed his philosophy of life. He devoted his life to **dhamma**.

Ashoka started to follow the principles and values of Buddhism—that of truth, charity, kindness, purity, and goodness. He prohibited sacrifices and the killing of animals. **Dhamma** was based on Buddhist scriptures. The word "*dhamma*" was derived from the Sanskrit word **dharma**, meaning religious duty. He spread his ideas based on Buddhism by engraving his principles on pillars erected throughout his kingdom. These

The Ashoka Pillar at Feroz Shah Kotla, Delhi.

306 Greek philosopher Epicurus (341–271 BCE) founds a school, *Ho Kepos* (The Garden), in Athens.
305 Ptolemy founds a new dynasty in Egypt.

301 Macedonian generals fight for control of Alexander's empire in Battle of Ipsus; divide empire between themselves.
c. 300 Cuicuilco in Mexico gains importance; has large buildings and circular pyramids.
• Kush kingdom expands in Africa.

edits were written in **Prakrit** language, except a few in Afghanistan, which were written in Greek. The purpose of these edicts was to propagate, and let people understand, Ashoka's reforms and to encourage them to practice generosity and kindness. He preached peace and harmony and tolerance toward the needy, slaves, and servants.

Sanchi Stupa.

Ashoka had become a **devout** Buddhist. He spread the religion to far-off places like Egypt, Syria, and **Macedonia**. He also sent his son **Mahendra** and daughter **Sanghamitra** on a journey to Sri Lanka.

Ashoka constructed many palaces, *stupas*, monasteries, and pillars. The most impressive of his pillars is at **Sarnath**. He also constructed *viharas* where monks could study and live. Caves were also carved from rocks for the shelter of meditating monks. He also built a large number of *stupas* which contained Buddha's **relics**. All these testify to the high standards of the Mauryan craftsmen in architecture and engineering. Agriculture was the most common occupation, even trade with South Asian countries developed.

Lauriya and Lion capital from Sarnath.

ADMINISTRATION OF ASHOKA

The administration of Ashoka, after his spiritual transformation, was focused solely on the well-being of his subjects. Over a period of time, the Mauryan Empire had developed a very well-defined administrative system which functioned mainly at four levels: Central, provincial, district, and village.

Under the system, the king was the supreme authority, the provincial capitals were headed by a royal prince, who represented the king and was assisted by governors.

Each province was divided into districts and each district had many villages. The entire administrative system within the Mauryan Empire was in line with bureaucracy as described by **Kautilya** *in the* **Arthashastra***.*

300–206 BCE

- Moche civilization begins in Peru.
- **c. 300 BCE–250 CE** Yayoi civilization begins in Japan.
- **c. 294–284** Chares of Lyndus builds the Colossus of Rhodes, a bronze statue of the Sun God Helios, 105 feet high, to commemorate victory over Macedonian invaders.
- **290** Ptolemy founds library at Alexandria, Egypt.
- **264–241** First Punic War begins between Rome and Carthage; Rome wins.

The Qin and the Han

A number of warring states existed in China until the ruler of the state of Qin created a united empire in 221 BCE, taking the name Qin Shi Huangdi, or "First Emperor of Qin." After his death in 210 BCE, Liu Bang or Liu Ji, an army officer, rose to power as emperor (202–195 BCE), and founded the Han dynasty. His strong imperial system, with Confucianism as the state ideology, was followed in essence for the next 2,000 years.

QIN SHI HUANGDI'S TOMB

The famous Terracotta Army, life-sized models of more than 7,000 warriors along with charioteers and horses, is only part of Emperor Qin Shi Huangdi's grandiose monument that he began to build for himself early on in his reign. Near the city of Xian, the tomb also contained a replica of an imperial palace, and skeletons of humans and horses were discovered in the complex.

The terracotta army of Qin Shi Huangdi.

Rome

Gradually, from 509 BCE Rome became the dominant state of the Western world. At first a kingdom, a popular uprising in 509 BCE saw the creation of the Roman Republic, which lasted to 27 BCE. Instead of a king at the helm, the Republic had two magistrates known as consuls, selected by the citizens and advised by the senate. A number of internal conflicts within the Republic ended when the politician-general Julius Caesar made himself dictator for life, but the senate was opposed to this, and Caesar was murdered by Longinus, Brutus, and other senators. There followed a period of transition before Octavius became the first emperor of Rome in 27 BCE.

250 Roman nobles begin collecting works of art.
• Arsaces founds kingdom of Parthia in eastern Persia.
247–183 Life of Hannibal of Carthage.

221 Antiochus III becomes ruler of the Syrian empire.
221–210 Shi Huangdi is first emperor of Qin dynasty in China; builds the Great Wall.
218–201 Second Punic War; Rome wins.
206 Liu Bang founds Han dynasty in China.

Julius Caesar.

The Romans eventually conquered a huge empire including: Syria; Macedonia; Greece; Spain; France; Pergamum in Asia Minor; and parts of North Africa, Germany, and Britain. Rome destroyed the North African state of Carthage, despite Carthaginian general Hannibal's expedition across the Alps to attack Rome with war elephants. After the conquest of Greece, Rome absorbed Greek culture, which became the foundation of its own culture.

The Roman empire, which lasted until 450 CE, was characterized by large houses, good roads, markets with rich produce, public baths, sports and games, as well as great literature, art, and culture: *The Aeneid*, composed by the poet Virgil (70–19 BCE), and the works of Horace (65–8 BCE) are Latin classics, while the senator Cicero (106–43 BCE) is remembered as Rome's greatest orator.

Greek philosophy

The foundation for all later Western philosophy was laid by the Greek thinkers who worked between about 600 to 200 BCE. Socrates (470–399 BCE), his disciple Plato, and Plato's student Aristotle, were the most influential Greek philosophers. Socrates sought truth through dialectical questions. He put forward the idea that *arete* (goodness or virtue) is an innate aspect of life, and is linked to self-knowledge. Socrates did not write anything himself, but his dialogues were recorded by others. Plato systematized Socratic

THE KUSH KINGDOM

In the Sudan region of Africa, the Kush kingdom, heavily influenced by Egypt, had its capital at Meroe, which became a trade center for northern Africa, the Middle East, and Europe. The Kush civilization was in decline by the first century CE.

Meroitic pyramids sitting amid sand dunes.

200–149 BCE

c. 200–50 Rock-cut Buddhist cave temples made in India along the western Ghat hills.
189 Romans defeat Antiochus III.
• Pushyamitra Shunga founds a new dynasty in north India.

171 Mithridates I becomes a Parthian king.
c. 166 Roman dramatist Terence writes his first comic play, *Andria*; the plots of his comedies influence later European writers.

philosophy, and defined the goal of the philosopher as that of knowing and understanding eternal forms, and instructing others in this truth. Plato's book, *The Republic*, presents a description of the perfect state. Aristotle wrote many works on logic, on the natural world, metaphysics, and ethics. His ideas were pervasive until modern times.

Aristotle.

Other great philosophers included Thales, Anaximander, and Heraclitus, who all provided explanations of matter; Pythagoras (582–500 BCE), who used mathematics to understand the natural world; and Anaxagoras, who introduced the concept of Nous—the mind or intellect that permeated all living beings—and believed matter was made up of tiny particles or atoms. In the fifth century BCE , the Sophists such as Protagoras focused on material success, as they believed understanding the ultimate truth was not possible. Cynics, Epicureans, Sceptics, and Stoics were other groups of ancient Greek philosophers, and overall, Greek ideas also influenced later politics and aesthetics.

Right: Michelangelo's rendering of Aristotle's Lyceum at Athens, on the Sistine Chapel ceiling in the Vatican.

165 Judas Maccabeus defeats Seleucids in Jerusalem, and rededicates the Jewish Temple.

c. 160 Bactrian Greeks begin rule in northwest India.

c. 150 Famous statue, Venus de Milo, is sculpted in Greece.

• Xitle volcano erupts in Mexico.

149–146 Third Punic War; Rome extends control over North Africa.

NEW IDEAS

Indian philosophy

Six classical systems of philosophy developed: Nyaya, Vaisheshika, Mimamsa, Samkhya, Yoga, and Vedanta. These laid the foundation for all future developments in Hindu philosophy, but at the same time, the new religions of Buddhism and Jainism were spreading. Jains follow the teachings of Mahavira and believe in strict non-violence and harming no living being, including insects.

Worshipping involved elaborate rituals, which had made practicing religion a very expensive affair. This had also made the priests, who performed the rituals, very wealthy. The common people could hardly ever have religious rituals as those had become virtually unaffordable. This prompted the thinkers among the common people to seek knowledge and enlightenment through meditation. They **renounced** worldly processions and retreated into deep forests to meditate. From these conditions, two great thinkers emerged—**Gautama Buddha** and **Mahavira**—who did not accept certain prevailing social rules and customs. They brought about a new balance in society which was more appropriate.

The preaching Buddha, Sarnath, India, fifth century.

Buddhism

Siddhartha Gautama, known as Lord Buddha or "the Enlightened One," founded the religion known as Buddhism. He was born a nobleman in Nepal, but in his 29th year, moved by sights of suffering, he became an ascetic, wandering and meditating until he reached enlightenment. His basic teachings are the Four Noble Truths that ascribe suffering to desire, and the Eightfold Path, which lay down the way of life that can lead one beyond material suffering.

146–73 BCE

146 Romans invade Greece.

141 Chinese emperor Wu-ti expands control of Han dynasty across East Asia.

138–78 Civil war takes place in Rome; ends with a dictatorship.

c. 112 Silk Route from China to the Mediterranean opens.

106–43 Life of Cicero, Roman scholar and orator.

THE UPANISHADS

Upanishad *broadly means sitting near somebody who is wise and illuminated. As per the Vedic scriptures, the Upanishad is the process of imparting knowledge by teachers to pupils sitting at their feet. The teachers mostly taught the pupils through sessions of questions and answers. There are around 108 Upanishads forming a very important part of Hindu philosophy. The ritualistic practices did not receive much importance in the Upanishads, which instead propounded the theory that the ultimate supreme power was* **Brahma**, *the universal soul. The Vedic belief was, when a person dies, his soul is reborn in another living entity, and deaths and births become a cycle. The Upanishads further say that the* **atma** *(soul) attains* **moksha** *(freedom from the cycle of birth and death) when it finally unites with Brahma. To achieve* moksha, *one has to attain complete understanding of Brahma.*

Although most often it was the domain of learned Brahmins to participate in the discussions pertaining to such philosophy, there are instances of women and people from lower castes participating in discourses. There were exceptions like **Gargi**, *a learned and an intelligent woman, and* **Satyakama Jabala**, *who was the son of a poor woman named Jabala.*

During the period of Upanishads, an upper-caste man had four stages of life called **ashramas**. *These were* **brahmacharya** *(student life),* **grihastha** *(family life),* **vanaprastha** *(retirement to the forest to meditate), and* **sanyasa** *(giving up everything).*

Jainism

The basic tenets of Jainism (the name derives from a Sanskrit word meaning "follower of the *Jina*, or conqueror") are not to kill, not to lie, and not to steal. Vardhamana, better known as Mahavira, was the founder of Jainism and also was the 24th and the last *tirthankara* of Jainism. He was a contemporary of Buddha and also preached during the sixth century BCE.

Lord Mahavira was born in Kundalpur, near Vaishali in Bihar. At the age of 30, Mahavira left behind all his family ties and started searching for spiritual truth. Rigorous *penance* and meditation for 12 years led him to attain enlightenment. He was called "*kaivalya*" meaning "one who knows all."

Statue of Lord Mahavira.

Mahavira traveled all over the Gangetic plains, the areas of modern Bihar, and parts of eastern Uttar Pradesh. His first sermon was given at Mount Vipul in Rajgriha. After traveling and teaching for about 30 years, Lord Mahavira attained Nirvana at the age of 72 at Pawapuri near Rajgir in Bihar.

Mahavira's teachings were simple—asking people to lead a pure and uncomplicated life and to practice self-control or the control of one's senses. Mahavira's five principles were *ahimsa, satya, asateya, aparigriha*, and *brahmacharya*. Mahavira denied the existence of God and believed that each individual soul controlled their destiny. The Jains believed that the soul is immortal and is constantly evolving. The present physical condition of the soul is based on past *karma* or deeds. Good deeds alone can lead the soul to freedom from the cycle of birth, death, and rebirth.

The Jain faith completely rejects the caste system. His followers are known as Jains.

Jainism is a philosophy which is based on love and respect for all living creatures. Mahavira advocated the three jewels necessary to attain *moksha*—Right faith, right knowledge, and right conduct.

The Dilwara Temple, Rajasthan.

63 BCE–5 CE

c. 63 Romans occupy Palestine.
59 Julius Caesar elected consul of Rome.
58–49 Caesar conquers Gaul and invades Britain.
51 Cleopatra VII becomes the queen of Egypt.

46 Caesar assumes rule of Rome as dictator.
44 Caesar is murdered.
43 Mark Antony, a statesman and general, and Octavian, nephew of Caesar, gain power in Rome.

Jainism gradually spread in all directions—from Bihar in the east to Gujarat in the west, to Mysore in the south, and Rajasthan in the northwest. The language used by Mahavira for preaching was Prakrit, which was the language understood and spoken by common people at that time. Jain sacred texts are called *Angas*. After the first Jain Council, Jainism was divided into two sects—*Swetambaras* (meaning "clad in white") and *Digambaras* (meaning "sky-clad or bare").

Xuanzang

In the seventh century CE, the Chinese Buddhist monk Xuanzang, who was a great traveler, scholar, and translator, visited India in search of Buddhist truths, as India was the birthplace of the Buddha. He stayed at Nalanda for a long time and participated in religious discussions. Xuanzang studied Sanskrit, Indian philosophy, grammar, and logic during his stay at Nalanda. He took back a large number of Buddhist texts, more than 600 written in the Sanskrit language, which he later translated into Chinese language.

A statue of Xuanzang.

Chinese philosophy

Confucius (551–479 BCE) lived in China at the time of the decline of Zhou dynasty, when corruption was rampant. In order to recreate an ideal state, he believed the principles of the ancient sages of China should be revived, and that society should be a heirarchy with both ruler and subjects behaving ethically, giving loyalty to superiors and justice for those below them. Confucius' philosophy became widely adopted and his teachings, collected in the *Analects*, are still popular.

Confucius.

At roughly the same time, the philosophy of Daoism developed. Dao (the Way) implied understanding the free-flowing, changeable nature of the world and of oneself, and being free of dogma.

NEW IDEAS

Tomb of Confucius in Shandong, China.

Confucius, original name Kongqiu, literary name Zhongni was born in 551, Qufu, state of Lu died in 479 BCE. He was China's most famous teacher, philosopher, and political theorist who became a huge influence on the civilization of East Asia.

He lead a simple life with no dramatic elements to it, which underlines that his humanity was not revealed truth but an expression of self-cultivation proving that human life is a result of its own efforts. The faith in the possibility of ordinary human beings to become awe-inspiring sages and worthies is deeply rooted in the Confucian heritage, and the insistence that human beings are teachable, improvable, and perfectible through personal and communal endeavour is typically Confucian.

Confucius is known for his effort of making education available in China. He established the art of teaching as a vocation, indeed as a way of life. Before him tutors were hired by most of the aristocratic background people. He worked for the transformation of the society by teaching the people the right way of life. He defined learning not merely as the acquisition of knowledge but also as character building, for Confucius the primary function of education was to provide the proper way of training exemplary persons (junzi), a process that involved constant self-improvement and continuous social interaction.

He said that learning was "for the sake of the self" (the end of which was self-knowledge and self-realization), he found public service integral to true education. Confucius was actively involved in politics, wishing to put his humanist ideas into practice through governmental channels.

1–43 CE

1–300 Cholas rule in part of south India; Sangam literature composed in Tamil language.

1–5 Tiberius, under the instructions of Augustus, puts down a revolt against Rome in Germania.

8 Julian calendar introduced in the Western world; used till 1582.

23 Greek historian Strabo completes 17-volume work on geography.

Basic concepts of Daoism

Certain concepts of ancient agrarian religion have influenced Chinese thought from before the formation of the philosophic schools until the first radical break with tradition and the overthrow of dynastic rule at the beginning of the 20th century. The most important of these concepts are: the continuity between nature and human beings, or the interaction between the world and human society; the rhythm of constant flux and transformation in the universe and the return or reversion of all things to the Dao from which they emerged; and the worship of ancestors, the cult of heaven, and the divine nature of the sovereign.

Daoism says anything that develops extreme qualities will invariably revert to the opposite qualities: "Reversion is the movement of the Dao" (Laozi). Everything issues from the Dao and ultimately returns to it; Undifferentiated Unity becomes multiplicity in the movement of the Dao. Life and death are a continuing transformation from Nothing into Something and back to Nothing without losing the underlying primordial.

For society, any reform means a type of return to the remote past. For the individual, wisdom is to conform to the rhythm of the cosmos. The Daoist mystics, however, not only adapt themselves ritually and physiologically to the alternations of nature but create a void inside themselves that permits them to return to nature's origin. Laozi, in ecstasy escaped the rhythm of life and death by contemplating the ineluctable return: "Having attained perfect emptiness, holding fast to stillness, I can watch the return of the ever active Ten Thousand Things." The number 10,000 symbolizes totality.

Daoists prefer to convey their ecstatic insights in images and parables; they should develop their male and female sides but "prefer femininity," "feed on the mother," and find within themselves the well that never runs dry. Much ancient Chinese mythology has been preserved by the Daoists, who drew on it to illustrate their views. Dreams of mythical paradises and journeys on clouds and flying dragons are metaphors for the attainment of the Dao, and the identity of dream and reality.

Lao Tzu or Laozi, the Founder of Taoism.

Buddhism

Siddhartha Gautama was the son of Shuddhodana, the king of Kapilavastu, now in Nepal, and chief of the **Shakya** clan. He was born in 563 BC at Lumbini. Gautama Buddha lost his mother within a week of his birth, and was brought up by his mother's sister, Gautami, with all the love and affection that could be given to any child. He is also called Shakyamuni as he belonged to the Shakya clan.

According to the Buddhist legend, fortune-tellers and pundits predicted that the young prince would be a great leader, who would lead the world on the path of righteousness. His father's attempt to bind him to his royal life by an early marriage to the beautiful **Yashodhara** did not work. He had a son named **Rahul**.

Gautama Buddha.

The Great Renunciation

As all his questions and queries to the priests and pundits in the palace were fruitless, he decided to give up the security of his palatial life and seek answers to life's greater mysteries. One day, Prince Siddhartha went along with his charioteer, Channa, to the city to see life closely.

Gautama saw a sick man, a dead man, and an ascetic. The sight of the sick man and corpse

Lord Buddha sees a sick man,
a dead man, and an ascetic.

46–118 CE

46 Plutarch, Greek scholar, born in Chaeronia.
54–68 Nero is emperor of Rome.
c. 56–c. 120 Life of Tacitus, Roman official; wrote historical works in Latin: *Germania*, on Germanic tribes; *Historiae* and

Annals, on different phases of Roman empire.
64 Large areas of Rome destroyed by fire.
79 Roman cities Pompeii and Herculaneum, in Italy, destroyed by eruption of Mt Vesuvius.

disturbed him immensely as he had never seen suffering before. He realized that no human being can escape suffering—everyone grows old and sick and dies. When he saw a sage with a calm and serene face, Gautama wondered at the secret of such peace in a world full of sufferings. He felt the urge to end the miseries of life. At the age of 29, he left the comforts of his home to lead the life of an ascetic. He practiced severe penance for 6 years, reducing his body to a mere skeleton. But he realized that enlightenment cannot be achieved by punishing the body. This, in Buddhist literature, is known as the **Great Renunciation**.

Gautama sat under a *peepal* tree or the *Bodhi* tree at Bodh Gaya and meditated for 49 days. At the end of this period he attained **enlightenment** or "saw the truth." Henceforth, he came to be known as Buddha or the "Enlightened One."

Gautama Buddha preached for about 45 years, traveling all over the **Terai region** (present day India–Nepal border area) to spread his ideas about eternal bliss. Buddha attained *parinirvan* at the age of 80 in Kushinagar, modern-day Uttar Pradesh.

Main teachings

Buddha gave his first **sermon** at the Deer Park in **Sarnath** to five men who had accompanied him. They became his first disciples.

Traveling far and wide for 40 years, Gautama Buddha spread his message. The Buddhist scriptures were written in Pali, the language of the common people, and were known as *Tripitakas*. Buddha preached the "**Four Noble Truths**" and the "**Eightfold Path**" or *Ashtangika Marga*.

The Four Noble Truths were as follows:

- The world is full of suffering.

Buddha, teaching his first five disciples.

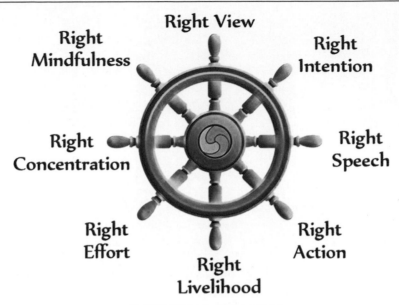

Right View

Right Mindfulness

Right Intention

Right Concentration

Right Speech

Right Effort

Right Action

Right Livelihood

The Eightfold Path, as taught by Lord Buddha.

- Suffering is due to the fact that we are never satisfied.
- In order to overcome suffering, one must give up desire.
- One must follow the Eightfold Path.

Buddha preached the Eightfold Path which emphasized the need to lead a good and pure life in order to free oneself from the cycle of rebirth and attain **nirvana** or salvation. The path advised by Buddha is often described as the Middle Path because he was against the two extremes of worldly pleasure and severe penance. It consists of eight ways of living—right views, right intention, right speech, right action, right livelihood, right effort, right mindfulness, and right concentration.

Killing of people and animals, stealing, and lying were against the teachings of Buddha. He emphasized the virtues of a pure and simple life for the attainment of nirvana. He made no mention of God. According to him, no one was an outcast by birth. He preached the path of **ahimsa**.

120–206 CE

c. 120 Kanishka I, Kushan king, begins rule in Central Asia, Afghanistan, and north India.

122–138 Hadrian's wall built to defend Roman province of Britain.

129–c. 216 Life of Galen of Pergamum (now in Turkey); synthesizes Greek and Roman medicine.

132–135 Jews of Judea, led by Simon bar Kokhba, revolt against Romans, but are defeated.

Sangha

Organizations set up by both Buddha and Mahavira were known as **Sanghas**. These *Sanghas* were for people who gave up worldly life in order to attain enlightenment. Buddhist monks were called *bhikshus* because they survived on alms. The *Sanghas* were organized on democratic lines. Initially, only male members (**bhikshus**) were allowed. Later, however, even women (called **bhikshunis**) were allowed to join *Sangha* that were specifically meant for women. Buddha organized his followers into the Buddhist **Sangha** or the monastic order to propagate his teachings.

Life in a *Sangha* was simple, chaste, and austere, and the monks led a life of celibacy. They wandered in areas allotted to them, preaching the doctrines of Buddhism.

The Buddhist *Sangha* of the time had sent **missionaries** to places like modern-day Burma (Myanmar) and Sri Lanka. The Buddhists who were not members of the *Sangha* were called *upasakas*.

After Buddha passed away, four Buddhist Councils were created to help establish the religion and its doctrines.

c. **150** Kingdom of Champa established in Vietnam.
198–217 Roman Emperor Caracalla rules; Roman citizenship extends to all free-born citizens.

c. **200** Bantu people move into central and southern Africa; cultivate cereal; from c. **300** herd cattle.
c. **200–650** Paintings made at Ajanta Caves, India.
206 Construction of Roman baths of Caracalla begins; comprise hot and cold rooms.

NEW IDEAS

Mahayana Buddhism

Second-century sculpture of a Bodhisattva, Mathura, India.

The Mahayana and the Hinayana are two forms of Buddhism. The Mahayana (the greater vehicle) is a form of Buddhism in which Buddha is worshipped as God. The followers of this form of Buddhism worshipped statues of Buddha and **Bodhisattvas** (Buddha-like beings). A Bodhisattva is a being who vows to help all and to take on the suffering of others. Each person who embarks on the Mahayana path is recognized as a Bodhisattva.

Most of the Buddhist literature is written in Sanskrit. This form of Buddhism spread in the Far East countries of Japan, China, and Korea. Buddhist art and shrines were found as far as Bamiyan in Afghanistan.

The Hinayana form (the lesser vehicle) or the Theravada form of Buddhism follows the original Buddhist philosophy. They do not believe in idol worship. They consider Buddha as their teacher and guide. They represent Buddha with symbols such as a pair of footprints or a lotus. The focus of Hinayana Buddhism is meditation and pilgrimage as a means to self-improvement. This form of Buddhism is found in Sri Lanka and Myanmar.

Basically, the fundamental difference between these two forms of Buddhism is that one worships an idol of Buddha as God (Mahayana) and the other (Hinayana) does not practice idol worship.

Role of universities

Buddhist monks founded the **Nalanda University** with the basic purpose of creating a place fit for meditation. It is believed that Gautama Buddha stayed at Nalanda several times and so various educational centers were erected there in order to provide the monks with a conducive and congenial learning and meditating environment.

Education was another important area of change that Buddhism brought in. The caste system was not acceptable to them, and along with it they rejected the practice of denying education to certain castes. They made their monasteries centers for education and encouraged research in all fields.

240–312 CE

c. 240 Mani establishes religion of Manichaeism in Iran; later spreads to other areas.

248 Trieu Au, Vietnamese woman patriot, leads to revolt against China; wins several battles, but finally defeated.

251–66 Plague epidemic spreads in the Roman world.

271–76 Aurelian walls constructed around Rome.

284–305 Diocletian is Roman emperor; brings in reforms, peace, and order; **294** divides empire

Universities such as Nalanda and Taxila attracted students and teachers from all over the world and from all religions. When Nalanda was at its peak, it hosted about 10,000 students and a world-renowned faculty of 1,500 teachers.

Getting admission was fairly difficult and the standard of education was very high. I-tsing, a Chinese traveler, wrote about the life of the monks at Nalanda in detail. Buddhism was thus spread by the foreign students who studied at these Indian universities and other Buddhist educational centers.

Ahimsa and the martial arts

Buddhist and Jain monks were required to travel far and wide, which meant that they had to travel through jungles and other hostile places. They were often attacked by thieves and wild animals.

Their monasteries, too, ran a risk of attack as they were situated in remote areas. To counter this, the monks developed a system of unarmed combat techniques in which the law of **ahimsa** is adhered to, yet the opponent is defeated. We know these today as kung fu, judo, and karate.

PADMASAMBHAVA

Buddhist ideas are believed to have spread to Tibet by the second century, but gained prominence from the seventh and eighth centuries, especially through the Buddhist monk Padmasambhava's efforts. By way of his teachings, debates, and magical demonstrations, Padmasambhava convinced the adherents of the prevailing animistic Bon religion of the "superiority" of Buddhism. Various schools of Tibetan Buddhism developed later, some incorporating deities.

Padmasambhava, a typical Tibetan Buddhist image.

c. **300** Tiridates III of Armenia makes Christianity the official religion; Armenia becomes the first Christian state.
- Yamato clan extends control over Japan.
- Early eastern Polynesian culture begins.

305 The Palace of Roman Emperor, Diocletian is built at Split (Spalato), Croatia, for his retirement.
312 Constantine becomes the emperor of the Western Roman empire.

Buddhism evolves

Buddhism became the state religion of Japan in 594 CE. New schools emerged in both China and Japan. In India, Mahayana Buddhism, which had emerged around the first century BCE, declined around the seventh and eighth centuries, and Vajrayana, a new form, gained prominence. Vajrayana incorporated several aspects of Mahayana, such as the worship of Buddhist deities, along with elements of Tantra, a Hindu religious philosophy. Buddhism grew in Tibet, and with the efforts of the monk Padmasambhava (c. eighth century), the Vajrayana form was firmly established in the region.

Hinduism

The Hindu religion, mostly prevalent in India, developed over time, and consisted of both high philosophy and popular practices. It has no single founder or canon. Among its features is the belief in deities, who represent aspects of a supreme being. It also embodies the concepts of *dharma*, or right action; *karma*, or action and its results; reincarnation; and the division of society into castes related to birth and occupation.

The form of Hinduism that developed during 1–500 CE was similar to that practiced today: Images, temples, and the worship of major deities such as Vishnu and his incarnations, as well as Lakshmi, Shiva, Parvati, Ganesha, and Kartikeya. Their myths and stories were consolidated in the *Puranas*, a series of religious texts in Sanskrit. Other texts, including the *Dharma Shastras*, or "great law books," were written, which described and explained customary laws and practices. At the same time, philosophy continued to develop.

Vishnu, one of the prominent deities of the Hindu religion.

324–345 CE

324 Constantine becomes sole emperor of both Western and Eastern empires.
319 Arius of Alexandria puts forward doctrine of Arianism; distinguishes between God and Christ.

320–550 Gupta empire begins in north India.
325 First Council of Nicaea; founds Nicene Creed, on the divine nature of Jesus Christ.

The Sasanians

Bas-relief, showing the investiture of Ardashir I by Ahuramazda, Naqsh-e-Rustam, Iran.

In Iran, Ardashir I defeated the Parthians in c. 224 CE, and established the Sasanian dynasty. The Sasanian empire soon extended from the Euphrates river up to northwest India. Iran's position as a gateway of trade and commerce between the Western and Eastern worlds was reflected in its wealth and abundance of luxury items such as silver plates, stucco panels, glassware, silk, and fine wool textiles. Elaborate gems and stone seals were carved and impressed on clay to seal documents. Huge reliefs of scenes of royalty, hunting, and battles, were hewn on rocky mountain cliffs. Zoroastrianism was made the state religion.

Gold coin of Samudragupta.

The Sasanid empire came to an end with its defeat at the hands of the Arabs in the seventh century.

Kushans and Guptas

After the decline of the Mauryan Empire, the two most powerful kingdoms that arose in India were those of the Satavahanas, who had ruled the Deccan, and the Kushans, who had ruled the north. The Central Asian Kushans gradually acquired a large territory, extending to the Tarim Basin in northwest China and through Afghanistan to north India. In the third century, the Kushans in Afghanistan were subjugated by the Iranian Sasanids. In north India, they were succeeded by the Gupta dynasty. The greatest Gupta king, Samudragupta (c. 335–80 CE), established a vast empire. Art and culture flourished under the Guptas. Beautiful and refined sculptures were produced, particularly at Sarnath and Mathura. Gold coins were used, and great literature composed. Kalidasa, one of the greatest writers in Sanskrit, lived at this time. Other small kingdoms were constantly fighting among themselves and had become disintegrated. As soon as the Gupta dynasty came to the throne, they united India and brought an empire under their rule.

c. **326–56** First Basilica of St. Peter constructed in Rome.

c. **329–79** Life of St. Basil; founds order of monks.

c. **330** New city of Constantinople founded on the site of Byzantium.

c. **345–405** Life of artist-Gu Kaizhi of China.

GREAT EMPIRES & CIVILIZATIONS

Kushans

Kanishka was the greatest Kushan ruler, whose huge empire was widespread and included distant places like Afghanistan, Peshawar, Varanasi, Gorakhpur, Mathura, and some areas of Central Asia. His capital was Peshawar, then known as Purushapura. He was highly influenced by Buddhism. Mahayana Buddhism was promoted by Kanishka, who built monasteries and also put up statues of Buddha in public places.

Guptas

After the fall of the Mauryan Empire, a new dynasty rose to power in the Ganges valley, the imperial Guptas. They established their rule over north India, central India, and Bangladesh.

Chandragupta I (320–30 CE) was the first Gupta emperor and was the grandson of Sri Gupta, the founder of the Gupta ruling dynasty. He died in 335 CE and was succeeded by his illustrious son Samudragupta.

Samudragupta is considered the epitome of an "ideal king" of the golden age of Hindu history. He was a great conqueror and his conquests are inscribed on the Ashoka pillar at Allahabad fort.

Having waged many wars, Samudragupta is also called the "Napoleon of India," as he politically unified India and brought it under his power.

Samudragupta's territories extended from the

Iron pillar at Kutub Minar.

Himalayas in the north to the Narmada River in the south and from the Brahmaputra River in the east to the Yamuna River in the west. He was an accomplished musician and could play the harp; he wrote poems as well. Samudragupta was an excellent warrior, a capable ruler, a scholar, a musician, and a poet.

350–400 CE

c. 350 *Panchatantra*, a book of fables, composed in India, in Sanskrit.

360s Huns of Central Asia invade Europe.

372 Huns drive Ostrogoths and Visigoths out of Ukraine.

378 Visigoths defeat Romans at Adrianople.

c. 378 Maya city Tikal captures rival Uaxactin.

Samudragupta was succeeded by his son Chandragupta II, also known as Vikramaditya or "as powerful as the sun". Chandragupta II was one of the most powerful rulers of the Gupta Empire.

The inscription on the Iron Pillar at Qutub Minar in Delhi states that it was erected to honor the Hindu god Vishnu and also to commemorate Vikramaditya's victory against the Vahilakas. The pillar, made of 98 per cent wrought iron, has stood there for more than 1,600 years without rusting or decomposing. Vikramaditya was the first ruler to issue silver and copper coins besides issuing gold coins. Vikramaditya patronized learning, and his court was adorned by nine gems; among the scholars at his court were the astronomer Varahamihira and the Sanskrit poet and dramatist Kalidasa.

Gupta administration

To show their power, the rulers of the period assumed high-sounding titles and performed the *rajasuya* and *ashvamedha yagyas* to show their power. The kings were powerful and ruled according to *dharma* or the law of the land, which was in the form of **Dharmashastras**.

These were compiled by learned brahmins. The division of the empire and the administrative hierarchy are shown in the table given below.

Empire (*Rajya*)	King (*Samrat*)
Provinces (*Bhuktis*)	Council of ministers (*Amatyas*)
Districts (*Pradeshas*)	Governors of provinces (*Uparikas*)
Villages (*Gramas*)	District heads (*Ayuktas*) Village head (*Gramapati*)

Justice was given in accordance with the laws of **Manusmriti**. Punishments were generally mild. The Gupta Empire maintained a large army consisting of 500,000 infantry, 50,000 cavalry, 20,000 charioteers, and 10,000 elephants. Chariots receded into the background and cavalry came to the forefront. Infantry archery became prominent in

c. 387 St Augustine of Hippo begins composition of *De Musica*, on musical aesthetics.
391 Library at Alexandria in Egypt destroyed by fire.

399–414 Chinese Buddhist pilgrim Faxian travels through India and records what he observes.
c. 400 Use of iron spreads in East Africa.

military tactics and rose to be one of the most advanced of the period. The bow was one of the predominant weapons of the army. They also used siege craft, catapults, and other sophisticated war machines.

The Gupta also maintained a powerful navy with more than 1,200 ships to control the regional waters. Chandragupta II controlled the entire Indian subcontinent. The Gupta Empire was considered to be one of the most powerful empires in the world during Chandragupta II's reign.

Society and religion

The life of the people is known from the literary works of Kalidasa, Banabhatta's *Harshacharita*, and the accounts of foreign travelers like Xuanzang.

Fa Hien spoke in glowing terms about society during the time of the **Guptas**. However, he mentioned the caste system as a widely prevalent practice and said that untouchability was rampant. Child marriage and *sati* (the immolation of a widow) were also practiced.

Guptas were mostly **Vaishnavas** or worshippers of *Vishnu and Shiva*. The rulers performed elaborate rites and rituals, including the *ashvamedha yajna*. The concept of **bhakti** or personal devotion to God without rituals or ceremonies began during this time. The Gupta rulers continued to be tolerant toward Buddhism and Jainism.

Trade

During the Gupta period, both internal and external trades flourished. The chief port in the east was Tamralipti, which handled trade with Southeast Asian countries like Suvarnabhumi (Myanmar) and Java. as well as trade developed with west Asian countries such as Afghanistan, Arabia, and Iran. This also led to widespread cultural exchange. For instance, the influence of the Sanskrit language, architecture, and religion on some Southeast Asian countries can be seen today.

The main items of export were spices, precious stones, textiles, sandalwood, indigo, herbs, and ivory, while the main item of import was gold. Various industries like weaving, carpentry, metallurgy, and pottery flourished.

406–450 CE

406 Vandals, Alans, and Sciri (Germanic tribes) cross the Rhine; Roman power collapses.
410 Visigoths loot Rome; Huns force Rome to pay tribute.

428 Gaiseric becomes the king of Vandals.
429 Vandals conquer Carthage; later annex Corsica, Sardinia, and Sicily.

Literature, art and architecture

The Gupta rulers themselves were accomplished scholars, and their courts were adorned with talented scholars and artists. Sanskrit was the court language of the Gupta kings. Kalidasa, the greatest gem in the court of Chandragupta II, had written the famous play *Abhijnanshakuntalam* and the epic poem *Meghaduta*.

During this period, a collection of fables known as *Panchatantra* was written by Pandit Vishnu Sharma. Probably the two epics, *Ramayana* and *Mahabharata*, were given their final form under the Guptas. The *Bhagvad Gita* was also compiled and the **Puranas** too were given their final shape during this age. During this period, the greatest work on Sanskrit grammar, Panini's **Ashtadhyayi**, was written. Drama, poetry, and prose reached their zenith under the Guptas.

The great centers of art were located at Mathura, Varanasi, and Pataliputra. The **Vishnu** temple at Deogarh and the brick temple at Bhitargaon are great specimens of the "Sarnath School of Art."

The art of painting reached the zenith of its splendor under the Guptas as is testified from the cave paintings seen in the wall **frescoes** of the temple of Ajanta Caves in Maharashtra.

The entrance of a Vishnu temple in Uttar Pradesh, India.

Science and education

During the Gupta period, great progress was made in the field of mathematics, **astronomy**, and medicine. Aryabhata was an astronomer and mathematician who had come to the conclusion that the Earth revolves around the Sun and rotates on its own axis. In the 16th century, the people in the West still believed that the Earth was the center of the universe. Aryabhata also worked out scientific reasons for eclipses.

Aryabhata.

c. 430 St Patrick arrives in Ireland; spreads Christianity.

434–53 Attila is the leader of Huns; attacks Europe, defeats Visigoths, Ostrogoths, and Alans.

451 Attila defeated by the Romans.

c. 450 Buddhaghosha of India compiles *Vishuddhimagga*, on teachings of Theravada Buddhism.

GREAT EMPIRES & CIVILIZATIONS

The concept of zero, as well as the system of writing numbers using zero and the numerals one to nine were formulated by him. The Arabs who carried it to Europe adopted this system. This is the reason why these numerals are called Indo-Arabic. The Indians also used the decimal system.

Vagabhatta and Balabhatta, who wrote treatises on medicine, were two great physicians of the Gupta period. The **Ayurveda** system developed medicines to cure various diseases using herbs.

The Maya

Possibly the greatest of the elaborate civilizations of South America, dating back to at least 1500 BCE, was the Maya. The Maya covered a very large area, including parts of Mexico, the Yucatan peninsula, and northern Central America. The civilization reached its height between *c.* 250–900 CE, with about 80 city-states, each with a distinct line of kings. The states practiced large-scale agriculture and had urban and religious centers, with palace complexes, pyramids, and temples. Tikal, Caracol, Dos Pilas, and Calakmul were among these centers.

An illustrated version of the Maya calendar.

The Maya are known for their architecture, art, pottery and ceramics, system of writing, calendar, and complex mathematical and astronomical systems. They also practiced human sacrifice, and most cities contained a court for a ritual ball game. The Maya calendar, beginning with a date equivalent to 3114 BCE, predicts a great change in 2012.

Han dynasty

In China, the Han dynasty overcame a usurper and reestablished itself in 25 CE as the Eastern Han, ruling from a new capital at Luoyang. Trade flourished and new inventions of the period included paper, water clocks, astronomical instruments, and a seismograph. The Han declined by *c.* 220 CE, giving way to the Period of the Three Kingdoms.

An Eastern Han pottery soldier, *c.* first century CE..

455–496 CE

455 Rome sacked by Vandals.
475–76 Romulus Augustulus becomes the last Roman emperor; expelled by Odoacer, Germanic invader.

c. **476–550** Life of Aryabhata of India, astronomer and mathematician; writes *Aryabhatiya* in Sanskrit.
477–84 Humeric becomes the Vandal king in North Africa.

The Roman empire

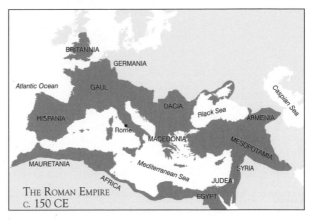

THE ROMAN EMPIRE
c. 150 CE

The greatest empire in the world at this time was that of Rome. The empire reached its height between the first and second centuries CE, with provinces in Europe, Asia, and Africa enjoying a period of peace and prosperity that ended about 180 CE. Rome was known for art, architecture, and literature, and for its vibrant social life. In 285 CE, Emperor Diocletian divided the empire into the Western and Eastern empires for easier governance. The empire was twice reunited for brief periods, but after 395 remained permanently divided, with the Eastern capital at Constantinople (Byzantium). In the fifth century, Rome's continental provinces were invaded by the Visigoths, Huns, and Vandals, but while the Western Roman empire declined, the Eastern Roman empire, also known as the Byzantine empire, continued to exist.

481 Clovis I becomes the king of Franks, founds Merovingian dynasty.
486 Occupies northern Gaul.
496 Converts to Christianity.

493 Theodoric, King of Ostrogoths, conquers Italy from Odoacer.
c. 496 Shaolin temple built in China.

GREAT EMPIRES & CIVILIZATIONS

ROMAN RELIGION

The Romans worshipped several deities, some, such as Jupiter and Mars, originating in early Etruscan and Latin traditions, and others, such as Diana, Minerva, Hercules, and Venus, derived from Greece and Iran. Mithra or Mithras, originally an Indo-Iranian deity, became the center of a mystical cult.

The emperor was also the Pontifex Maximus (chief priest), the head of the Roman state religion and guardian of the old Roman cults. In the first century, Paul of Tarsus (c. 10–67 CE) began to propagate Christianity, but the Roman state responded with fear and persecution until Emperor Constantine converted and enforced Christianity in parts of his empire. Earlier deities and the Mithra cult declined.

Emperor Constantine.

Roman cities

Ruins of the Roman Forum, Rome, Italy.

Among the empire's many cities, Rome itself was the greatest. Rome was dominated by the Forum, originally an open space for public functions, later the site of huge buildings, temples, and archways. Begun in 600 BCE, and added to by many emperors, the Forum was the center of public life. Political discussions, victory processions, sacrifices, worship in temples, games, amusements, and theatrical performances took place here. Wheeled vehicles were prohibited within till 4 p.m., and it was surrounded by huge market centers. Later, there were separate forums for legal and administrative matters, and for markets.

499–531 CE

c. 499 Angles and Saxons conquer parts of Britain.

c. 500 Thale people occupy Alaska.

• Polynesians settle on Hawaiian islands and Easter Island.

508 Clovis I of Merovingian dynasty occupies most of France and Belgium; Paris becomes the capital.

510 Huns invade India.

c. 520 Indian monk Bodhidharma reaches China; considered founder of Chan (Zen) Buddhism.

Each city in the empire had public buildings, forums, theaters, amphitheaters, bridges, aqueducts, arches, and statues, all modeled on Rome, though the architecture varied in different regions. Public baths, where men met to discuss various issues, were another common feature.

A typical Roman home.

AKSUM

Many different societies at varying levels of development existed in Africa at this time. The coastal regions of the north were under the Roman empire. The Kush kingdom, with its capital at Meroe, was declining, and in c. 300 CE it was taken over by the state of Aksum. In the fourth century, Aksum became a Christian state, and finally declined in the seventh century with the spread of Islam in Africa.

Mosaic of Jesus Christ at the Hagia Sophia museum, Turkey, 13th century.

Jesus, a Jew born in Bethlehem in Judea, was the founder of the religion later known as Christianity. Around the age of 30, he gathered 12 disciples (also known as the Apostles) who would be his main companions, and began to teach people about love, forgiveness, and compassion. He is also said to have performed miracles. He came to be known as "Christ," a term meaning "messiah," and his followers came to be called Christians. Threatened by his growing stature, the Jewish clergy pressed the Roman administration to sentence him to be crucified. The office of the pope, first at the head of the entire Christian Church, and later exclusively of the Catholic Church, is traced to St. Peter, the leader of the Apostles.

Christianity's basic text is the Bible, consisting of the Old Testament and the New Testament. The four Gospels of the New Testament, the Gospels of Matthew, Mark, Luke,

c. **523** Boethius (c. 484–524), Roman philosopher and statesman, writes *De Consolatione Philosophiae* (The Consolation of Philosophy).

525 Kaleb of Aksum conquers Yemen; builds churches.

529 St. Benedict establishes monastery of Monte Cassino at Nurse, Italy.

531–79 Hussar I of the Sasanian dynasty extends Persian empire.

and John, record the life and teachings of Jesus, and were composed sometime in the first century. They chronicle the Sermon on the Mount, a message of love and forgiveness, which is the essence of Jesus's teachings. In c. 380 CE, Christianity became the religion of the Roman empire, and by this time it had also reached North Africa, Armenia, Persia, India, and some other areas.

Developments in Judaism

Judah, to the south of Israel, was occupied by the Romans in 63 BCE. In 70 CE, the Jewish temple was destroyed by the Romans and many Jews left their homeland and settled in different parts of the world.

In the first century CE, Jewish scribes divided into two camps following the ideas of scholars Shammai or Hillel. Toward the end of the century, the patriarch Gameliel II unified the community, and allowed a lenient interpretation of Jewish law. The Jewish calendar was standardized. By 136 CE, Jewish resistance to the Romans had collapsed and instead, led by the rabbis, they began to develop their scripture. This included the Mishnah, on various Jewish laws, and the Talmud, with commentaries and elaborations on the Mishnah. After Christianity became the official religion of the Roman empire, the Jews retained freedom of worship, but suffered some limitations, for instance in collecting taxes from other Jews or building synagogues. The office of the Jewish patriarch was abolished in c. 425.

Hillel, the elder.

Temple Mount, the most sacred place of Judaism.

534–563 CE

534 Byzantine military commander Balearics defeats Vandals in North Africa.
541 Plague sweeps through Europe.
c. 550 David brings Christianity to Wales.

• Kalabhras, a group of unknown origin, defeat kings of south India.
• Tendai Buddhism established in Japan by Zhiyi.
550–600 Nubians in Sudan become Christian.

Indian dynasties

The ruins of Nalanda.

Kingdoms rose and fell. The Gupta empire declined after attacks by the Huns, while Harsha (r. 606–47) of the Pushyabhuti dynasty established control over much of northern India. In the south, the Chalukyas, Pandyas, and the Pallavas were among the most powerful dynasties. The great Buddhist monastery of Nalanda thrived at this time, with 10,000 monks affiliated to it.

The Suis and Tangs

Although the Chinese Sui dynasty ruled for a short period (581–618), it is remembered for starting the Grand Canal, the longest in the world, and for reconstructing the Great Wall. The succeeding Tang dynasty (618–907) saw an increase in urban centers and trade, along with cultural developments in literature and art. Woodblock printing was developed, and medical texts were compiled.

EMPRESS SUIKO

Empress Suiko was the first reigning empress of Japan, the wife of the emperor Bidatsu (r. 572–585) and the daughter of the emperor Kimmei. When Suiko assumed the throne, it was a milestone in the history of Japan, as although Japan had been ruled by many women, around that time the ruling line had been male, and she toppled her brothers in the conflict for the throne.

Buddhism grows in Japan

Empress Suiko (r. 593–628) made the Asuka valley in Yamato province her capital. Her nephew and regent, prince Shotuku, reformed the administration and drafted the first Japanese constitution, consisting of 17 principles of good government. He also promoted Buddhism throughout Japan, building a Buddhist temple complex with 41 buildings at Horyu-ji, southwest of Nara, which became the capital in 710.

c. 550–1190 Rule of various Chalukya dynasties in west and central India.

553 Justinian I holds Second Christian Council of Constantinople (Fifth Ecumenical Council).

560–636 Life of St Isadore, Archbishop of Seville, Spain; composes *Etymologiae*, an encyclopedia.

563 St Columba begins conversion of Picts in Scotland to Christianity.

CULTURAL DEVELOPMENTS

Americas: Hohokam and Huari cultures

Among the several Native American cultures of North America, the Hohokam flourished between 300 BCE and 1400 CE in central and southern Arizona. During 500–900 CE, they lived in villages with pit houses, and cut deep irrigation channels to grow corn and cotton. They had several varieties of pottery, mainly buff ware, decorated in iron red.

South America had a number of civilizations, among which were the Moche and Nazca cultures, and the Huari and Tiahuanaco civilizations. The Huari, in the highlands of modern Peru, reached its height between 600–1000, with an urban site that was probably the center of an empire. Large stone structures, temples with naturalistic sculptures, and metal artifacts, including gold masks, have been found there. The "Doorway God," a figure with a rectangular face and headdress with rays, is often depicted on their pottery. Huari artistic styles were closely linked with Tiahuanaco, near lake Titicaca in Bolivia, and also influenced the Late Nazca culture.

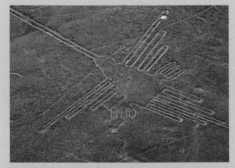

Nazca Lines, Peruvian desert.

NAZCA LINES

The Nazca civilization of Peru (200–700) drew mysterious lines in the Nazca desert, creating giant drawings of birds, plants, lizards, and geometric figures, some of them 400 feet long. Formed by removing surface stones to reveal a lighter layer beneath, the lines' purpose remains unknown. While some see them as extra-terrestrial landing spots, anthropologists believe that they are connected with ancient water rituals and that the lines may mark underground aquifers.

The Tegai gate at Todai-ji Buddhist temple, Nara, Japan.

570–605 CE

c. 570–632 Life of the Prophet Muhammad who receives the message of Islam and inspires the creation of the Arab Empire.

581–617 Yang Jian of Sui dynasty rules China; reunites country, known as Emperor Wen-di.

584 Kingdom of Mercia founded in England.

590 St. Gregory the Great elected pope.

595 Indian mathematicians use decimal system.

The Merovingians and the Carolingians

Charlemagne.

After the decline of the Western Roman empire, new rulers and kingdoms emerged in the region. The Frankish King Clovis I of the Merovingian dynasty ruled in Gaul up to 511 CE. However, on his death, the empire was partitioned among his four sons, and later among their sons, causing frequent wars. Monks and missionaries brought Christianity to the Franks at the time of the Merovingians.

The Merovingians were followed by the Carolingians, who officially took power under Pepin in 751. Their greatest king was Charlemagne, who ruled from 768–814. He united much of western Europe, and was made Holy Roman Emperor by Pope Leo III in 800. (The Holy Roman Empire's actual foundation is considered to be under king Otto II, in 962.) The title was based on the concept of a Christian empire which would revive the glory of the Western Roman empire, as well as establish papal sovereignty in Italy. Charlemagne's empire included France, northern Italy, and parts of Spain and Denmark. The blossoming of literature, education, art, and architecture during his reign and the succeeding period has been called the Carolingian Renaissance.

THE MIDDLE AGES

Beginning in the fifth century and lasting up to the Renaissance, the Middle Ages in Europe saw the decline of the advanced culture of the Western Roman empire. Political and economic developments were largely local, although some areas then saw a limited and static feudal society develop, which gradually changed into the dynamism of the Renaissance.

Charlemagne's gold and silver casket.

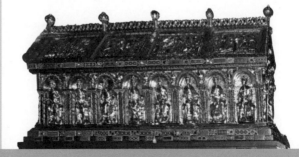

597 St. Augustine of Rome reaches England to convert Anglo-Saxons to Christianity; becomes first Archbishop of Canterbury.

c. 600–700 Welsh bard Aneirin composes *Book of Aneirin*.

c. 602 Slavic tribes begin to settle in the Balkans.

c. 605–10 Canal built in China, linking Yangtze river with the capital, Changan.

CONQUESTS AND INVASIONS

A folio from the *Lindisfarne Gospels*.

Anglo-Saxons in England

Numerous invasions and internal wars were a feature of this period. By around 600 CE, the Angles and Saxons from Germany had occupied most of England. According to a 12th-century source, there were seven separate kingdoms of Kent, Sussex, Wessex, Mercia, East Anglia, Essex, and Northumbria, though research shows these emerged at different times and were not equal in power, and that, in addition, other kingdoms existed. Anglo-Saxon kings and chiefs were sometimes buried in ships, which were pulled onto land. These ship-graves such as at Sutton Hoo were filled with elaborate ornaments and other goods. Religious art flourished, a fine example being the illustrated Lindisfarne Gospels of the eighth century that was bound in leather and encrusted in jewels and metals.

Justinian I and the Byzantine empire

Meanwhile, the Eastern Roman, or Byzantine, empire flourished from Constantinople, with a widespread trade network. Under Justinian I (r. 527–65), it expanded to include parts of Spain and Italy, the Balkan peninsula, Asia Minor, and Palestine, as well as Egypt and other areas in North Africa. Justinian is remembered for his codes of law, and the grand church of Hagia Sophia (Church of the Holy Wisdom) was constructed during his reign.

THE GHANA EMPIRE

One of Africa's numerous kingdoms was the Ghana empire, south of the Sahara (nowhere near modern Ghana). Well established by the eighth century, around 700 it was ruled by the Soninke or Serahule people, with their capital at Kumbi Saleh, a leading trading center. The empire was first called Wagadou or Aoukar, but came to be known as Ghana as this was one of the titles of the king. Gold was the most valuable product of this rich and powerful state.

608–641 CE

608–42 Reign of Pulakeshin II, king of Chalukya dynasty, in India.

617–86 Life of Wonhyo Daisa, an influential Korean Buddhist.

618 Tang dynasty begins in China under Li Yuan; unites China; **628** adopts Buddhism.

629 Dagobert I of Merovingian dynasty unites Frankish lands.

Advancement of Christianity

In the sixth century, Christianity reached Wales and Scotland, and spread through England over the next two centuries. Pope Gregory the Great (590–604 CE) reformed the structure and administration of the Church. Between 500 and 800 CE, three Christian Councils were held during which bishops decided on matters of Christian doctrine and practice.

The advent of Christianity

Christianity emerged, spread, and was accepted as the official religion of the Roman Empire in one of the most remarkable developments in history.

Christianity was preached by Jesus, who was a Jew and was born about 5 or 4 BCE in Bethlehem in Judaea. Jesus Christ, who was also considered as the Messiah and the Son of God by the Christians, began his ministry at the age of 30. He could perform miracles with his healing power, according to the Gospels.

The Silver Star marks the site where Jesus was born in the Church of the Nativity.

c. **632** Queen Sondok begins rule in Silla kingdom of Korea.

632 King Penda of Mercia takes control of northern Britain after killing King Edwin of Northumbria.

636–713 Life of Huineng, Sixth Patriarch; most important figure of Chinese Zen Buddhism.

640–41 Arabic Caliph Omar conquers Egypt.

641 Last Sasanid king Yazdgird III defeated by Arabs.

NEW IDEAS

Teachings of Jesus Christ

Jesus Christ.

The Old Testament, which was simplified and summarized from the Jewish Bible, called the Torah, was the basis of the teachings of Jesus. He taught that we should have unconditional love for God and that good should triumph and prevail over evil. Jesus professed that the virtues of compassion, courage, and tenderness are of great importance. He himself possessed the virtues that he preached. He despised pretence and hypocrisy in any form and lived a simple life. According to him, all human beings are equal.

Crucifixion of Jesus Christ

Jesus was arrested by the ruling Romans on charges of sedition, on the instigation of the Jewish authorities, as they considered him a threat to their authority and power. In 30 CE, he suffered death by *crucifixion.*

By 300 CE, Christianity had spread through the entire Roman Empire and beyond, to places like Persia and Armenia, due to the efforts of St. Paul and other **apostles.**

Spread of Christianity

Constantine, the Roman emperor, was tolerant of Christianity and by the fourth century, Christianity became the official religion of the entire Roman Empire and the Greek initials for the cross became symbols on the shields and banner of Emperor Constantine.

In the fifth century CE, the Roman Empire fell. The Christian Church, being the only organized institution which could emerge as an alternative at that time, took over many of the responsibilities of the government.

646–700 CE

646–700 Political and social reforms in Japan.

c. 650–888 Later Pallava dynasty in south India erects temples at Mamallapuram.

650–1150 Sri Vijaya kingdom of Sumatra dominates the Malay region.

c. 651 Arab traders bring Islam to China.

661–750 Umayyads rule Arab Caliphate; continue rule in Spain up to **1031**.

c. 675 Bulgars from Russian steppes settle south of Danube river.

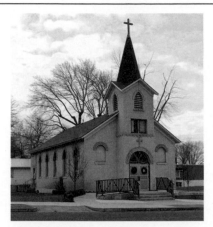

The historic Our Lady of Limerick Catholic Church (built 1915), located at 113 West Arthur Street in Glenns Ferry, Idaho, United States, is listed on the US National Register of Historic Places.

In the Middle Ages, from CE 500 to CE 1500, the most prominent and important cultural institution was the Christian Church, and the head of the Catholic Church, the Pope who was based in Rome, was recognized as the head of the Church in the west. He had the support and friendship of the kings of the time.

Monasteries

Christian churches were set up almost all over Western Europe by the fifth century CE. Religious rites and ceremonies were performed by priests living among the people. Some of them also chose to live as ascetics in monasteries, and were called monks.

Giving up a worldly life, some women, known as nuns, started living in convents and nunneries. The monks and nuns lived a Spartan life, shunning all luxuries and comforts, and also the institution of marriage.

The Church was the only source of education during the medieval period. The sick, the poor, and the destitute were looked after by the monks and nuns. Many of the monks and nuns were outstanding scholars.

Many divisions developed within the Christian Church by the late 16th century. The Protestant Church and the Eastern *Orthodox* Church were the most important divisions.

The Cathedral of Christ the Saviour in Moscow, Russia, the world's tallest Orthodox church.

NEW IDEAS

Emergence of Islam

Muhammad, the founder of Islam, was born in Mecca (in today's Saudi Arabia) in 570 CE. In 610 CE, he began to receive messages from god through the angel Jibril (Gabriel). Muhammad began to spread these messages, but facing hostility in Mecca, left for Medina in 622 CE. This departure, known as the Hegira, is the beginning of the Islamic era.

Muhammad's influence spread, and he re-entered Mecca in 630 CE, setting up the Kaaba as the center of Islamic pilgrimage. This cube-like shrine originally contained several pagan idols, which Muhammad destroyed in order to promote the worship of one god, Allah. By the time of his death in 632 CE, most of Arabia was unified under Islam.

The caliphs

Spiritual successors of Muhammad, the caliphs (Arabic *khalif*), also held political power in the Arab empire. The early caliphs were:

- Abu Bakr (632–34 CE)
- Umar al-Khattab (634–44 CE)
- Usman (644–56 CE)
- Ali (656–61 CE)
- The Umayyads (661–750 CE)
- The Abbasids (750–1258 CE)

The Quran

The word of god, as conveyed to Muhammad, forms the Quran, Islam's sacred text. Consisting of 114 suras or chapters, the Quran defines the nature of god, and explains beliefs, religious duties, and right actions.

SUNNIS AND SHIAS

After his death, some of Muhammad's followers elected Abu Bakr–a faithful disciple and father of Aisha, one of Muhammad's favorite wives–as the caliph. This group later became known as Sunnis (people of custom and community). Others felt Muhammad had wanted Ali, his cousin and son-in-law, to be his successor. They became known as Shias (partisans) of Ali.

BATTLE OF KARBALA

In 661, Ali's son Hasan was chosen as his successor, but was opposed by Muawiya, governor of Syria, who founded the Umayyad dynasty. The succession of Muawiya's son Yazid was opposed by Husain, brother of Hasan, leading to the battle of Karbala in Iraq in 680 CE. There Husain was killed and his followers were defeated by Yazid's forces.

700–729 CE

- **c. 700–92** Life of Wu Daozi of China, painter of Buddhist frescoes.
- **c. 700–900** Pueblo people in Arizona, North America, build houses above the ground.

- **710–70** Life of Du Fu, Chinese poet.
- **712** Arab Muhammad bin Kasim conquers Sind (now in Pakistan).
- **715** Islamic forces conquer most of Spain.

Rule of the caliphs

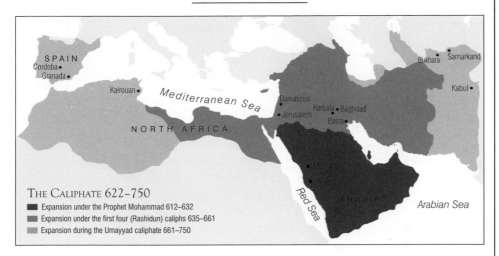

THE CALIPHATE 622–750
- Expansion under the Prophet Mohammad 612–632
- Expansion under the first four (Rashidun) caliphs 635–661
- Expansion during the Umayyad caliphate 661–750

Map labels: SPAIN · Cordoba · Granada · Kairouan · Mediterranean Sea · NORTH AFRICA · Damascus · Jerusalem · Karbala · Baghdad · Basra · Bukhara · Samarkand · Kabul · Mecca · Medina · ARABIA · Red Sea · Arabian Sea

In Asia, the Arab Abbasid caliphs overthrew the Umayyads, and shifted their capital to Baghdad, but the political and religious authority of the caliphs began to decline after about 850 CE. The 800–1000 CE period was known for developments in science, technology, medicine, philosophy, education, and culture. Among the caliphs, Haroun al-Rashid (r. 786–809 CE) encouraged arts, culture, and scholarship. An embellished account of life at his court is given in *The Thousand and One Nights*. Another notable caliph was Haroun's son Al-Mamun (r. 813–33 CE) who set up the Baitul Hikmah or the House of Wisdom. Here, literature from various parts of the world was translated into Arabic.

The Arab world was known as a melting pot of different cultures and ideas. Philosophers like Al-Kindi, Al-Farabi, and Ibn Sina imbued Islamic thought with ideas from Greek philosophy. In addition, the Arabs disseminated algebra, Arabic numerals, and knowledge from other parts of the world, such as paper-making and gunpowder (both from China).

Politically, however, other dynasties began to assert themselves. A branch of the earlier Umayyads ruled independently from Spain. Cordoba, in Spain, was a great center of learning and culture, and, during the 10th century, it was the largest city in Europe. Iran, Afghanistan, and North Africa were among other areas over which the Abbasids gradually lost control.

c. 716 Traditional date for arrival in India of a group of Zoroastrians from Iran; came to be known as Parsis.

c. 718–1492 Period of Reconquista: attempt of Spain and Portugal to regain control of territories in Iberian peninsula from Arabs.

721–c. 815 Life of Jabir, Arab alchemist.

729 Kingdom of Nanzhao founded in western Yunan, China; declines after **836**.

CONTINUITY AND CHANGE

Main tenets of Islam

The basic tenets of Islam have been compiled in the Quran. Some of these tenets are as follows:

- Allah is one and powerful and only He is to be served and worshipped. Image worship is forbidden.
- Belief in Angels: Allah created invisible beings called angels, who work to administer Allah's wishes. These angels are all around us, recording our words and deeds.
- Allah communicates through human prophets. The main message of all the prophets has always been that there is only One true God and He alone is worthy of being worshipped.
- Allah has revealed wisdom and instructions through "books" to some of the prophets. They believe that the *Quran* is Allah's final revelation which was revealed to Prophet Muhammad.
- Belief in the Day of Judgment: There is life after death. One will be rewarded with life in Heaven or punished in Hell according to one's deeds. Allah will show mercy and fairness in judgment. According to Islam, those who reject faith in Allah will be eternally punished in the fire of Hell.
- Belief in Destiny and Divine Decree; Allah is the Sustainer of all life and Muslims believe that nothing happens except by His Will and with His full knowledge. This belief does not contradict the idea of free will. As Allah has full knowledge of our choice beforehand, He does not force us because His knowledge is complete. This recognition helps the believer through difficulties and hardships.

One should observe the Five Pillars of Islam which are:

Kalma (reciting hymns from the *Quran*), *Namaz* (praying), *Zaqat* (charity), *Ramzan* (the holy month of fasting during which one should stay away from drinking, gambling, etc.), and *Haj* (the pilgrimage to Mecca, which is in Saudi Arabia, at least once during one's lifetime).

731–788 CE

731 Benedictine monk, the Venerable Bede, completes *Historia Ecclesiastica Gentis Anglorum* (Ecclesiastical History of the English People).

c. 740–1000 Rashtrakuta dynasty rules in central India.

746 Greeks reoccupy Cyprus, drive out Arabs.

c. 750 *Beowulf*, epic poem in Old English, composed.

765 Ismaili sect founded in Islam.

773 Charlemagne annexes Lombard kingdom.

Trade

Trade led to economic prosperity, which in turn led to development in various other fields. Certain important trade routes linking the Mediterranean Sea with China and India were controlled by Abbasids. Trade between Europe and the East was completely in the hands of the Arabs for about 700 years, until the discovery of the sea routes around Africa by the Europeans in the 15th century.

Baghdad became a flourishing and rich city as it stood at the meeting points of trade routes. The Arabs, by and large, traded in commodities and items like ivory from Africa, linen from Egypt, silk, jewelry, spices from the East, and fur and honey from Russia. A slave trade was also widely prevalent among the Arabs.

Intellectual progress

New styles in architecture, literature, and poetry were created and introduced by Arabs. The *Rubaiyat* of Omar Khayyam, *Shahnama* by Al-Firdausi, and the *Arabian Nights* were some of the famous works of the Arabs.

Omar Khayyam was a renowned poet, mathematician, and astronomer. The Indian system of numerals in Europe was introduced by the Abbasids; hence the phrase "Arabic numerals" was coined. The word **algebra** is also of Arabic origin.

Omar Khayyam.

Omar Khayyam wrote: "By the help of God and with His precious assistance, I say that Algebra is a scientific art. The objects with which it deals are absolute numbers and measurable quantities which, though themselves unknown, are related to 'things' which are known, whereby the determination of the unknown quantities is possible." (*Treatise on Demonstration of Problems of Algebra*, 1070 CE). The Abbasids were open to learning. They translated many works of literature from Greek, Chinese, Egyptian, and Sanskrit into Arabic. The Arabs learnt about the manufacturing of glass, paper, and use of the mariner's compass (from the Chinese), geometry (from the Greeks), and mathematics (from the Indians). They first showed the use of the **astrolabe** for navigation. They were successful in diagnosing the cause of diseases such as smallpox and tuberculosis.

CONTINUITY AND CHANGE

Tangs to Sungs

In China, the Tangs saw their authority reduced by the rise of regional military governors. In 907 CE, the dynasty was overthrown, and a period of unrest followed, until the founding of the Sung dynasty in 960 CE.

The Fujiwara regents

The Japanese capital shifted to Heian-kyo (Kyoto) in 794 CE, the start of the Heian period. Members of the Fujiwara clan began to dominate the government, ruling as regents on behalf of the emperor. There was a great flowering of art and culture. Distinctively Japanese paintings, different from the earlier Chinese-influenced styles, depicted court life and stories of gods. Japanese Buddhist art was heavily influenced by Shingon beliefs, depicting mandalas or cosmic diagrams. Two types of Japanese script developed.

Despite clashing with other powerful clans, such as the Taira and the Minamoto, the Fujiwara continued to control the throne until the mid 11th century.

Indian dynasties, Shankara's philosophy

From around 700 CE, a number of dynasties rose in north India who called themselves Rajputs (from "*raja putra*," or "sons of kings"). In the south, the Chola dynasty became the most prominent. Both in the south and the north, great temples

were built. Perhaps the greatest and most influential philosophy of India, known as Advaita Vedanta, was propagated at this time by the saint Shankara (c. 788–820 CE). In essence, it states that there is only one true reality known as Brahman, the Absolute: Uncreated, unchanging, and eternal.

Chola temple at Pudukkottai, Tamil Nadu, India.

794–827 CE

794 Emperor Kammu unites Japanese islands.
c. 800 Compositions of woman poet, Ono-no Kamachi of Japan.
• First castles built in western Europe.
800 Charlemagne crowned Holy Roman Emperor.

800–909 Aghlabid dynasty rules in Tunis, North Africa.
c. 800–950 Aksum empire declines, but Christianity continues in Ethiopia.
c. 801–73 Life of Al-Kindi, Islamic philosopher.

THE SUFIS

Tracing their origin to an inner circle around the Prophet Mohammad, the Sufis are esoteric Islamic sects. Over time, many different Sufi schools developed. Meditation, asceticism, devotion, repetition of the word of God, music, and specific breathing techniques are used by Sufis to unite with the "god within."

Rabia al-Adawiyya, the first female Sufi saint.

SUFI MOVEMENT

An offshoot of Islam, the **Sufi movement** was led by mystics from Persia in 11th century CE. The Sufi saints believed that there is only one God and all human beings are his children. Their beliefs and convictions were like *Bhakti* saints, in terms of equality and love for fellow beings. They discarded the ritualistic practices of feasts and fasts. Their emphasis was on approaching God through love and devotion and hence a form of devotional music (*qawwali*) emerged. Religious tolerance was prevalent and they mingled freely with Hindus. The *Sufis* were categorized into 12 *Silsilahs*, that is, orders.

MOIN-UD-DIN CHISTI

A Sufi saint, Khwaja Moin-ud-din Chisti, came to India in CE 1192. He lived in Lahore and Delhi for a short period of time and then shifted to Ajmer. His *dargah* at Ajmer is visited by thousands of pilgrims including a very large number of Hindus from within the country and beyond. He died in 1235.

BABA FARID

In the Chisti Sufi Order, **Baba Shaikh Farid** was one of the founding fathers. He was a disciple of Khwaja Qutubuddin Bakhtiyar Kaki, who was a disciple of Sheikh Moin-ud-din Chisti. The area he chose to preach in was Haryana and Punjab, and he convinced many people that by loving God's people one can love God Himself. His followers included both Hindus and Muslims. Some of his verses have been included in the Adi Granth.

NIZAMUDDIN AULIYA AND SALIM CHISTI

Nizamuddin Auliya of Delhi and Salim Chisti of Sikri were the other famed Sufi saints from the Chisti order. They preached that '*Ishwar*' and '*Allah*' are the two different names of the same **Superior Being**. The basic theme of their teaching was love for humanity and religious tolerance.

809–17 Wars between Byzantine empire and Bulgars.

c. 815–77 Life of philosopher John Scotus Erigena; introduces Neoplatonism in Christianity.

827–69 Life of St Cyril, a Byzantine monk; creates Glagolitic, a Slavonic alphabet; along with his brother St Methodius, converts Danubian Slavs to Christianity.

CONTINUITY AND CHANGE

Dargah at Ajmer.

EFFECTS OF SUFI MOVEMENTS

The Sufi Movement was widespread in India, embracing almost the whole country. This had far-reaching effects:

Amir Khusrau.

- The Movement taught the people the concept of equality, brotherhood, and religious tolerance.
- As a result of the efforts put in by the Sufi saints, Hindus and Muslims started coming closer to each other which resulted in social and cultural amity between them.

During the Sultanate period, a great deal of progress was made in literature, not only in Sanskrit but also in other regional languages, including Persian. Significantly, the language of the nobles and the court was Persian. Learning was patronized by the Sultanate rulers, and Amir Khusrau was the most famous literary figure of the period.

830–868 CE

830–70 Life of Al-Bukhari, compiler of *Al-Sahih*, a collection of hadiths, or sayings of Mohammad.

843 Treaty of Verdun; sons of Louis I agree on division of Carolingian empire.

c. **845–925** Life of Al-Razi, Islamic physician from Rey, Iran; wrote *Al-Hawi*, a medical encyclopedia.

c. **850** Borubodur, large Buddhist temple, constructed near Magelang, in Java, Indonesia.

- Louis II becomes Holy Roman Emperor.

c. **850–900** Early Cyrillic alphabet, related to Glagolitic, devised by a follower of St Cyril.

MUSIC AND DANCE

Music in India was vastly enriched through the Indo-Islamic collaboration, and the Hindustani style of music was born. New musical instruments, such as the rabab and the sarangi, were introduced in India, and new musical traditions were brought by the Turkish rulers from Arabia, Iran, and Central Asia.

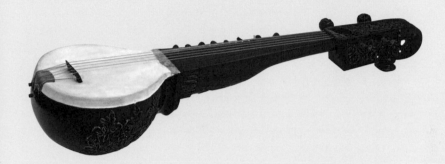

Rabab.

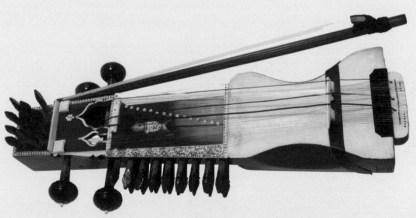

Sarangi.

850–1846 Kanem-Bornu empire flourishes in Africa.

c. 858–929 Life of Al-Battani, Arab astronomer and mathematician.

858 Fujiwara clan begins to control Japanese emperors.

862 Vikings rule north Russia.

c. 865 Vikings conquer parts of England.

868 Tulunid dynasty founded in Egypt.

• Buddhist text *Diamond Sutra* printed in China with wood blocks; oldest extant printed book.

CONTINUITY AND CHANGE

AMIR KHUSRAU

Apart from being a great poet, Amir Khusrau was a renowned musician as well. It is believed that he invented the sitar and the *tabla*.

It is also said that he introduced many ragas of Indo-Arabic genre. A new tradition of musical gatherings started to flourish under the patronage of the rulers. The Mughal rulers, with the sole exception of Aurangzeb, were extremely fond of music. The development of Hindustani music, with the amalgamation of Indian and Persian styles, was a major event which resulted in the creation of different styles of vocal music renditions such as **Thumri, Khayal,** and **Ghazal**.

Amīr Khusrau was born in 1253 in Patiali [which is now in Uttar Pradesh, India]. He was a great poet and historian, and is considered to be one of India's greatest Persian-language poets.

The son of a Turkish officer in the service of Iltutmish, Sultan of Delhi, Amīr Khusrau was showered with respect throughout his life by the Muslim rulers of Delhi and he enjoyed the patronage of them, especially Sultan Ghīyās-ud-Dīn Balban and his son Muhammad Khan of Multan. Muhammad Nizam-ud-Dīn Awliya was his guiding light during his youth, and he became a dedicated follower of the saint of Delhi of the Chishti Dervish order. He was buried next to the saint's tomb.

Interestingly, Amir Khusrau was sometimes known as "the parrot of India." He wrote numerous works, including five divans, which were compiled at different periods in his life. His *Khamsah* (Pentalogy) is a group of five long idylls. Apart from his poetry, he is known for a number of prose works, including the *Khaza in al-futuh* (The Treasure-Chambers of the Victories), also known by the title *Tarikh-e Alai* (The History of Ala). Two historical poems for which he is well known are *Nuh Sipihr* (The Nine Heavens) and the *Tughlaq-namah* (The Book of Tughlaq). The great poet breathed his last around 1325 AD in Delhi.

Whirling Dervishes performing the dance called the sema, a religious dance performed to express emotion and achieve the wisdom and love of the almighty.

868–907 CE

c. 868–1000 Vikings colonize Iceland, Greenland, and parts of North America.

873–950 Life of Al-Farabi, Islamic philosopher; proposes universal approach to religion.

875 Charles the Bald is Holy Roman Emperor.

878 Alfred the Great allows Danes to occupy parts of England.

881 Pope John III becomes Charles III, Holy Roman Emperor.

886–1267 Chola dynasty rules in south India.

After the death of Charlemagne's son Louis the Pious in 840 CE, the Carolingian empire in western Europe began to decline and disintegrate. The Byzantine empire was still flourishing, and reached its height under Basil II (963–1025).

The Vikings

A Viking longboat.

Much of Europe at this time was dominated by Viking raids. Also known as Norsemen or Northmen, the Vikings were warriors from Scandinavia who crossed the seas in their longships, invading and setting up trading centers. In England, the Vikings began to plunder coastal towns and settle in some areas in the late eighth century. They settled in Iceland from around 900 CE, and then colonized Greenland. They also settled in Ireland and in Normandy, and even reached Russia. Viking raids died out by the end of the 11th century.

NORSE GODS AND LITERATURE

Thor and Hymir in an 18th-century Icelandic manuscript.

Thor, the god of thunder, and Odin, a wizard and warrior god, were among the main Viking deities. Dating back to an earlier period, the gods attained their full form at the time of the Vikings, though most accounts of them were written down later. Viking myths and legends were composed in Iceland and Scandinavia, in works known as "sagas." Two main works of this type are known as Eddas. Snorri Sturluson (1172–1241) of Iceland compiled the Prose or Younger Edda, consisting of a prologue and three parts. The first two parts provide instruction on earlier meters used in poetry, so that the poems of the oral tradition could be understood. The third part includes a number of Norse myths. The Poetic, or Elder Edda, is contained in a manuscript of the 13th century, but has a collection of poems on heroes and gods composed between 800–1100.

Magyar invasions

Other European invaders during this period were the Magyars from Romania and Hungary. They penetrated Germany, northern Italy, and France, but were defeated by Otto, king of Germany, in the Battle of Lechfield, in 955. In 962, Otto was crowned Holy Roman Emperor, and later became king of Italy.

891 *Anglo-Saxon Chronicle*, a history of England, written by monks.
895 Magyars settle in present-day Hungary and part of Romania.
c. 900 Liturgical polyphony known as organum has developed; important step in growth of western music.
• Post-classic period of Maya civilization begins.

• Kingdom of Chimor established in Peru.
900 Settlers from Cook Island reach New Zealand.
906 Annam (Vietnam) frees itself from Chinese rule.
907–26 Khitan Mongols conquer Inner Mongolia and part of north China.

Kievan Rus

The name Russia derives from Rus, a people whom some scholars believe were Vikings, although others think they were Slavic. Slavic tribes had occupied western Russia from around the seventh century, but Vikings came to the region evidently as traders. According to the *Primary Chronicle*, a 12th-century account, a Viking named Rurik became the elected ruler of Novgorod in *c.* 860. His successors extended their territory to Kiev, and Kievan Rus became a large and prosperous state in the 10th and 11th centuries. A differing opinion says that Kievan Rus was a Slavic state, only briefly occupied by Vikings, who were later absorbed by the

A painting showing the baptism of Vladimir I, *c.* 1890s.

Slavs. Vladimir the Great (980–1015) adopted Byzantine Christianity, and Byzantine art styles influenced Russia.

Alfred the Great.

England, Scotland, and Wales

England began to unite under Athelstan, king of Wessex (r. 925–39), who was the first to rule the whole of England after he gained control of Northumbria in 927. In Scotland, the Picts, Scots, Britons, and Angles were the four main groups, and in 843 the Scot, Kenneth MacAlpin, conquered the Pictish lands, creating a kingdom known as Alba. In 940, Malcolm I of Alba expanded the territory, and during the next two centuries the whole of Scotland was united. Meanwhile, Rhodri Mawr (d. 878), prince of Gwynned, defeated the Vikings and the English, and became king over most of Wales.

909–950 CE

909–1171 Fatimid dynasty rules North Africa and Sicily.

910 Benedictine Abbey of Cluny founded in France.

911 Rollo, Viking chief, settles in France.

912–61 Abd Al-Rahman III, Umayyad caliph, rules in Cordoba, Spain.

915–65 Life of Arab poet Al-Mutanabbi; also writes political satires.

925 Athelstan becomes king of Wessex; unites all the English kingdoms into one.

933 Jewish scholar Saadia Ben Joseph writes *Book of Opinions and Beliefs* on Jewish religion, law, and traditions.

The Caliphate loses its hold

Al-Azhar mosque, Cairo, Egypt.

Parts of North Africa remained under the Abbasid caliphs, while some areas asserted their independence. Sicily was conquered during the time of emir Ziayadat Allah I (817–38). Kairouan (Al-Qayrawan), the Aghlabid capital, flourished in the ninth century. Its great mosque, first constructed in the seventh century, was rebuilt at this time, and still stands today.

In northern Algeria, the Rustamid state, known for its learning and religious tolerance, was independent from 761–909. Other independent states were the principality of Banu Midrar, and the Idrisid state, in southern and northern Morocco, respectively. A new Shia Muslim dynasty, the Fatimids, emerged under Abaidullah in 909, and annexed Ifriqiyah and the other states in the region. The Fatimid dynasty reached its height under Al-Muizz (r. 953–75), who conquered Egypt, Palestine, and part of Syria, and founded the town of Al-Qahirah (Cairo). The great Al-Azhar mosque, as well as Al-Azhar University, was constructed in Cairo. Fatimid power began to decline after 1100. In West Africa, Ghana remained prosperous. There were several other states in the rest of the continent.

The Anasazi

Various groups lived in settlements across North America, including those later known as Pueblos. The early Pueblos, sometimes referred to as the Anasazi, date back to about 100 CE, but their society began to increase from around 700. Their houses had circular underground rooms, probably used for ceremonial purposes.

Anasazi pottery had black painted designs on a white or grey background, while petroglyphs and pictographs were other artistic forms. After about 1050, the Anasazi built extraordinary stone and molded-brick houses along cliff walls.

An Anasazi pot.

c. 935–c.1002 Life of German woman poet and chronicler Hrosvitha; best known for her moral comedies.

935 Koryo dynasty founds a united kingdom in Korea.

937 Battle of Brunanburh in northern England; Athelstan of England defeats Scots, Irish, and Danes.

939 Ngo dynasty founded in Vietnam; marks end of Chinese supremacy.

942–50 Welsh law codified and written down.

950 *Njal's Saga* composed in Iceland.

950–1050 Igbo-Ukwu culture in eastern Nigeria.

• Temples with erotic sculptures built at Khajuraho, India.

CONTINUITY AND CHANGE

The Toltecs

The Maya civilization began to decline around the 10th century, and most of their temple complexes were abandoned. However, in the Yucatan peninsula, cities like Chichen Itza, Uxmal, Ednza, and Coba, still flourished. A group of new people, the Nahuatl-speaking Toltecs, appeared. Probably an agglomeration of several different ethnic groups, they migrated from northern Mexico, and reached central Mexico around 900 or even earlier. With their capital at modern Tula, they probably occupied some Maya centers.

According to traditional accounts, the Toltecs under the leadership of Mixcoatl sacked and burned Teotihuacan. His son, Toplitzin, united a number of states into an empire, and established the cult of Quetzalcoatl. Skilled in medicine, astronomy, and craft, the Toltecs constructed huge statues, monumental porticoes, serpent columns, and reclining Chac-Mool figures.

The Mixtecs

The Zapotecs, who had been in southern Mexico from the first century BCE or earlier, were replaced by the Mixtecs. The latter flourished from the 9th to 16th centuries. The Mixtecs specialized in stone and metal work, polychrome pottery, feather mosaics, and fine embroidered textiles. They used a calendar similar to the Aztecs. Monte Alban, in the Oaxaca valley, has both Zapotec and Mixtec remains, including plazas and pyramids, a ball-game court, and a number of tombs.

QUETZALCOATL

A god of the Toltecs and Aztecs, his name is usually translated as "feathered serpent." The god was earlier worshipped at Teotihuacan and by the Maya under the name Kukulcan. Under the Toltecs, he was god of the morning and evening star, and the central deity in ceremonial worship.

The ruins of Monte Alban in Oaxaca, Mexico.

959–997

959 Edgar, king of Wessex, becomes the king of England.
960 Sung dynasty reunifies China.
962 Otto the Great of Germany crowned Holy Roman Emperor.
• Alptigin founds Ghaznavid dynasty in Afghanistan.

963 Mieszco I founds kingdom of Poland.
c. 964 Great Mosque (Mezquita) constructed in Cordoba.
970 Paper money introduced in China.
970s Fatimids annex Egypt from Tulunids.
c. 973–1050 Life of Arab Al-Biruni; writes over 100 works, mostly on various branches of science.

Two seemingly contradictory trends were a feature of this period. On one hand, there was the growth in long-distance trade and new ideas, while on the other hand, some groups were stagnant and tied to the land. New routes were discovered, and roads were built across borders, facilitating economic activity. Towns increased in number, and, with universities opening in Europe, there was a new impetus to learning.

Feudalism

Manuscript illustration of emperor Charlemagne accepting the fealty of his vassal, Roland.

Wars and unrest gave rise to a static organization of society with a hierarchical framework of land ownership that came to be called feudalism. This structure existed in western Europe between *c.* 800 and 1400, and in other areas of the world at different times. Feudalism involved the grant of large tracts of land by the king—who was at the apex of the structure—to people of high standing, such as noblemen, important officials, rich merchants, and influential lawyers. Monasteries were also beneficiaries.

In return, the landowner paid rent or taxes to the king, and provided certain services, including an army in times of war. The landlord maintained peace and dispensed justice within the area under his control. His manor or estate was the economic and social unit of life, and included the manor house, tracts of cultivated and forest land, and one or more villages. Castles were built by kings and lords for the defence and protection of their lands.

The two types of land in the estate were those which the landowner cultivated himself, and those he sublet to vassals, who could cultivate or further sublet them. In return for the land (a fief), the vassal had to pledge allegiance (fealty) to the lord.

The 12th-century Bamburgh castle on the coast of Northumbria is a typical example of a medieval castle.

980–1037 Life of Ibn Sina (Avicenna), Iranian philosopher.

983 *Taiping yulan*, a 1000-volume encyclopedia, produced in China.

985–1014 Chola king Rajaraja I rules in south India.

c. 986 Viking Eric the Red sets up colony in Greenland.

987 Hugh Capet becomes the king of France; founds Capetian dynasty.

990–92 Aelfric, English abbot and writer, composes *Catholic Homilies* in Old English.

c. 994 Japanese court lady Sei Shonagon composes *Pillow Book*, anecdotes of her life.

997 Stephan I becomes first king of Hungary.

KNIGHTS

Symbol of the Knights Templar.

Initially, "knight" was just a term for a horseman, but gradually it came to indicate warrior nobles. In the early feudal period, the vassals of a manor were usually knights. In battle, knights wore heavy armor and helmets, and were identified through painted designs on their armor and shields. There were also military knights who had no individual land holdings, but were organized into orders to which land grants were made. Among these orders were the Teutonic Knights, Knights Templar and Knights Hospitaller. Stories of knights, such as the legends of King Arthur and his Knights of the Round Table, were popular in medieval days.

The Knights of Christ, an offshoot of the Knights Templar.

Peasants and serfs

In England, two types of peasants lived in the manor villages: Those who were free and those who were serfs. Free peasants had a hard life but were better off than serfs, who were peasants tied to the land and under the rule of the lord. In the highest category of serfs were villeins, who voluntarily entered into an arrangement with the landlord to gain land and his protection. The institution of serfdom was probably the successor of the Roman slave system, though some serfs were granted the use of land by the lord, and, in return, had to provide a certain amount of free labor, and some produce. The system was not uniform, and functioned in varying degrees in different parts of the world. In much of Europe, serfdom died out between the 14th and 16th centuries, although it continued in Austria, Hungary, Russia, and some parts of eastern Europe till the 19th century. In Asia, some elements of feudalism existed in several countries.

A 14th-century painting showing serfs tilling the land around a French lord's castle.

997–1025

997–1030 Mahmud of Ghazni rules in Afghanistan.

c. 1000 Chinese invent gunpowder.

• Maoris settle in New Zealand.

1000 People speaking Bantu languages form kingdoms in South Africa.

1000–38 Under Stephen I, Christianity becomes state religion of Hungary.

c. 1000–1200 Italian towns Rome, Venice, Florence, and others become city-states.

c. 1008–20 Court lady of Japan, Murasaki Shikibu, writes *Tale of Genji*, a novel.

1010–1225 Ly dynasty rules territory of present-day Vietnam.

In Asia, the Arab empire was breaking up, though the Abbasids continued to be the caliphs of Baghdad. The Buyids or Buwayids (945–1055) from Iran captured Baghdad and seized political power, but allowed the caliph to retain his title.

The Kharaghan twin towers (1067): Seljuk tombs in Qazvin, Iran.

Seljuk Turks

Among the rising powers were the Seljuks, a group of Turks originally from Central Asia. Tughril (Togrul) Beg, their leader, conquered most of Iran and Iraq, including Baghdad, in 1055, and became protector of the caliph. His successors, Alp Arslan and Malik Shah, extended control into Syria, Palestine, and Anatolia (Rum). Alp won a great victory in the Battle of Manzikert in 1071 against the Byzantine empire. The Seljuks, with their capital at Isfahan, Iran, were great patrons of Persian art and literature. After the death of Malik Shah, the empire was divided among his sons, and different lines of Seljuk sultans ruled from Hamadan, Kerman, Syria, and Anatolia.

Muslims and Cholas in India

The Rajput dynasties were prominent in north India. Like the European knights, Rajputs had a tradition of chivalry and protection of the weak. From the region of Afghanistan, Mahmud of Ghazni (997–1030) made several raids into India, followed in the next century by Muizuddin Muhammad of Ghur (1173–1206), who defeated the combined Rajput kings in the Battle of Tarain (1192), and paved the way for the rule of Muslim sultans in north India.

South India was dominated by the Chola dynasty which had a strong army and navy, and an efficient administration, with self-government in the villages. Devotees of the god Shiva, they built a number of temples, the greatest being the Brihadeshvara at Thanjavur.

SELJUKS OF ANATOLIA

By the end of the 12th century, only the Anatolian line of Seljuks remained. They lasted till 1308, and are known for their art and architecture. More than 100 caravanserais, trading posts and shelters for traveling caravans, were established on roads across their territories. The largest of these, the Sultan Han, built in 1229 between Konya and Aksaray, covers an area of 42,000 sq. ft.

1016–35 Canute (Knut) II of Denmark is the king of England; 1018 becomes king of Denmark; 1028 of Norway.

1019–30 Airlangga becomes the king of Java; frees country from rule of Malay Sri Vijaya kingdom.

c. 1021–58 Life of Spanish Jewish philosopher and poet Solomon ibn Gabirol; writes Neoplatonic treatise *Mekor Chayim* (The Fountain of Life).

1023–91 Muslim Abbadid dynasty rules from Seville, Spain; known for opulence and patronage of arts.

c. 1025 Italian Benedictine monk Guido d'Arezzo develops musical notation.

THE RISE AND FALL OF DYNASTIES

Advances under the Sung

Chinese movable type.

In China, the Sung dynasty came to power in 960. Kaifeng was the capital under the Northern Sung (960–1126). The Southern Sung (1127–1279), with their capital at Hangzhou, controlled southern China. The Sung period saw a growth in the economy, and new techniques in agriculture and craft production. Double-cropping began in rice cultivation, and iron and textile production increased. Varieties of pottery were made. A highpoint was reached in art, particularly in landscape painting. Poetry and music flourished, and in printing, movable type was invented, leading to the production of books.

Shoguns and samurai

The power of the Fujiwaras declined in Japan, and the Minamoto family gained supremacy. In 1192, Yorimoto declared himself shogun, or military ruler, at Kamakura. The samurai, the hereditary warrior class, became powerful. At the end of the 12th century, Zen Buddhism was introduced in Japan, and soon became the religion of the samurai. The modern Japanese language began to develop at this time.

A samurai warrior.

SHAH NAMAH

Firdausi, a Persian Muslim, resented the Arab and Turk occupation of Iran. He wrote the Shah Namah *(Book of Kings) in 1010. The epic story, in 60,000 couplets, has semi-mythical and historical accounts of pre-Islamic Persia.*

An illustrated folio from the *Shah Namah*.

1027–1075 CE

1027–1137 Traditional dates of life of Indian philosopher Ramanuja; puts forward philosophy of qualified non-dualism.

1037 Spanish kingdoms of Castile and Leon unite.

1044 King Anawrahta establishes kingdom of Pagan (Burma), uniting northern Burmese

and Southern Mon people of present-day Myanmar.

1046 Clement II appointed the pope by German king Henry III; crowns Henry Holy Roman Emperor.

c. 1050 Port of Mombasa established in East Africa.

The Holy Roman empire, in the west, and the Byzantine empire, in the east, dominated Europe and parts of Asia and Africa. Their borders were not static, and were constantly changing. Although the court language of the western empire was Latin, the eastern empire used Greek, and their views on Christianity also varied. A formal split between the Western and Eastern branches of the Church took place in 1054. There were also conflicts between the pope and secular authorities of both empires.

Robert Curthose (c. 1051-1134), Duke of Normandy, at the seige of Antioch in the First Crusade.

The Crusades

After the Turkish victory at the Battle of Manzikert in 1071, the Byzantine emperor Alexius I (1081–1118) appealed to Pope Urban II (1042–99), who authorized a holy war to recapture Jerusalem. A series of wars then began, known as the Crusades. Though ostensibly motivated by religious factors, the Crusades were also fought for economic reasons and the control of valuable lands. The First Crusade succeeded in capturing Antioch and Jerusalem; however, the Second Crusade (1147–49) ended in disaster. The Seljuks re-established their hold on Anatolia in 1176. Saladin (Salah ad-din), the Kurdish prime minister of Egypt, overthrew the Fatimid dynasty in 1171, and formed a kingdom from the Nile to the Tigris rivers. In 1187, he invaded the Latin kingdom of Jerusalem and the Frankish states. The Third Crusade (1189–92) did not succeed in recapturing Jerusalem. More Crusades took place in succeeding centuries.

TOWNS

Despite the wars and battles, trade increased, and numerous urban centers emerged by the 11th century. Some of the great cities were London, Paris, Cordoba, and Venice. Town dwellers, who were artisans, merchants, and craftsmen (often organized into guilds), paid a tax to the lord who owned the land, but otherwise did not owe him service or obedience. Some towns in Europe were autonomous.

1051–1107 Life of Mi Fei, Chinese landscape painter; introduces ink-splash technique.

1058–1111 Life of Islamic philosopher and theologian Al-Ghazali.

1066 Norman conquest of England.

c. 1070 Somadeva of India composes *Katha Sarit Sagara* in Sanskrit, a collection of stories and fables.

1070 Tilantongo kingdom, a Mixtec state in Oaxaca, expands.

1073 Gregory VII becomes pope; introduces Church reforms.

c. 1075–1141 Life of Judah Ha Levi, Jewish physician and philosopher of Judaeo-Arabic school; composes religious and secular verse.

William, and Brian Boru

The Normans, under William the Conqueror, won the Battle of Hastings against Harold II of England in 1066, thus beginning a new era in English history. A land survey was carried out during William's reign to assess the amount of taxes he could raise. The *Domesday Book*, as the compilation is called, is an invaluable source for English history of that period.

In Ireland, Brian Boru, king of Munster, began to unite the different kingdoms, making himself high king. He was killed in 1040 fighting Vikings.

Romanesque and Gothic architecture

Art, architecture, literature, and philosophy flourished. Universities were established at Bologna, Paris, and Oxford. Romanesque architecture, typified by strong pillars and rounded arches, emerged around 1000. Another new style, Gothic, developed from around 1135. It was expressed particularly in religious themes: Cathedrals were built with tall spires, flying buttresses, and vaulted ceilings, and were decorated with stained glass windows. Arches were pointed and pillars were tall and slender. In art, strong and bright colors were used.

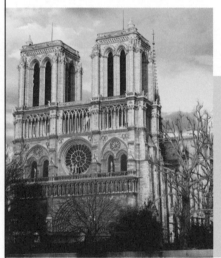

MONASTERIES, CENTERS OF CHRISTIANITY

Christianity and the Church formed an important part of life in Europe, and also provided an impetus to learning, art, and music. New monastic orders were formed, building monasteries where monks or nuns could devote themselves to the service of Christ, and where monks studied, preserved, copied, and illustrated manuscripts. Music was composed for church services, leading to the development of polyphony.

The Gothic-style Notre Dame cathedral, Paris, France.

1078–1110 CE

1078 Philosopher St. Anselm composes *Proslogium* (Discourses), containing ontological proof of the existence of god.

1079–1142 Life of Peter Abelard, French philosopher; Paris becomes center of religious learning.

1080 Toledo in Spain captured by Christians as part of Reconquista; **1118** Saragossa.

1084 Kyanzittha becomes king of Pagan dynasty in Burma; strong and tolerant rule.

1086 *Domesday Book* provides detailed land survey of England.

The Viking Leif Ericson sailed from Greenland and established a settlement in Newfoundland. Elsewhere in North America, there were numerous cultures, including the early Pueblos (Anasazi), the Mississippi, and the Mogollon. In Mesoamerica, Maya and Toltec cities continued to be occupied.

Several changes were taking place in Africa, as dynasties and kingdoms rose and fell. The Shia Fatimid dynasty was overthrown by Saladin in 1171. Shewa, on the central Ethiopian plateau, was an independent kingdom from c. 950–1400. In South Africa, Bantu peoples set up kingdoms. In West Africa, the kingdoms of Tukrur and Gao flourished on the back of the gold trade.

Mississippi culture

Large towns and intensive maize cultivation were features of this widespread culture, which had emerged along the Mississippi river around 750. It existed in the Midwestern, eastern, and southeastern United States up to 1500. The central point of each town was a ceremonial plaza. Around this, there were earthen oval or pyramidal mounds, on which temples or important houses were built.

A painting by Herbert Roe (2004) of the Kincaid site in Illinois, an important center of the Mississippi culture.

CAHOKIA

The most important city of the Mississippi culture, Cahokia possibly had a population of 50,000 by around 1200. The grand plaza of Cahokia measured 16 hectares (40 acres). One of the Cahokia mounds contained the remains of a man in his 40s, who could have been a ruler. He was buried on more than 20,000 marine-shell disc beads, arranged in the shape of a falcon. There are several other burials at the site, some of which seem to be of sacrificial victims.

1088 Chinese Su Sung constructs a water-powered mechanical clock.

1095 Pope Urban II asks Christians to fight a crusade against Muslims; **1096** First Crusade starts.

1095–1139 Life of Avempace, philosopher in Islamic Spain; combines ideas from Neoplatonism and logic.

1099 Jerusalem captured by Christians in the First Crusade.

c. 1100–1200 Jayadeva in India composes *Gita Govinda*, devotional poem on the god Krishna, in Sanskrit.

1100–1200 Hohokam people in Arizona, North America, make platform mounds.

CULTURES AND KINGDOMS

Mogollon culture

Located mainly in western Texas, Arizona, and New Mexico, in high altitude desert regions, the Mogollon culture had several branches, the most distinctive being the Mimbres Mogollon. It began around 200 BCE, along the Mimbres river in New Mexico, and reached its height during 1000 to 1200. From around 1000, the earlier pit houses were followed by two- to three-story-high structures made of adobe and masonry, built on the surface. The Mimbres Mogollon are known for their distinctive pottery, black with geometric lines on a white background. Pottery bowls are often found along with burials.

The Almoravids

The Almoravids, a Berber Muslim dynasty, rose to power in 1040 in the Sahara region of Africa, and soon spread to include a large area of northwest Africa, as well as Spain and Portugal. In 1076, Ghana was conquered. Marrakesh, in Morocco, was founded in 1062 as the Almoravid capital. It became one of the largest and richest cities of North Africa, with markets selling goods from all parts of the empire. The Almoravids declined by 1147, when Marrakesh was conquered by the Almohads (1121–1267), another Berber dynasty.

St Giorgis church, Lalibela, Ethiopia.

The Zagwes

According to traditional accounts, a non-Christian queen named Gudit took over the Aksum state (approximately the same area as Ethiopia) around 960, and her descendants continued to rule until 1137. The Agew, one of the subject people of the Aksum, founded a new dynasty, the Zagwe, and ruled Ethiopia between 1137 and 1270. The Zagwe were staunch Christians. One of their greatest kings was Lalibela (r. c. 1185–1225), who created 11 churches carved out of rock, below ground level.

1100–1120

1100 Sufi movement led by mystics from Persia.

1100s Polynesians settle on Pitcairn Island in the south Pacific.

c. 1100–1300 *Mabinogion*, a collection of Welsh stories, including those on Arthurian legend, are composed.

1114–c. 1186 Bhaskara of India composes works on mathematics; uses decimal system.

Western North Africa (The Maghrib)

Art of the Fatimid Period.

Autonomous Muslim Berber powers define the late medieval period (1000–1400 A.D.) in western North Africa. Despite periods of struggle among different dynasties, the entire region is united under Almohad rule. Later, under the Hafsids in the east and Marinids in the west, the Maghrib enjoys stability. Patronage and the creation of metropolitan centers such as Fez, Marrakesh, and Tunis stimulate developments in philosophy and the arts.

Two Berber dynasties, the Zirids and Hammadids, control Tunisia and eastern Algeria, as Fatimid vassals. A Zirid rebellion against the Fatimids in 1050 and subsequent retaliation by the Hilali Bedouin under Fatimid orders bring devastation, including the destruction of Kairouan.

The Hammadids found a fortified citadel (Arabic: qal'a) in the Maadid Mountains of Algeria which is rapidly populated and develops into the first capital (destroyed 1152). The site, known today as the Qal'a Bani Hammad, is an important example of a medieval Muslim city, and its congregational mosque is among the largest in North Africa.

The Almoravids (al-Murabitun), another dynasty of Berber origin, conquer Morocco and found Marrakesh as their capital. They rule parts of the Sahara, Morocco, Algeria, and Spain and control important North African ports as well as trans-Saharan trade. Due to their interest in reviving Islam and strengthening orthodoxy, the arts and architecture in the early period are simple, in contrast to developments in later periods. The mosques of Algiers (ca. 1097), Tlemcen (1136), and Qarawiyin in Fez (1135) are important architectural examples from the Maghrib during this period.

Following their conquest of Almoravid Morocco and Spain, the Almohads (al-Muwahhidun), another Berber dynasty, add Hammadid and Zirid territories (in present-day Algeria and Tunisia) to their realm (1152–60). Religious reformation is integral to Almohad establishment, and their courts in Marrakesh and Sevilla become centers of Islamic learning. The integration of all of the Maghrib as well as Islamic Spain under one rule creates a unified artistic sphere. Developments in architecture include the walls of Fez, Rabat, and Marrakesh and the mosques of Taza (Marrakesh, 1142), the Kutubiyya (Marrakesh, 1147–58), Tinmal (1153–54), the Qasba (Marrakesh, 1195), and Hasan (Rabat, 1199; unfinished).

CULTURES AND KINGDOMS

The Mongols

In 1206, the nomadic Mongol tribes chose Temuchin (c. 1155–1167) as their Khan or leader. Temuchin, the son of Yesugei, a member of one of the royal clans, took the title Gengis (lord). With his capacity to gain the loyalty of different groups, Gengis unified the tribes of Mongolia. Karakoram was established as his capital. He then embarked on a series of conquests, and by the time he died in 1227, his empire occupied a vast territory from the Caspian Sea to the Sea of Japan. Apart from being a great conqueror, Gengis was an efficient organizer. After Gengis's death, the empire was divided among his sons, from whom separate Mongol dynasties arose. However, all owed allegiance to one leader known as the Great Khan, chosen through election by an assembly of Gengis' descendants.

In 1260, Kublai became the Great Khan. He extended control over China, defeating the Southern Sung dynasty in 1279, and founding the Mongol Yuan dynasty. Other Mongol dynasties were those of Greater Iran, Central Asia or Turkestan, and Russia. Kublai reorganized China and built roads throughout the country. He made Buddhism the state religion, and introduced paper money. Porcelain, metalwork, and textiles were produced. His capital was at Dadu (Beijing); the wealth of his summer capital at Shangdu was described by the traveler Marco Polo. After the death of Kublai, in 1294, the power of the Mongols in China began to wane. In 1368, they were replaced by the Ming dynasty. The great Mongol

Gengis Khan. Kublai Khan.

THE MONGOL EMPIRE, c. 13TH CENTURY

GOLDEN HORDE

CHAGHATAI KHANATE

EMPIRE OF THE GREAT KHAN

IL KHANATE

THE TRAVELS OF MARCO POLO

Marco Polo (1254–1324), a Venetian, along with his merchant father and uncle, reached Kublai Khan's court at Shangdu in 1275. Marco was employed by the emperor as his agent. All three Italians came back to Venice in 1295. In the war between Venice and Genoa, Marco served as commander of a Venetian fleet. He was captured and imprisoned, during which time he dictated an astounding account of his travels.

1122–1150

1122–79 First three Lateran Councils held in Rome.
c. 1126–90 Life of Persian poet Anvari; composes elegy *Tears of Khorasan*.
1126–98 Life of Ibn Rushd (Averroes), Islamic philosopher.

c. 1128–1203 Life of theologian and philosopher Alain de Lille, a Flemish Cisterian monk; writes allegorical poem *Anticlaudianus*.
1133–41 French theologian and philosopher Hugh heads monastery school at St. Victor, Paris.

nation covering over 33 million km, with an amazingly large population of over 100 million people was founded by Gengis Khan in 1206. At its height the nation encompassed the majority of territories like from Southeast Asia to central Europe.

Mongol leader Genghis Khan never allowed anyone to paint his portrait, sculpt his image or engrave his likeness on a coin. The first images of him appeared after his death.

During the 13th and 14th centuries the Mongol empire existed and it became over a period of time, the largest land empire with the unification of nomadic tribes of Mongol and Turkic.

The empire expanded its territories in almost every direction through invasions.

The raids conducted by the Mongols were notorious for cruelty in human history. These invasions ultimately connected the east with the west through a treaty called Pax Mongolica (Mongol Peace). This agreement facilitated trade, commodities and exchange of ideologist throughout Eurasia.

The Mongols used a very useful and also very successful tactics of wiping out urban populations which refused to surrender. During the invasion of Kievan Rus', almost all major cities were destroyed. However, in the event of people deciding to surrender, they were spared and treated leniently. In addition to the intimidation policy, the reason behind the rapid expansion was a special skill of invading hostile territories during bitterly cold winters. Among the Mongol commanders, Subotai was one who considered winter as the best time for war as the common people did not venture out of their houses hiding from the bitter cold. The Mongols had the skill of using frozen lakes and rivers as highways for their horsemen.

The Mongol Empire had a lasting impact, unifying large regions. The Mongols were also assimilated into local populations after the fall of the empire which started disintegrating after the demise of Kublai Khan.

Archaeologists discover a city ruled by Gengis Khan's heirs.

1136 Church of St. Denis, France, constructed in new style; marks beginning of Gothic architecture.

c. 1150 Angkor Wat temple constructed in Cambodia.

• Kamban writes Tamil *Ramayana* in south India.

c. 1150–1200 Life of French poet Chretian de Troyes; composes *Percival* and other works on Arthurian legend.

1150 Paris University founded in France.

• Hopewell culture in North America ends.

The Il khanate and the Mongol invasion of the Islamic world

The Mongol invasions of the Islamic world began in 1221 with the conquest of eastern Iran. A more devastating wave of conquest, however, came with Genghis Khan's grandson Hülegü, when Mongol forces subjugated all of Iran and by 1258 had also taken Baghdad, thus bringing to an end the Abbasid caliphate (750–1258). Establishing rule over most of West Asia, including Iraq, Iran, Khorasan, the Caucasus, and parts of Asia Minor, Hülegü (r. 1256–65) assumed the title of "Il-Khan," meaning lesser Khan, subordinate to the Great Khan ruling in China. This branch of the Mongol dynasty, which became known as the Il khanids (1256–1353), centered its power in northwest Iran.

East Asian elements absorbed into the existing Perso-Islamic repertoire created a new artistic vocabulary, one that was emulated from Anatolia to India, profoundly affecting artistic production.

During the Il khanid period, the decorative arts—textiles, pottery, metalwork, jewelry, and manuscript illumination and illustration—continued along and further developed established lines. Popular subjects, also sponsored by the court, included well-known stories such as the Shahnama (Book of Kings), the famous Persian epic. Furthermore, the widespread use of paper and textiles also enabled new designs to be readily transferred from one medium to another.

Along with their renown in the arts, the Il khanids were also great builders. The lavishly decorated Ilkhanid summer palace at Takht-i Sulayman (ca. 1275), a site with pre-Islamic Iranian resonances, is an important example of secular architecture. The outstanding Tomb of Uljaytu (built 1307–13; r. 1304–16) in Sultaniyya, is the architectural masterpiece of the period. Following their conversion to Islam, the Il khanids built numerous mosques and Sufi shrines in cities across Iran such as Ardabil, Isfahan, Natanz, Tabriz, Varamin, and Yazd (ca. 1300–1350). After the death of the last Il khanid ruler of the united dynasty in 1335, the empire disintegrated and a number of local dynasties came to power in Iraq and Iran, each emulating the style set by the Il khanids.

Religion under the Mongols

At the time of Gengis, Tangri, a sky god, was the major deity of the people of the Asian steppes. Like the Mongol rulers that followed him, Gengis was tolerant of all religions. His followers included Buddhists, Nestorian Christians, and a few

1152–1170

1152 Frederick I becomes the king of Germany; crowned Holy Roman Emperor; dies during Third Crusade.
- Henry II is the king of England.
- c. 1154 Arab geographer Al-Idrissi draws world map and writes commentary on it.

1154 Nicholas Breakspear becomes the only English pope, Adrian IV.
1154–91 Life of Al-Suhrawardi, Islamic Sufi philosopher.
c. 1159 Spanish rabbi Benjamin of Tudela begins travels through Europe and Asia to contact dispersed Jews.

Turkish Muslims. Later, Kublai Khan became a Buddhist, though he was also influenced by Christianity. Ghazan of the Il khanate accepted Islam.

The Delhi sultanate

From 1206, northern India was ruled by various Muslim dynasties based in Delhi. The Delhi sultanate lasted for 320 years, during which five dynasties ruled India. Under Alauddin Khilji, the sultanate reached its greatest extent. Mosques and tombs were built, introducing new styles in architecture, particularly the true arch and dome. The Qutb Minar, a 73 meter high tower at Delhi, is a signature structure of this period.

The Qutb Minar, Delhi, India.

Muhammad Ghori's invasions

Muhammad Ghori, a Turkish ruler of a small kingdom of Afghanistan, laid the foundation of Turko-Afghan rule in India. Between 1191 and 1194, he conquered territories in India, but left India leaving behind his Indian territories in the charge of his trusted slave and able general, Qutb-ud-din-Aibak who established the **Slave** or the Mamluk **Dynasty** (the Arabic word mumluk means "slave" or "owned"). The slave dynasty was the first Muslim dynasty to rule India.

The facade of Alai Darwaza (Alai Gate), a magnificent gateway built by Ala-ud-din Khilji of the Delhi Sultanate, Delhi, India.

1159 Alexander III becomes the pope.
1164 Henry II of England issues Constitutions of Clarendon and laws to restrict power of the Church.

c. 1170–1240 Life of Leonardo Fibonacci, Italian mathematician; contributes to algebra and number theory.
1170 Thomas Becket, Archbishop of Canterbury, murdered.

Qutb-ud-din Aibak (1206–10)

Qutb-ud-din-Aibak was the first slave ruler who reigned as the sultan of Delhi for 4 years, from 1206 to 1210. He initiated the construction of the Qutb Minar, which was later completed by Iltutmish. He also built two famous mosques—the Quwwat-ul-Islam, at Delhi, built from the remains of 27 demolished Hindu and Jain temples, and the other, at Ajmer, called Adhai Din Ka jhonpra (hut created in two and a half days). In the year 1210, he fell from a horse while playing polo, and consequently, lost his life.

Iltutmish (1210–36)

Coins issued by Iltutmish.

Iltutmish, also known as Shamsuddin, was one of the most powerful rulers of the slave dynasty and was the son-in-law of Qutb-ud-din-Aibak. Muslim law forbade slaves from becoming kings, but Iltutmish, a former slave, was the first Sultan of India who got his claim to the throne approved by the **Khalifa.** In 1221, Iltutmish had refused to give shelter to the Shah of Persia and, with his diplomatic skills, saved the country from Mongol invasion. He saved the Islamic state in India from disintegrating. Iltutmish made Delhi his capital. Iltutmish was a great administrator and issued gold and silver coins to encourage trade. He also built good roads. He was a great lover of art and education and completed the Qutb Minar and the Qutb mosque started by Qutub-ud-din-Aibak. Great scholars, like Minhaj us Siraj, Ruhani, and Usmanin, lived in his court. Iltutmish ruled for 25 years and died in the year 1236. After his death, there was political instability in Delhi.

Razia (1236–40)

Iltutmish had announced that after his death, his daughter Razia Sultan would become the *sultana* (female ruler) of Delhi, because his sons were not capable enough to rule

A sketch of Razia Sultan.

1171–1190

1171 Saladin seizes Egyptian throne.

1173–74 The construction of Leaning Tower of Pisa, in Italy, begins.

1177 Chinese Xhu Xi writes commentaries on Confucian texts, founding Neo-Confucianism.

c. 1180 Chartres cathedral constructed in France, in Gothic style.

• Philip II becomes the king of France.

1183 Peace of Constance leads to agreement between Lombard League and Holy Roman Emperor Frederick I.

the kingdom. The nobles were not happy with a female ruler; hence they made Rukn-ud-din Feroze Iltutmish, the eldest son of Iltutmish, an heir to the throne. But he proved to be an incapable ruler, so, finally Razia became the ruler of Delhi. Razia was the first and only female ruler of the Delhi Sultanate. She was a very wise and capable ruler and brought many reforms in the state. But Razia was killed in 1240, along with her husband, the Turkish noble Ikhtiyar-ud-din.

Ghiyas-ud-din Balban (1266–87)

In 1246, the influential Turkish nobles, known as the Chalisa or the "Group of Forty", made the youngest son of Iltutmish, Nasir-ud-din Mahmud, the sultan. However, being only 17 years old at that time, he left the entire administration in the hands of his prime minister, Balban (originally his slave). Balban, who was also his father-in-law, served his sultan faithfully. Nasir-ud-din died in 1265 and Ghiyas-ud-din Balban ascended the throne in 1266. He was a great ruler, a strict disciplinarian, and led a simple life.

Tomb of Ghiyas-ud-din Balban in Delhi.

He was murdered in 1287 by Jalaluddin Khilji, who became the founder of the Khilji dynasty. After the death of Balban, the slave dynasty came to an end. His grandson, the last ruler of the slave dynasty, was murdered in 1290.

Khilji dynasty (1290–1320)

The Khilji dynasty was founded by Jalaluddin Firoz in 1290. He was an old man of 70 when he ascended to the throne. In 1296, his nephew and son-in-law Alauddin Khilji captured the throne and murdered him.

1184 New Canterbury cathedral constructed.
1187 Saladin wins Battle of Hattin against Christians; takes Jerusalem; unites Egypt, Syria, Palestine, northern Mesopotamia.
• Richard the Lionheart becomes the king of England.

c. **1190** Jewish philosopher Maimonides writes *Guide for the Perplexed*; attempts to reconcile Greek and Jewish philosophy.
1190 Teutonic Order of Knights set up in Germany.

CULTURES AND KINGDOMS

Alauddin Khilji (1296–1316)

A sketch of Alauddin Khilji.

Alauddin was the second ruler of the Khilji dynasty. His name was Juna Khan and proclaimed himself as the Sultan of Delhi. In 1296, he attacked and defeated Raja Ramchandra of Devagiri in Deccan, and returned with fabulous riches. In order to win over the nobles he distributed the booty that he had got in Devagiri among the people.

Apart from conquering Gujarat and Malwa in 1297, he also captured Ranthambhor and Chittor in Rajasthan. Alauddin faced more than a dozen Mongol invasions during his reign but he was successful in countering them. Alauddin's empire extended from the Brahmaputra in the east to the Arabian Sea in the west, and from the Himalayas in the north to Madurai in the far south.

Alauddin was the first ruler, after Ashoka, who controlled the whole of India under one administration. He wanted to conquer the whole world, and called himself the second Alexander. His administration was based on centralized government and he became the absolute ruler.

Chittorgarh Fort in Rajasthan.

1191–1209

1191 The first battle of Tarain between Prithviraj Chauhan, ruler of Delhi and Ajmer, and Muhammad Ghori.

1191 Henry VI becomes Holy Roman Emperor.

• Chinese Buddhist Ensai spreads Zen Buddhism in Japan.

1192 Second battle of Tarain took place between Prithviraj Chauhan and Muhammad Ghori.

1192 Khwaja Moin-ud-din Chisti comes to India.

1194 Muhammad Ghori defeats the ruler of Kanauj.

Alauddin undertook various economic measures to maintain a large **standing army**. and supervised the functioning of markets ensuring low and stable prices in all conditions, even during famines.

Alauddin was a great lover of art and music, and Amir Khusrau was a member of his court. He built the Alai Darwaza, which served as a beautiful entrance to the Qutb Minar He also built the Siri Fort and the Palace of Thousand Pillars. Hauz Khas, a big tank for royal baths, was also constructed during his rule. He died on 1316 due to an illness. His son Qutb-ud-din Mubarak held the reins for 4 years but proved to be an ineffective ruler.

Tughlaq dynasty (1320–1412)

Ghazi Malik became the sultan and changed his name to Ghiyas-ud-din Tughlaq. He built a new city near Delhi, which was named Tughlaqabad, after the dynasty. This dynasty became very popular because their rule extended all the way to the south. Bengal was also invaded and some parts of it were annexed to the empire. Ghias-ud-din died in 1325, when the pavilion built for his reception by his son Juna Khan, collapsed in a planned accident.

Muhammad-Bin-Tughlaq

(1325–51)

Muhammad-Bin-Tughlaq was the son of Ghiyas-ud-din Tughlaq. Before ascending the throne, his real name was Juna Khan. After killing his father and one of his brothers, he became the sultan of Delhi in the year 1325. Stories of his success and failure run

Siri Fort, built by Alauddin Khilji.

CULTURES AND KINGDOMS

side by side. He is, however, better known for his administrative disasters. He is sometimes also referred to as a wise but foolish king. He was an accomplished poet and a versatile scholar in the field of Astronomy, Physical Sciences, and Medicine. He ruled Delhi for 26 years.

A sketch of Muhammad bin-Tughlaq.

In 1327, Muhammad bin-Tughlaq shifted his capital from Delhi to Devagiri in Maharashtra, 700 miles in the Deccan, which he renamed as Daulatabad. He felt it would keep him safe from the constan Mongol invasions. The plan was a disaster, due to the Mongol attack in the north and inadequate water supply in Daulatabad, which forced him to move back his capital to Delhi.

Daulatabad fort built by Muhammad bin-Tughlaq.

1210–1236

- German prince Otto IV invades Italy; is crowned Holy Roman Emperor.
- **1210** Qutb-ud-din Aibak falls from a horse and dies while playing polo.
- **1216** Llewellyn the Great is recognized as ruler of Wales.

c. **1220** German epic poem *Nibelungenlied* composed on mythical hero Siegfried.
1220–44 French scholar Vincent of Beauvais compiles encyclopedia, *Speculum Majus.*

The failure of his schemes and the hardships suffered by the people made him very unpopular. He died in 1351 while suppressing a revolt. Historians call Muhammad-bin-Tughlaq the "wise fool".

Firoz Tughlaq (1351–88)

After Muhammad Bin Tughlaq, Firoz Shah became the ruler. He did not contribute much to the expansion of his territory. He ruled for 37 years. He tried to re-conquer the territories of Bengal and Sind, but failed and only resulted in the draining of the state treasury.

Firoz Shah Kotla fort in Delhi.

He according to the Shariat law; he abandoned all the taxes that were unlawful by the Shariat. He was very kind towards the peasants, and all their taxes and loans were exempted.

He founded several cities like Jaunpur, Ferozpur, Hissar, Fatehabad, and Firozabad on the banks of the Yamuna River near Delhi.

He was murdered in 1389 and was succeeded by Abu Baker. After him, the dynasty began to disintegrate. Timur, a Mongol invader, ended the Tughlaq dynasty.

Timur's Invasion

Timur Lang (Timur the Lame) was the head of the Chagatai Turks around Samarkand in Central Asia. He invaded India in 1398 and occupied some territories in the north-west. He then plundered

Bust of Timur Lang.

CULTURES AND KINGDOMS

Delhi. He appointed Khizr Khan as his governor in India. Thus, the country's stability was disrupted and finally led to decline of the Tughlaq dynasty.

Tomb of Timur Lang in Samarkand.

Sayyid dynasty (1414 to 21)

The founder of Sayyid dynasty was Khizr Khan. Unlike other rulers, he never waged any wars till it became an absolute necessity. He was an able ruler and a very kind hearted person. He fought wars against, and defeated the Hindus of Doab, Chandawar, and Kalithar as they had stopped paying him tributes. No other major event is recorded during this period and nothing much is known about this period.

Lodi Dynasty (1451–1526)

Bahlol Lodi was the founder of the Lodi dynasty. He was the only Afghan ruler of the Delhi sultanate. Before him, all the other rulers were Turkish rulers. He conquered Jaunpur. He died in the year 1489.

Sikandar Lodi (1489–1517 AD)

After the death of Bahlol Lodi, his son Sikandar Lodi assumed the throne. Ibrahim Lodi was the last king of the Lodi dynasty, defeated and killed by Babur in the first battle of Panipat in the year 1526. Thus in 1526, the rule of the Delhi sultanate came to an end, and paved the way the Mughal dynasty.

1237–1258

1237 Mongol khanate of Golden Horde formed in Russia by Batu Khan, grandson of Gengis.
1238 Nasrid dynasty established in Granada, Spain.
1240 Razia was killed, along with her husband.

1240 Alexander Nevsky of Novgorod, Russia, defeats Swedes; **1242** defeats Teutonic knights in the Battle of Lake Peipus.
1241 German cities Lubeck and Hamburg unite; beginning of Hanseatic League.

The Magna Carta

A 14th-century manuscript of the Magna Carta.

England faced unrest in the 12th century, and the king increasingly came to depend on the support of the barons, the owners of landed estates. They requested king John (r. 1199–1216) to sign the Magna Carta, a charter or list of demands, and he finally did so in 1215. It regulated the relationships between the king and his barons, and the latter and their tenants. It also stated that even the king was subject to the law of the land.

This document is considered significant as it marked the beginning of constitutional government in England, placing limits on the right of the king.

The Hanseatic League

The rise of towns and trade led to the Hanseatic League in Europe, a group of towns to protect trade. The League began with Hamburg and Lubeck, where a hansa (association) was created for self-protection, as the government was weak. By the middle of the 14th century, the League had around 70 towns across Northern Europe.

GREAT LITERATURE

Dante Alighieri (*c.* 1265–1321), Francesco Petrarca (1304–1374), also known as Petrarch, and Giovanni Boccaccio (1313–1375) are the three great Italian writers of this time.

Dante's most famous poetic work is *Divina Commedia* (The Divine Comedy), which describes a journey through hell, purgatory, and paradise. Petrarch wrote sonnets which provided a model for later literature. Boccaccio's masterpiece is the prose *Decameron,* consisting of stories narrated by 10 characters.

Fresco of Dante Alighieri at the Uffizi gallery, Florence, Italy.

- Holy Roman Emperor Frederick II invades papal states.
- 1245 Westminster Abbey, London rebuilt.
- 1246 The youngest son of Iltutmish, Nasir-uddin Mahmud, assumes the throne.

1253 Amır Khusrou is born in Patiali, Uttar Pradesh, India.

c. 1258 Persian poet Sadi composes his masterpiece, *The Rose Garden.*

1258 English House of Commons formed.

CULTURES AND KINGDOMS

Also called Hansa, German Hanse, organization founded by north German towns and German merchant communities abroad to protect their mutual trading interests. The league dominated commercial activity in northern Europe from the 13th to the 15th century. (Hanse was a medieval German word for "guild," or "association," derived from a Gothic word for "troop," or "company.")

Painting of a Hanseatic league port.

After its capture by Henry the Lion in 1158, Lübeck became the main base for Westphalian and Saxon merchants expanding northward and eastward; Visby, on the Swedish island of Gotland, was soon established as a major transshipment centre for trade in the Baltic and with Novgorod, which was the chief mart for the Russian trade. From Visby, German merchants helped establish important towns on the east coast of the Baltic: Riga, Reval (now Tallinn), Danzig (now Gdansk), and Dorpat (now Tartu). Thus, by the early 13th century Germans had a near-monopoly of long-distance trade in the Baltic. In the meantime, merchants from Cologne (Köln) and other towns in the Rhineland had acquired trading privileges in Flanders and in England.

The decisive steps in the formation of the Hanseatic League took place in the second half of the 13th century. While overseas, the German merchants had tended increasingly to form associations ("hanses") with each other in order to secure common action against robbers and pirates. From the mid-13th century this cooperation became much more extensive and regularized, and by 1265 all the north German towns having the "law of Lübeck" had agreed on common legislation for the defense of merchants and their goods. In the 1270s a Lübeck-Hamburg association that had acquired trading privileges in Flanders and England united with its rival Rhenish counterpart, and in the 1280s this confederation of German merchants trading in the west was closely joined to the association trading in the Baltic, thus creating the Hanseatic League.

1260–1275

c. 1260 Nicola Pisano, Italian architect and sculptor, integrates classical art into Gothic style.

1260 Sufi poet Rumi, founder of Mevlevi sect, composes *Masnavi*, spiritual couplets.

1265–73 St Thomas Aquinas composes *Summa Theologica*, influential work on theology.

1266 Ghias-ud-din Balban ascends the throne to the Delhi Sultanate.

1270 Navigational charts used in Europe.

The Reconquista

The Umayyad Muslims had conquered much of Spain in the eighth century. The few remaining Christian states were keen to reconquer the region, and by the 13th century had achieved some success. The Reconquista (reconquest) continued, and the great cities of Cordoba and Seville were recaptured by the Christians

The Alhambra palace in Granada, Spain.

in 1236 and 1248, respectively. Granada, ruled by the Nasrid dynasty, remained the only Muslim state. In 1238, it became a tributary of Castile, and continued to exist till 1492. The grand Alhambra palace complex was built during the Nasrid period.

BLACK DEATH

Possibly originating in Central Asia, the virulent bubonic plague known as the "Black Death," struck China and India and reached Constantinople in 1347. From here it was transmitted to Sicily, France, England, and then to the rest of Europe. In Europe, the first and worst phase of the Black Death ended in 1351, although there were later epidemics. Some saw the plague as the wrath of god, some blamed it on beggars and the poor who lived in unhygienic conditions, and others on the Jews. The latter belief led to the massacre of Jews in some cities. The population of Europe was much reduced after the epidemics. As a result, there were temporary benefits for the survivors: Wages rose for the remaining available workforce, the rents for tenants on the landed estates fell, and food prices were lower.

Plague victims being blessed by a priest, manuscript detail c. 14th century.

1271 Edward I becomes the king of England; introduces administrative and legal reforms.

1273 Rudolf I crowned Holy Roman Emperor; is the first Habsburg king of Germany.

1274 Second Council of Lyons brings short reunion of Eastern and Western Churches.

1275 Ramkhamhaeng is the king of Sukothai (Thailand); expands kingdom.

CONFLICT AND CHANGE

European rulers continued to organize Crusades, and fought other wars in Europe, such as the Hundred Years' War. At the same time, new trade routes opened and commercial towns emerged.

The Crusades continue

Five Crusades took place during this period.

1. The Fourth Crusade (1202–1204) aimed to reconquer Jerusalem, but ended in a conflict among Crusaders and an attack on Constantinople.

2. The Fifth Crusade (1218–1221) called for by Pope Honorius II, ended in failure.

3. The Sixth Crusade (1228–1229) was led by Frederick II (1194–1250), the Holy Roman Emperor. He negotiated a 10-year truce, which allowed Christians to return to Jerusalem. Frederick made himself the king of Jerusalem in 1229. However, the Templar and Hospitaller knights fought each other over territory, and mercenary Turks seized Jerusalem in 1244.

4. The Seventh Crusade (1248–1254) was begun by Louis IX of France (1215–1270). He attacked Cairo, but was taken a prisoner. A ransom was paid to free him, and he rebuilt Jaffa and Acre, making peace with Muslim leaders.

5. The Eighth Crusade was initiated by Louis IX in 1270, but he died at Tunis. Prince Edward of England then went to Acre and negotiated an 11-year truce. However, in 1289 the Mamluks took Tripoli, and in 1291 captured Acre.

EASTER ISLAND STATUES

This southeastern Pacific island was first settled by the Polynesians in the sixth century. Around 700–850, they built rectangular platforms, known as ahus, along the coasts. Medium-sized stone

statues, probably depicting important people, were erected on them. These were destroyed later, and stronger platforms constructed. Between 1200 and 1680, more statues, this time much bigger, were dragged on to the platforms with the help of ramps. More than 600 such sculptures have been found. Between 10 and 40-feet-high, some weigh over 80 tons.

1280–1300

c. 1280 Kabbalah, the Jewish mystical philosophy, emerges in Spain and Portugal.

1282 Pedro III of Aragon becomes the king of Sicily.

1284 Edward I of England annexes Wales.

c. 1285 Florentine painter Cimabue (Bencivieni di Pepo) creates naturalistic paintings.

1287 Ghias-ud-din Balban murdered by Jalaluddin Khilji, founder of Khilji Dynasty in Delhi.

Hundred Years' War: the first two phases

Born in 1312, Edward III of England was the son of Edward II of England and Isabella, daughter of Philip IV of France. When he laid claim to the throne of France in 1337, a series of wars started between England and France, generally known as the Hundred Years' War. This war had three main periods of conflict. In the first phase, known as the Edwardian War (1337–1360), England gained control over Calais, in the northeast, and a part of southwest France. A new weapon, the longbow, helped England to win the first phase of the war. During the second phase, termed the Caroline War (1369–1389), Charles V of France regained most French territories. A truce was signed in 1389.

The English longbow

Edward III of England.

An interrogation under the Inquisition: a priest exhorts the condemned to confess as he is being tortured.

THE INQUISITION

Christian Councils were held from the fourth century onwards to define the essentials of Christian belief. Anyone who differed was considered a heretic and was excommunicated. Then, in 1231, Pope Gregory IX set up the office of Inquisitor to pressurize Christians into accepting Church doctrines. Often torture was used, and those who refused were executed. In some regions, the Inquisition lasted up to the early 19th century.

1290 Osman I is leader of Seljuk Turks from Central Asia; **c. 1300** founds Ottoman empire.
1290–1320 Khilji Dynasty in Delhi, India.
1292 Edward I of England chooses John de Balliol as king of Scotland; **1296** conquers Scotland.

1296 Alauddin Khilji of Delhi attacks and defeats Raja Ramchandra of Devagiri in Deccan.
1297 Alauddin Khilji conquers Gujarat and Malwa.
c. 1300 Kingdom of Majapahit emerges in Java; expands over Indonesia and Malay territory.

NEW EMPIRES

The empire of Mali

In 1240, Ghana was absorbed into the growing empire of Mali, which had developed from the earlier state of Kangaba on the upper Niger river. Under Mansa Musa (*c.* 1307–1332), Mali reached its greatest extent, incorporating the great trading centers of Timbuktu and Gao. Mali traders dominated West Africa, ambassadors were sent to Egypt and Morocco, and Egyptian scholars were brought to the kingdom. The empire broke up by 1550.

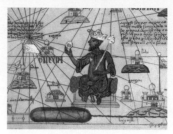

Mansa Musa of Mali holding a gold nugget, Catalan Atlas c. late 14th century.

The Mamluks

In 1250, the Mamluks, originally Turks or Circassian slave-soldiers, overthrew the Ayyubid sultanate founded by Saladin in Egypt. In 1260, though Baghdad was taken by the Mongols and the caliphate ended, it was restored by the Mamluk sultans in Cairo. The Mamluk state continued till 1517. During its height under the Turkish sultans who ruled till 1382, Mamluk control extended to Syria and Palestine. Egypt and Syria became great commercial and trading centers, rich in art and craft. The Mamluk period was known for its woven carpets, and metal and glass work. Its architectural achievements were vast; more than 3,000 buildings, including mosques, tombs, and seminaries were constructed.

Mamluk enameled lamp, c. 13th century.

CHIMU CULTURE

The Chimu state came into being along the coast of Peru around Chan Chan (c. 1200–1400), the capital. This was divided into separate areas, one for the ruling lords and priests and another for the common people. The Chimu built roads, wove textiles, and made fine pottery. In 1465–1470, they were conquered by the Incas.

A Chimu mantle, c. 14th century.

1300–1314

c. **1300–77** Life of French poet and musician Guillame de Machaut; composes masses, vocal ballads, rondeaux in polyphonic form.

1301–08 Civil war in Hungary.

1302 Papal bull *Unam Sanctam* issued by pope Boniface VIII, stating the pope's supremacy over kings; Boniface later imprisoned.

1303 University of Rome founded under papal control.

Mayas, Incas, and Aztecs

Manco Capac, founder of the Inca dynasty.

Maya power in the Yucatan had shifted to the new capital city of Mayapan. In other areas, there were independent Maya city states. The *Popul Vuh*, a famous Maya work of myth and history, was composed by the Kiche Maya.

Of uncertain origin, the Incas settled in Peru, South America, with their chief center at Cuzco, around 1200. They had a dynasty of kings with the title Sapa Inca, or "unique Inca," who was considered a descendant of Inti, the Sun God. According to tradition, the Incas began to expand in the 14th century. In c. 1390, King Hatun Tapac called himself Viracocha, after the supreme creator deity.

Inca rulers wore gold-threaded garments, decorated with brightly-colored feathers. Quipus, knotted strings in bundles, were used to record information and for accounting purposes. Roads were constructed throughout their territories. Textiles with intricate motifs were woven; painted ceramics and gold and silver objects were crafted. The Incas cultivated potatoes, maize, squash, tomatoes, peanuts, and cotton, among other crops, in their mountainous kingdom.

The Aztecs, also known as the Mexica, probably arrived in the valley of Mexico in the 12th century, when Toltec power was declining. A Nahautl-speaking community, they settled at various places in the northwest of the valley. In 1325, the city of Tenochtitlan was founded on a swampy island at the edge of Tezcoco lake. Tlatelulco was a sister settlement to the north. The Aztecs did not at first control the region. There were other city-states—Azcapotzalco was one—and, for some time, the Aztecs were subject to them. In the 15th century, Aztec power rose to dominate the rest. Their calendar of 365 days was divided into 18 months of 20 days each, and 5 extra days.

The pyramids at the Aztec capital at Tenochtitlan.

- Chinese mathematician Zhu Shijie develops algebra.
- **c. 1305** Italian artist Giotto di Bondone develops realistic style in paintings and frescoes.
- **1306** Jews expelled from France and England.

1309–77 Period of Avignon papacy.
1314 Scots under Robert the Bruce defeat Edward II in Battle of Bannockburn; Scotland becomes independent for the next 300 years.

THE MUGHALS

An illustration from the *Akbarnama* (the biography of Akbar), showing the author Abul Fazl presenting a copy of his work to the emperor.

Explorers set out to discover and settle in new areas. Empires declined and new dynasties emerged. New crops were grown, and different parts of the world were linked through trade, commerce, and adventure.

Among the great dynasties of Asia were the Mughals in India, the Safavids in Iran, and the Mings in China. The power of the Ottoman Turks crossed beyond Asia to Europe and Africa.

The Mughals

The Muslim dynasty of Turkic-Mongol origin that ruled most of northern India from the early 16th to the mid 18th century was called Mughal. The Delhi Sultanate was declining. Meanwhile, in 1494, Babar, a 12-year-old boy, became king of Ferghana, in Central Asia. Babar extended his sway over Kabul, and invaded north

1316–1330

1316 Alauddin Khilji of Delhi dies due to an illness.

c. 1320–80 Life of Welsh bard Dafydd ap Gwilym.

1320–1414 Tughlaq Dynasty in Delhi, India.

c. 1325 Kachina cult established in Colorado river valley by Native Americans.

c. 1325 Amır Khusrou, the great Sufi poet and musician dies in Delhi.

1325 Ghias-ud-din Tughlaq of Delhi dies.

1325 Muhammad-Bin-Tughlaq becomes the sultan of Delhi.

India, founding the Mughal dynasty. Babar's grandson, Akbar, was the greatest Mughal ruler. Akbar (reigned 1556–1605) defeated the Hindu usurper Hemu at the Second Battle of Panipat (1556) and, thereby, reestablished his dynasty in Hindustan. Through his conquests, he united much of North India. He divided his territory into provinces. Stone and ivory carved into fine objects, brocades, and embroidered textiles, were among the goods produced. Trade and commerce prospered, and large cities emerged. At the time of Akbar's death in 1605, the empire extended from Afghanistan to the Bay of Bengal and southward to modern-day Gujarat and the northern Deccan region (peninsular India).

Origin of the Mughals

The Mughals were descendants of the Mongols from Central Asia. The Mughal period, unlike the Delhi Sultanate that was ruled by many dynasties, witnessed rule by a single dynasty for nearly two and a half centuries. It was broken only by Sher Shah Suri's family's in from 1540 to 1555. The Mughals established an empire which roughly coincides with the present Indian territory.

Babur (1494–1530)

Zahir-ud-din Muhammad Babur was born in 1483 in Ferghana, a small state in Transoxania in Central Asia. He became the king of Ferghana at the early age of 12, upon his father's death. Within a couple of years, he fulfilled his dream of conquering Samarkand. He was a descendent of Timur from his father's side and had kinship with Genghis Khan on his mother's side. He referred to himself and the dynasty he established as Timurids (meaning "descendents of Timur"). He turned eastward and conquered Kabul in 1504.

Babur marched toward Delhi and occupied the throne in Delhi.

Babur.

1326–27 Queen Isabella kills her husband Edward II; makes her son the king of England, as Edward III.
1327 Muhammad-Bin-Tughlaq decides to move the capital from Delhi to Devagiri or Daulatabad in Maharashtra.

1328 Philip VI begins Valois dynasty in France.
1329 French rabbi Gersonides writes *The Wars of the Lord*, a study of philosophical theology.
c. 1330–36 Italian sculptor Andrea Pisano founds Florentine school of sculpture.

THE MUGHALS

Babur was an orthodox Sunni Muslim and loved architecture. He wrote the autobiography *Tuzuk-i-Baburi* or the *Baburnama*.

Babur went on to suppress the Rajputana and other kingdoms up to the regions of Bengal and Bihar. By 1530, he had acquired a large empire in the north in the richest area in India, the Ganga-Yamuna Doab. However, before he could consolidate his empire, Babur died at the age of 48 in 1530.

Babur watching his gardeners at work.

Humayun

(1530–40 and 1555–56)

In 1530, Babur was succeeded by his eldest son Humayun. Sher Shah, the Afghan ruler of Bihar, defeated Humayun in the Battle of Chausa in 1539 and again in the Battle of Kanauj in 1540. In order to save his life, Humayun was forced to wander through Rajasthan and Sind. At Amarkot, he married a young girl called Hamida Banu and a son was born to him who later on became the greatest Mughal emperor ever—Akbar.

At Amarkot, Humayun met Bairam Khan, who became his faithful friend and later the guardian of his young son, Akbar. It was with the aid of the Persian forces that Humayun was able to

Emperor Humayun.

1331–1351

1331 First Swabian League formed by 22 cities in southwest Germany to unite against local rulers.

c. 1333 In Japan, Emperor Go Daigo removes shoguns (hereditary warlords) and restores power to imperial line.

1338 Muromachi period begins in Japan.

c. 1338–39 Sienese painters Ambrogio and Pietro Lorenzetti create naturalistic art.

1340 Kimono, Chinese robe, introduced in Japan.

Sher Shah's tomb at Sasaram, Bihar.

consolidated his position in Afghanistan and regained his lost empire in Delhi after a gap of 15 years.

Unfortunately, he was not able to enjoy his rule for more than a year. He met with an accidental death after falling from the staircase of his library in 1556.

Humayun's tomb in Delhi.

Sher Mandal (Library) in Purana Quila.

1343 Hanseatic League, N. European trading cities, set up in 13th century, gains power.

1348–50 Black Death kills millions in Europe.

c. 1350 African kingdom of Kongo founded in region of Angola.

- Thai kingdom of Ayutthaya established; continues till 1767.

1351 Muhammad-Bin-Tughlaq of Delhi dies while suppressing a revolt.

THE MUGHALS

Akbar (1556–1605)

Jalaluddin Muhammed Akbar was born to the second Mughal Emperor Humayun and his teenage bride Hamida Banu Begum on October 14, 1542 in Sind, now in Pakistan. Akbar came to the throne in 1556 at the age of 13. Initially, he was guided by his tutor and Humayun's faithful general, Bairam Khan. Akbar later became the Shahanshah (king of kings).

Jalaluddin Muhammad Akbar.

It was under Akbar that the Mughal Empire established itself and Bairam Khan's contribution to creating a successful empire was tremendous. Under his guidance, Akbar defeated Hemu, the Afghan general, at the Second Battle of Panipat in 1556, thus crushing the Afghan power completely.

Akbar assumed control of the state as the emperor after Bairam Khan's assassination while on a pilgrimage to Mecca. Then he went about subduing the Rajputs and regaining the territories that had been lost during Humayun's reign.

In a short span of time Akbar's empire extended from Hindu Kush in the north-west to the Brahmaputra in the east and from the Himalayas in the north to the Godavari in the south. Buland Darwaza at Fatehpur Sikri was built to commemorate Akbar's conquest of Gujarat.

Akbar was not only a great warrior and a statesman but also an efficient administrator. Akbar continued with Sher Shah Suri's impressive administrative methods.

Akbar's administrative policies were continued by his successors and, later, also served as the basis of the administrative set up in British-India. He was the Supreme Commander of the army. He established a centralized administration with himself as the highest court of appeal.

Akbar introduced a unique system known as the Mansabdari system where every officer or noble had a rank which was indicative of his hierarchy and was called a **mansabdar**.

1356–1370

1356 Golden Bull, edict on electoral procedures, issued by Charles IV, Holy Roman Emperor.

1361 Murad I becomes Ottoman sultan; expands empire.

1366–67 Statutes of Kilkenny restrict the use of Irish language and customs among English settlers.

1368–70 King Waldemar IV of Denmark defeated by Hanseatic League.

Buland Darwaza at Fatehpur Sikri was built to commemorate Akbar's conquest of Gujarat.

There was no Mughal land revenue system before Akbar. Raja Todar Mal, the revenue minister of Sher Shah Suri, was appointed by Akbar as his revenue minister. He framed the land-revenue policy of Akbar which was followed till the arrival of the British. Land was divided into three grades—good, average, and bad. Assessment was based on the average produce prevailing over the past 10 years. The share of the state was one-third of the produce, which could be paid in cash or kind. Akbar ensured that no farmers were harassed by officials. In times of natural calamities, farmers were also given loans. Trade

1369 Timur, of Mongol descent, occupies Samarkand in Central Asia.

c. 1370 Construction completed of palace of Comares at Alhambra, residence of

Islamic rulers of Granada (entire complex dates between 11th and 14th centuries).

1370–1430 Life of Andrei Lubyov, Russian monk and icon painter.

Diwan-i-Aam.

Diwan-i-Khas.

developed with China, Central Asia, and Europe and both inland and overseas trade was encouraged. Textiles, saltpeter, spices, and indigo were the commodities exported. Gold coins, called *mohur*, were issued. Silver and copper coins were also used.

Akbar's cultural contributions

Akbar was a great patron of learning. He had a marvellous memory and learnt a lot by listening. He held frequent discussions with religious thinkers, scholars, and writers. Akbar's court was adorned with nine gems or the **Nine Jewels**, who were highly accomplished and distinguished in their respective fields–

1. Abul Fazl was the official briographer who wrote an autobiography of Akbar's life, and an account of the various laws and revenue system of the empire.

Abdur Rahim Khan-i-Khanan, famous for his couplets.

1372–1382

1372 Tezozomoc is the ruler of Azcapotzalco, most powerful city-state in Mexico.
1375 Scottish poet John Barbour writes epic poem, *The Bruce,* on king Robert the Bruce.

1376 Second Swabian League formed.
1378 Byzantine icon painter Theophanes the Greek creates frescos.
1378–1417 Great Schism of Christian Church; two rival popes claim authority.

2. Faizi was a poet who translated the Ramayana and Mahabharata into Persian. The Bhagvad Gita, the Bible and other famous Arabic and Greek works were also translated into Persian for benefit of the common man.

Nine Jewels along with Akbar.

3. Abdur Rahim Khan-i-Khanan (son of Bairam Khan) was famous for his couplets in Hindi.
4. Todar Mal excelled as revenue minister.
5. Bhagwan Das, brother of Akbar's wife Jodha Bai, and Man Singh were great generals.
6. Birbal's witticism and intelligence have now become a part of Indian folklore.
7. Tansen, the greatest singer of the period, enriched the Hindustani classical music with compositions of new *ragas* like the *Raga Darbari* in honor of Akbar's empire.
8. Humam was a well-known physician.
9. Mulla Do Piaza was known for his ready wit.

Akbar established a policy of great tolerance toward all which was was followed by his descendants with the exception of Aurangzeb.

In 1582, Akbar started a new state religion called the **Din-i-ilahi** which was an amalgamation of Sufism and Hinduism. It involved worship of the Sun, fire, and light. However, propagation of this faith was not very successful.

Ibadat khana.

1379 John Wycliffe, English theologian, attacks accepted Church doctrines.

c. 1380 Japanese actor and playwright Zeami develops Noh theatre, writes 50 plays.

1380 Tarot cards begin to appear in Italy and France.

1381 Peasant revolt in England.

1382 Poland's Baltic provinces conquered by Teutonic Knights.

Jahangir (1605–27)

In 1605 Akbar died, and his son Muhammed Sultan Salim (who was named after the great Sufi saint, Sheikh Salim Chisti), succeeded him to the throne.

Jahangir inherited the largest and most powerful empire in the world. Jahangir was married to Nur Jahan, daughter of Itmad-ud-daulah, a noble in the court of Akbar. Nur Jahan was an intelligent, clever, and competent ruler and had creative abilities. Jahangir left the running of the kingdom to his wife Nur Jahan.

Empress Nur Jahan and Emperor Jahangir.

In 1627, Jahangir became seriously ill and died on October 28, 1627. Shah Jahan, with support from his father-in-law Asaf Khan, became the emperor.

Shah Jahan (1628–58)

Prince Khurram was 35 years old when he ascended the throne at Agra as Shah Jahan 'king of the world' in 1628. He built the Taj Mahal at Agra for his beloved wife Mumtaz Mahal. He shifted the capital from Agra to Delhi and started the construction of a new city called Shahjahanabad. He also built the Red Fort which has many beautiful buildings. This was the Age of Magnificence. The Mughal Empire

A painting of Shah Jahan and Mumtaz Mahal.

reached its zenith during this period. Shah Jahan fell ill and a fierce conflict broke out among his sons Dara, Shuja, Murad, and Aurangzeb. Shah Jahan was imprisoned in the Agra fort by Aurangzeb.

1386–1397

1386 University of Heidelberg (Ruprecht-Karls Universitat) founded; oldest in Germany.
- Jagellion dynasty of Poland and Lithuania established.

- Construction of Milan cathedral begins; is completed in the 20th century.
1389 Turks invade Serbia and win Battle of Kosovo Polje; execute King Lazarus of Serbia.

Aurangzeb (1658–1707)

Aurangzeb announced himself as the emperor of India in AD 1658. Aurangzeb's reign lasted for 49 years until his death in 1707.

Aurangzeb was intolerant toward other religions which made him an unpopular ruler. His cruelty toward the Sikhs ruined the empire's relations with them, which had been established during the rule of Akbar, and his anti-Hindu stand angered the majority of his subjects.

This paved the way for the rise of the Maratha power. The Marathas gained great support from the common people and carved out a huge autonomous area within the Mughal Empire.

After Aurangzeb, the Mughal emperors never rose to any great stature again, and the empire began to disintegrate. In 1707, his eldest son Bahadur Shah Zafar II ascended the throne. But he failed to control the Marathas and the Jats. He died in 1712.

The Safavids

Ismail I.

Ismail I established the Safavid dynasty in Iran in 1502. They were the descendants of Sheikh Ṣafī al-Dīn (1253-1334) of Ardabīl, head of the Sufi order of Ṣafavīyeh (Ṣafawiyyah), but about 1399 they beforehand their Sunni affiliation for Shiism. In August 1514, Ismā'īl was defeated by his Sunni rival, the Ottoman sultan Selim I, at Chāldirān. As a result of the long struggle against the Sunnis—the Ottomans in the west and the Uzbeks in the northeast— the before lost Kurdistan, Diyarbakır, and Baghdad; the Safavid capital was relocated at Eṣfahān, at first temporarily but permanently by about the early 17th century. Under Abbas I (1587-1628), a period of peace and prosperity began. The capital was moved to Isfahan, the administration was reorganized, and literature, art, and architecture flourished. Isfahan was said to have 500,000 residents, and beautiful gardens. The Safavid period is particularly known for miniature painting, textiles, and intricately woven carpets.

THE MUGHALS

The Mings

The first Ming emperor had to reestablish control over the country. As stability was restored, China's prosperity increased and trade expanded. The tributary position of several other East Asian states was restored. Admiral Zheng He (1371–1433) made seven expeditions to far flung ports for trade, including those in Thailand, India, and Iran, Jeddah in Saudi Arabia, and along the coast of East Africa. Silk, textiles, and ceramics were among the products exported from China. Around 1400, their capital Yintiang (Nanjing), with a population of around one million, was the largest city in the world. In 1421, the capital was moved to a reconstructed Beijing.

Chinese culture flourished under the Mings. Books, including novels, were written. New styles in painting developed. Wars against the Mongols and Japan, weak emperors, and rival factions in the government contributed to the Mings' decline. The dynasty finally came to an end in 1644.

The establishment of the Ming dynasty in 1368 marked the return of native rule over all of China for the first time in centuries. An interest in cultural restoration characterizes the first part of the dynasty, when the court sets the style for ceramics, lacquers, textiles, painting, and other arts. The delicate porcelain bodies and elegant underglaze cobalt blue decorations on imperial wares made for the Xuande (r. 1426–35) and Zhenghua (r. 1465–87) emperors are among the most famous blue-and-white wares in ceramic history. Painters, working at the court, or professionally, or as a means of self-cultivation, derive inspiration from earlier traditions found in the sixteenth century, the development of massive manufacturing industries, such as those for porcelains and textiles, spurs great prosperity and the rise of a more educated populace, particularly in southern China. New

Ming dynasty Sutra box with dragons amid clouds.

1398–1414

1398 Timur Lang invaded India.

1400–1511 Kingdom of Malacca established in Malaya; becomes important trading center.

1402 The Yongle emperor is Chinese Ming emperor; constructs palace complex of Forbidden City in Beijing; dynasty reaches its pinnacle.

1405 Timur dies; his empire disintegrates.

regional centers came up in response to the private patronage of arts by wealthy officials and merchants in cities such as Nanjing and Suzhou. The widespread printing of books and the development of new types of painting and less formal designs in the decorative arts reflect these economic and cultural changes.

Exotic porcelain punch bowl.

The reign of the authoritative and expansionist Yongle emperor was marked by five massive expeditions against the Mongols to the north, as well as campaigns in Vietnam. It is also a period of artistic flowering noted for elegant porcelains and textiles, and for the production of numerous Buddhist icons for use at the court and as gifts to Tibet.

Muslim Grand Eunuch Zheng He (1371–1435) lead seven grand naval expeditions, some totaling 300 ships and 27,000 sailors, reaching India and Persia in the first four expeditions and Africa in the last three. His concerns were primarily diplomatic, seeking to establish ties with other nations. However, exotic products and animals, such as giraffes, rhinoceroses, and lions, were also brought back to China.

It was during this time that construction of the Forbidden City started, an imperial complex at the heart of Beijing, which will remain the home to China's emperors until 1912. Orientation of the complex and the surrounding city followed a rigid north-south axis, and all of the most important buildings face south in the traditional manner. The Yongle emperor first uses the Forbidden City in 1420.

A selection of Confucian texts known as the Great Compendium of the Philosophy of Human Nature is published. In conjunction with the Great Compendium of the Five Classics and Four Books of 1415, it serves as the standard for all scholarship, particularly which needed to pass the imperial examination that led to coveted roles in the government bureaucracy.

The Temple of Heaven is built. It was the site for an important rite, held at the winter solstice, in which the emperor reported on the state of the nation to the heaven and paid his homage. Enlarged during the reign of the Jiajing emperor (1522–1566), the temple was last used in 1915 by Yuan Shikai (1859–1916), president of the short-lived Chinese Republic.

c. 1410 Andrei Rublev (c. 1360–1430), Russian icon painter, paints *Old Testament Trinity*.
1410 Kiche Mayas of Central America expand kingdom.

• Battle of Tannenberg; Polish and Lithuanian armies defeat Teutonic Knights.
1414–92 Life of Nuruddin Jami, Iranian Sufi poet; writes *Haft Aurang* (The Seven Thrones).

THE AGE OF DISCOVERY

The reign of the Xuande emperor is marked by active patronage of the arts. He replaces the early informal manner of administering court painters with a more rigorous system in which they are appointed duty at the Renzhi Hall. The latter, due to its visibility, is known informally as the Huayuan, or Painting Academy. An imperial foundry for the production of fine bronze and copper vessels was also established, as is the system of marking ceramics with reign dates to indicate their period of production.

Suzhou in Jiangsu Province and other cities in the southeast flourished as economic and cultural centers. Wealthy families lived in elegant garden homes amassing important collections of paintings, calligraphy, bronzes, and other antiquities and supported professional painters and other craftsmen. In addition, Suzhou was home to scholar-amateur artists such as Shen Zhou (1427–1509) and Wen

Ming dynasty bronze Buddha.

Zhengming (1470–1559), who are noted for their calligraphic ink paintings of landscapes, flowers, and figures. They and their circle are often categorized as the Wu School after the ancient name for the city.

Arts also flourished during the reign of the Zhenghua emperor, himself a proficient painter. Known as doucai (contrasting colors), porcelain decorated with images outlined first in cobalt blue under the glaze and colored with enamels over the glaze reaches its peak of development. Luxury textiles were produced in large quantities in the southern cities of Suzhou and Hangzhou.

The life of Wang Shouren (also Yangming), one of the most important intellectuals of the Ming dynasty, noted for his idealistic and intuitive approach to moral cultivation. Wang's "teaching of the mind," or xinxue, system argues that knowledge is innate, immediately apprehensible, and can be acquired in many pursuits.

Mongol incursions into northern China help spur the addition of extensions to the "Great Wall." This work continues

1414–1430

1414–1451 Sayyid Dynasty in Delhi, India.
1416 Ottoman Turks defeated by Venice at Dardanelles.
1419 Philip III (Philip the Good) becomes the Duke of Burgundy; creates a powerful state in Europe.

c. 1420–1506 Life of Japanese Zen Buddhist artist Sesshu, master of ink painting.
c. 1425 Pueblo people in New Mexico build multi-storied buildings with stone and Sun-dried bricks.

Ottoman–Venetian Treaty of 1416

15th Century Venetian trading Galley.

The Ottoman–Venetian Maritime Treaty of 1416 was signed between the Ottoman Empire and the Republic of Venice, ending a short conflict between the two powers. On 29 May 1416, the Venetian fleet defeated the Ottoman fleet laying the foundation for the maritime treaty under the mediation of the Byzantine Emperor Manuel II Palaiologos. The treaty was the base of their future maritime trade. Under this treaty the Ottoman Empire had to give many concessions to the Venetians as well as both sides returned each other's prisoners. It was also agreed that both the kingdoms would together fight piracy.

Ottoman Turks

Osman, who died in 1326, founded the Osmanli or Ottoman state, northeast of Turkey. His dynasty lasted for 600 years as his successors extended their realm into Byzantine lands through war and diplomacy. By 1398, the Ottomans controlled Anatolia, Thrace, Macedonia, and parts of Bulgaria and Serbia. Bayazid was defeated by Timur in 1402, but later the Ottomans regained their lands and continued to expand their territories. The political, economic, and social institutions of the classical Islamic empires and those of Byzantium and the great Turkish empires of Central Asia were merged and reshaped in the new forms that were to distinguish the area. Their greatest victory was the capture of Constantinople in 1453, thus bringing the declining Byzantine Empire to an end. Under the Ottomans, great literature was composed in Persian and Turkish, while Arabic was used for scientific and religious works.

OTTOMAN ART AND ARCHITECTURE

Glazed pottery and silver and gold metalwork reached a high degree of excellence. Intricate designs were woven on textiles and carpets. The great Topkapi palace in Constantinople (formally renamed Istanbul in 1930), as well as mosques and tombs, were constructed. Heavy domes were raised on square bases and brilliantly colored tiles decorated the buildings.

The Suleimaniye mosque, built in the 1550s in Istanbul by the Ottomans.

1428–29 Orleans in France rescued from the English by Joan of Arc.

1429 Cosimo de Medici is head of Medici banking house in Florence; richest man of his time.

1430 Order of Golden Fleece, an order of knights, founded by Philip the Good of Burgundy.

c. 1430–1435 Italian sculptor Donatello (c. 1386–1466) creates bronze image of David;

THE AGE OF DISCOVERY

There were wars between England and France in Europe, and civil war within England. The Byzantine empire fought its last battle against the Turks. In Russia, the state of Muscovy began to expand; in 1480, Ivan III declared himself grand prince of all Russia. Among the Scandinavian countries, Sweden asserted her independence in 1523.

At the same time, Europe saw a flowering of culture. Protestantism developed within Christianity; urban centers flourished along with trade and commerce; and Europeans went on voyages of exploration, establishing colonies and settlements around the world.

Hundred Years' War: the final phases

There was political confusion in France and England before the third phase of the Hundred Years' War (1415–1435). Eventually, the French regained lost territory. In 1435, peace negotiations began with Charles VII of France. However, due to this, Philip the Good of Burgundy, who had supported the English, withdrew support, and France regained Paris in 1436. Using the mobile cannon to its best advantage, France wrested back more territories. A 5-year truce was signed in 1444, but hostilities were resumed. Eventually, the Hundred Years' War ended after the Battle of Castillon, in 1453. In France, only Calais remained under the control of the English.

The Battle of Castillon, by the French painter Charles-Phillippe Larivière, 19th century.

1431–1450

first sculpture in Western Europe cast in the round, and first nude, since ancient times.

1431 Angkor, capital of Khmer kingdom in Cambodia, invaded and destroyed by people from Thailand; new capital at Phnom Penh.

1438 Emperor Pachacuti in Peru expands Inca empire: Machu Picchu probably built for him.

c. 1441 Maya city of Mayapan destroyed; region divided into separate city-states.

JOAN OF ARC

Born in 1412 in France to a poor farmer's family, Joan of Arc spent her day taking care of the animals. Joan of Arc is said to have had visions of St. Michael and St. Catherine asking her to become the savior of France and encouraging her to work with Charles, who was next in line to the throne. She was directed to send the English people back to England and take his position as the rightful king. In the course of the Hundred Years' War, Joan of Arc, also known as "The Maid of Orléans," led the French army toward victory over the English. She was called the national heroine of France; later, she was burnt at the stake for being a heretic by the English and their French collaborators. On May 16, 1920, after almost 500 years she was pronounced as a Roman Catholic saint.

Joan's visions asked her to go to Vaucouleurs and meet the garrison commander and a supporter of Charles by the name of Robert de Baudricourt. Joan was first criticized with a z and rejected for her claims but, with over, people started believing in her visions, which is when, in 1429, they agreed to give her claims her a horse and an escort of several soldiers. She had to chop off her hair before undertaking the journey, which took her 11 days.

Joan won the trust of Prince Charles by identifying him among a crowd of members of his court, where he came dressed in a manner that would conceal his presence among the others. During their conversation, Joan revealed the prayer he had to say in order to save France. At the age of 17, she received her armor and a horse and was allowed to accompany the army to Orléans, the site of an English siege.

In the battle that took place between May 4 and May 7, 1429, the French took control over the English. Charles VII was crowned on July 18, 1429, after entering Reims, on Joan's advice, immediately after the war. Joan stood by his side at the time of his crowning.

However, Charles did nothing when she was captured by the English and a tribunal announced Joan of Arc guilty of heresy on May 29, 1431. She was 19 years old when she was taken amid a crowd of 10,000 people and burned at the stake. Her heart is said to have survived the fire.

- The Portuguese bring first African slaves to Lisbon.
- **1448** Portuguese navigator Dinis Dias discovers and names Cape Verde, the western-most part of Africa.

- **c. 1450** French painter Jean Fouquet (c.1416–80) paints the Melun Diptych.
- Vatican Library, originating from earlier papal collections of books and documents, established.

THE AGE OF DISCOVERY

The Wars of the Roses

The Hundred Years' War had hardly ended when a civil war, known as the War of the Roses, was fought between the Houses of York (white rose emblem) and Lancaster (red rose emblem) in England. The main battles took place between 1455 and 1485. Henry VI of Lancaster, backed by his powerful queen, Margaret of Anjou, was challenged by Richard, Duke of York. Both sides were descended from King Edward III, and were aided by feudal lords, their vassals, and mercenaries. The worst battle was that of Towton, in 1461, when 28,000 men were killed in a single day. Edward, son of Richard, was crowned king as Edward IV after this battle, but the Wars were not over. Richard, the Duke of Gloucester, seized the throne from Edward V (son of Edward IV) and became King Richard III. The Lancastrian, Henry Tudor, then defeated Richard III at the Battle of Bosworth and was crowned Henry VII. He united the factions through marriage and established the Tudor dynasty in England.

The red rose of the House of Lancaster (extreme left). The white rose of the House of York (middle). The Tudor rose symbolizing the union (extreme right).

ELIZABETH I

The queen of England and Ireland (1558–1603), Elizabeth I was the last ruler of the Tudor dynasty founded by Henry VII. She faced numerous problems during her reign, including a conflict with Mary, Queen of Scots, war with Spain and the French Catholic League, and rebellion in Ireland.

Arguably the most famous English before, Elizabeth I was a long-ruling queen of England, with an era named after her (Elizabethan era). She governed with prosperity for 44 years. Born on September 7, 1533 in Greenwich, England, Queen Elizabeth I was a princess but was initially beforeillegitimate through political machinations. She eventually claimed the throne at the young

1451–1470

1451–1526 Lodi Dynasty in Delhi, India.
1452–1519 Life of Italian polymath Leonardo da Vinci.
1453 Hundred Years' War between France and England ends.

1455 Civil war, Wars of the Roses, in England.
• Johannes Gutenberg of Germany prints first book in Europe using fully moveable type.
1458 Matthias Corvinus becomes king of Hungary; recognized by Holy Roman Emperor in 1462.

age of 25. she held it for 44 years. During her reign, England saw glorious days and she led it through wars, and political and religious turmoil.

Elizabeth I was the daughter of King Henry VIII and his second wife, Anne Boleyn, who was beheaded on the orders of Henry VIII on adultery and conspiracy charges, when Elizabeth was only 2 years old. As a consequence, Elizabeth and her older half-sister Mary were declared to be illegitimate by her father though they were later reinstated as potential heirs. Their half-brother Edward was born in 1537 to Henry VIII's third wife, Jane Seymour.

Raised as a royal child, Elizabeth was taught by tutors and she was good at languages and music. After Edward's death in 1553, her cousin, Lady Jane Grey, was appointed as a successor, but her reign proved to be short-lived. After only 9 days on the throne, she was unseated by Mary, Elizabeth's older sister, who had gained the support of the English people.

After the death of Mary in 1558, Elizabeth took over the reins of her country. At that time, the country was at war with France. Thanks to Mary, there was also great tension between different religious factions, as Mary had wanted to restore England to Roman Catholicism.

Elizabeth soon showed her talents as a diplomat, managing the country with deft hands. Although she saw troubled times marking the end of her reign, Elizabeth is largely remembered as being a queen who supported her people. Owing to the long duration during which she held the throne, her subjects were happy, and thanks to her sharp wits and clever mind, the nation surged ahead in spite of religious and political challenges. Her reign has been referred to as the Golden Age of the English Renaissance. Writers of this time included William Shakespeare, Edmund Spenser, and Philip Sidney. Elizabeth herself was a scholar and linguist. She had a love for theater and plays were performed in her honor. She breathed her last on March 24, 1603.

1461 Louis IX becomes king of France.
1461–83 Reign of Edward IV of England.
1462 Ivan III is grand duke of Muscovy.
1466–77 Onin War between two rival clans in Japan.

c. 1469–70 Thomas Malory (d.1471), English writer, composes prose epic Le Morte d'Arthur (The Death of Arthur).
1470 Portuguese explorers reach Gold Coast in Africa.

THE AGE OF DISCOVERY

Martin Luther (1483–1546).

The Reformation

From the 14th century onward, some people openly challenged practices that had crept into Christianity. The before monk, Martin Luther published his *Ninety-Five Theses* on October 31, 1517, the eve of All Saints' a date, date that marks the beginning of the Reformation. Born on November 10, 1483, in Germany, Martin Luther became one of the most influential figures of Christian history. He began the Protestant Reformation in the 16th century. His followers started adopting Protestant traditions after he raised queried the beliefs of Roman Catholicism.

He received his master's degree in arts from the University of Erfurt. One moment in his life, when he was stuck in a storm, made him change his views on life. He gave up everything and chose to become a monk. He wanted salvation through an ascetic life in the monastery. However, he was soon disillusioned by the impious practices in the monastery. He could clearly see the level of corruption within the church. His experience left him full of sorrow. Afterward, he enrolled in the University of Wittenberg, where he received his doctorate. In 1513, while preparing lectures, he gained the real meaning of enlightenment. Later, while preparing a lecture on Paul's Epistle to the Romans, he read the line, "The just will live by faith." Which actually meant that fear was not a way of achieving salvation, but a deep faith was all that mattered. In his publication, he protested against various aspects of Church functioning. He believed that people should be freed from the authority of the pope, and should be able to gain direct experience of God themselves through the Bible. Martin Luther claimed that what distinguished him from previous reformers was that while they attacked corruption in the life of the church, he went to the theological root of the problem. His views had a huge impact, and other reformers began to preach similar ideas. Among them were Huldrych Zwingli in Zurich, and John Calvin, a French theologian settled in Geneva. Gradually, entire groups, and even countries, broke away from the Roman Catholic Church. They came to be known as Protestants, and set up their own churches. Despite attempts to reform the Catholic Church, known as the Counter Reformation, Protestantism flourished and expanded. In England, the Reformation's roots were both political and religious. Henry VIII, incensed by Pope Clement VII's refusal to grant him an annulment of his marriage, repudiated papal authority and in 1534, established the Anglican Church with the king as the supreme head.

1471–1486

1471–1528 Life of German painter Albrecht Durer.
1475–1564 Life of Italian artist and sculptor Michelangelo.
1476 First English printing press set up by William Caxton, at Westminster.

1478 Tarascan and Aztec empires clash in Central America.
• Start of the Spanish Inquisition.
1483 Richard III becomes the king of England; he is the last of the House of York.

Explorers and traders

Flourishing cities and the expansion of trade led to a search for new lands. The occupation of Constantinople by the Turks forced Europeans to find different routes to the East. The early explorers and colonizers were largely Portuguese and Spanish, though the English and French also ventured into Africa, the Americas, and the East.

The Portuguese were the first Europeans to tap into Africa's lucrative trade of gold, copper, and slaves. Henry the navigator, prince of Portugal, organized numerous voyages of exploration from 1434 onwards. In the late 15th century, the Portuguese discovered the sea route around Africa. In 1497–98, Vasco da Gama followed the route around the Cape of Good Hope and reached India.

Vasco da Gama

Vasco da Gama was born in Sines, Portugal, to a noble family. He joined the navy at an early age, where he acquired the knowledge of navigation. He was sent by King John II of Portugal to the south of Lisbon and, then, to the Algarve region of the country, to seize the French-owned ships as a sign of Portuguese displeasure at the French government's act of halting Portuguese ships from sailing. After King Manuel took charge of the kingdom, the Portugese revived their earlier mission of finding a direct route toward India. Portugal was at the peak of its prosperity and power at this time. On July 8, 1497, Vasco da Gama captained a team consisting of four vessels, which included his flagship, the 200-ton *St. Gabriel*, to discover a sailing route to India and the East.

Vasco da Gama
(1460–1524).

Construction at the Kremlin under Ivan III.

The Kremlin

The citadel of a Russian city is known as a kremlin. Under Ivan III (r. 1462–1505), the Moscow kremlin was rebuilt with a new wall and towers, a new palace, and three new cathedrals. The great bell tower was built by Ivan's son Vasily III between 1505 and 1508.

• Dominican monk Tomas de Torquemada appointed to conduct Spanish Inquisition.
1483 Babur, founder of the Mughal Empire, born in, Central Asia.
1483–1520 Life of Italian painter Raphael.

1485 Jewish philosopher Joseph Albo writes *Sefer ha-Ikkarim* (Book of Principles), explaining the aspects of Judaism.
1485–1603 Tudor dynasty rules England.
1486 Aztecs defeat Guarrero and Oaxaca people.

THE AGE OF DISCOVERY

By taking advantage of the prevailing winds along the coast of Africa, he pointed his ships toward the south. Vasco da Gama sailed round the Cape of Good Hope and up the eastern coast of Africa, toward the uncharted waters of the Indian Ocean. They stopped at Mozambique, Africa, which was dominated by Muslim traders. They had to depart from there as the king was not pleased with the gifts he received from the explorers. They set foot upon after in southern India on May 20, mistaking the people there to be Christians. They were welcomed and they stayed there for three months. Muslim traders, however, were in no mood to accept the growing competition with the emergence of Christian traders. His first journey covered nearly 24,000 miles, taking almost 2 years, and out of the 170 who had set sail with him, only 54 people survived. He came back as a hero, opening the way to many more such trips to India. In 1502, he undertook the same journey with a greater number of people, with the idea of conquering more of India and removing the Muslim traders He reached home on October 11, 1502 with a firmer grip of authority over India. In 1524, King John III named da Gama the Portuguese viceroy in India.

The Renaissance

Michelangelo.

Italy, in the 14th century, saw the beginning of a period called the Renaissance (rebirth), characterized by a revival of interest in the arts of classical Greece and Rome. It is a period of history seen as a glorious age, whereas the Middle Ages were condemned for cultural stagnation. The renewed interest in the classical was combined with new concepts and ideas. The background for the Renaissance lay in economic change. Trade and commerce had led to the rise of wealthy cities in Italy, among which were Florence, Venice and Milan. Rich families such as the Medici of Florence, the Gonzaga of Mantua, the dukes of Urbino, and the Doges of Venice patronized Renaissance art and education. Although Christianity and the Church continued to be important, there was a growth of secular ideas. "Humanism" is a term used to describe these ideas, emphasizing the importance of the human

Leonardo da Vinci.

1488–1502

1488–1576 Life of Italian painter Titian.
1489 Bahlol Lodi of the Delhi Sultanate dies.
1490 Portuguese explorers reach Congo.
1492 Christopher Columbus sets sail for the East Indies.

1493 Askia the Great rules the Songhai Empire.
1494 Christopher Columbus reaches the Caribbean Islands.
1497 On July 8, 1497, Vasco da Gama sets sail to discover a route to India and the East.

Last Supper by Leonardo da Vinci.

being, rather than god. Secular histories, which did not incorporate Christian theories of creation and the Last Judgment, were written. Theological questions addressed by Humanists came to have an impact on Christianity.

In art, classical forms were revisited. A technique, called the linear perspective, which gave depth to a drawing or painting, was understood and adopted. Among the greatest artists of the Renaissance were Raphael, Leonardo da Vinci, and Michelangelo. In sculpture, the human body once again became important. There were fresh trends in architecture. Literature began to be composed in regional languages. Ancient Greek treatises were translated. Nicolaus Copernicus, Tycho Brahe, Johannes Kepler, and Galileo were among the pioneers who opened new dimensions in science.

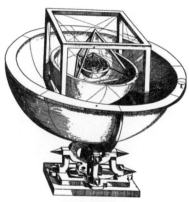

The solar system model developed by Johannes Kepler.

1497 Vasco da Gama sets foot upon Calicut on, south India and mistakes the people there as Christians.

1497–98 Spanish explorer Amerigo Vespucci explores North America; Americas are named after him.

1499 Plague epidemic kills thousands in London.

1500 Pedro Alvares Cabral reaches Brazil; makes it a Portuguese dominion.

1502 Safavid dynasty of Persia assumes power in Azerbaijan.

THE AGE OF DISCOVERY

Nicolaus Copernicus

stablishing the concept of a heliocentric solar system, in which the Sun, and not the Earth, is the center of the solar system, was one of the famous discoveries of Nicolaus Copernicus. Born on February 19, 1473, in Torun, Poland, he was the first one to propose that the Sun is at a fixed point to the motions of the planet Earth. According to his findings, Earth rotated around the Sun and also on its own axis.

It was only in 1514 that he shared his findings with the friends and fellow astronomers in the book *The Commentariolus* (*Little Commentary*). The final version of his book is known as *De Revolutionibus Orbium Coelestium Libri VI* (Six Books Concerning the Revolutions of the Heavenly Orbs), which was

Nicolaus Copernicus (1473–1543).

printed in 1543. Great scientists such as Galileo, Kepler, Descartes, and Newton referred to his work.

Copernicus was appointed a canon in the cathedral of Frombork, Poland, but this gave him less time for his own research work. In 1496, Copernicus traveled to Italy, where he studied religious law at the University of Bologna. This was the place where he met the astronomer Domenico Maria Novara. In 1501, moved to the University of Padua to study medicine, but then went to the University of Ferrara, from where he earned his doctorate. From 1510, he lived at the Frombork cathedral as a canon.

By 1508, he started developing his more repetition heliocentric planetary systemputting, putting the Sun at the center of the solar system. Copernicus also believed that the size and speed of each planet's orbit depends upon its distance from the Sun.

In 1513, Copernicus designed his own model based on which he assumed the planetary orbits to occur in perfect circles. Later, this was proved wrong by the German astronomer Johannes Kepler, who proved the planetary orbits to be elliptical in shape. Copernicus' theories challenged the Roman Catholic Church, which banned his book in 1616. Copernicus is said to have died clutching onto his book *De revolutionibus* on his death bed on May 24, 1543 in Frombork.

1504–1514

1504 Zahir-ud-din-Muhammad Babur conquers Kabul.

1505 The Portuguese conquer African kingdoms of Quiloa and Mombasa; reach India.

1507 Shaibanid dynasty established in Transoxiana area of Central Asia.

1508 Nicolaus Copernicus starts developing his own celestial model, a heliocentric planetary system.

Tycho Brahe

Tycho Brahe (1546–1601).

Tycho Brahe was a Danish astronomer who also developed astronomical instruments that were used in measuring and fixing the positions of stars. He made accurate observations of more than 777 fixed stars as well as of the planets of the solar system.

Born in 1546, Tycho Brahe studied at the **University of Copenhagen** in 1559–62. He predicted a total eclipse of the Sun on August 21, 1560, which was advanced work for a 14-year-old. He would take lectures on jurisprudence during the day and secretly live his dream of astronomy at night. His professors were helpful in providing him with books of astronomy and building globes where he would position his stars.

He completed his further studies at the University of Leipzig until 1565. Later, in August 1563, he made a significant observation on the overlapping of Jupiter and Saturn.

He traveled within Europe, studying at Wittenberg, Rostock, Basel, and Augsburg, acquiring knowledge. Then on November 11, 1572, he saw a star brighter than Venus itself and at the position in the constellation Cassiopeia where no star should have been.

For the world at that time, this was a revolutionary discovery, because according to the Aristotlian doctrine, the universe beyond the solar system was supposed to be fixed and unchanging. The news that stars could change their position had a major impact on human thinking.

Brahe coined the word "nova" for a new star, and published his observations in De nova stella in 1573.

The German king Frederick II gave Brahe the island of Hven near Copenhagen as a place to build an observatory. There, he made the most accurate astonomical observations of the time.

Brahe only accepted part of Nicolaus Copernicus' theory that the Sun is at the center of the Universe. He proposed that although the other planets did revolve around the Sun, the Sun itself revolved around the stationary Earth. He died in Prague in 1601, leaving his assistant Johannes Kepler to carry on his astronomical work.

1508 Pope Julius II finds League of Cambrai; fights against Venice.
1509 Henry VIII becomes the king of England.
1510 Portuguese conquer Goa in India.

1513 Italian Niccolo Machiavelli writes *The Prince.*
• Portuguese reach China via sea-route.
1514 Ottomans defeat Safavids of Persia; capture Persian capital Tabriz.

Johannes Kepler

Johannes Kepler was a German astronomer who is known for his discovery of the three major laws of planetary motion. Kepler's discoveries supported the heliocentric theory of Nicolaus Copernicus that the Earth and other planets revolve around the Sun, and his laws provided a foundation for much of our modern understanding of how the solar system works..

Kepler's ideas were published in his first work, *Mysterium Cosmographicum* (1596; Cosmographic Mystery).

Astronomers had long struggled to figure out why Mars appeared to walk backward across the night sky. No model of the solar system—not even Copernicus'—could account for the retrograde motion. Using Tycho Brahe's detailed observations, Kepler realized that the planets

Johannes Kepler (1571–1630).

traveled in "stretched out" circles known as ellipses. The Sun did not sit exactly at the center of their orbit, but instead lay off to the side, at one of the two points known as the focus. Some planets, such as Earth, had an orbit that was very close to a circle, but the orbit of Mars was one of the most eccentric, or widely stretched. The fact that planets travel on elliptical paths is known as Kepler's first law of planetary motion. His other 2 laws are:

2. An imaginary line from the center of the Sun to the center of a planet sweeps out equal areas in equal lengths of time. This means that planets move faster when closer to the Sun, and move slower when they are more distant from the Sun.

3. The squares of the sidereal periods (length of time of an orbit) of planets are directly proportional to the cubes of their mean distances from the Sun.

Apart from his laws on planetary motion, Kepler is also known for several other significant contributions to science. Among his other finds was that gravity was caused by two bodies, rather than one. Hence, the moon was the cause of the motion of tides on the

THE AGE OF DISCOVERY

Earth. These include the discovery that refraction drives vision in the eye and that using two eyes enables depth perception. For both near and farsightedness, he created eyeglasses and explained how a telescope works. He also described images and magnification, and understood the properties of reflection. He also coined the word "satallite."

Galileo

Galileo, or Galileo Galilei, was born on February 15, 1564 in Pisa, Italy. He was a physicist, an astronomer, a mathematician, and an inventor, building the first telescope powerful enough to observe the solar system in detail. He is known as the "father of modern science" since he pioneered the experimental, quantitative scientific method that is standard today.

Galileo is famous for dropping balls of different masses from the top of the Leaning Tower of Pisa. This may not have actually happened, but he did discover that falling objects of different mass have the same speed. Through his experiments he also developed his law of uniformly accelerated motion. He made many other discoveries, for example about pendulums and projectiles.

Galileo (1564–1642).

Galileo's telescope.

Through his astronomical observations, Galileo realized that Nicolaus Copernicus' heliocentric theory was correct, and the Earth did revolve around the Sun. Since the Catholic Church held that the Earth was at the centre of the universe, Galileo was called before the Inquisition in 1633, accused of heresy. The philosopher and scientist Giordano Bruno had been burnt at the stake in 1600 for heretical ideas, so Galileo recanted his views. He spent the rest of his life under house arrest.

Galileo died in Italy on January 8,1642, and 350 years later, in 1992, a papal commission admitted that the church had been wrong to suppress his work.

THE AGE OF DISCOVERY

By 1400, the population of North America, (north of Mexico) is estimated to have been between one and 10 million, with most people living in the area of today's USA and only about 250,000 living in the Canada region. There were about 240 tribal groups of Native Americans such as the Apache, Navajo, Iroquois, and others, most speaking different languages.

Christopher Columbus lands on an island in Central America (1492).

In South and Central America, where the empires of the Incas, Aztecs, and others thrived, the population would have been much higher.

Europeans reach the Americas

A population explosion in Europe as well as a desire to find new sources of wealth and gold prompted its inhabitants to seek new lands. In the late 15th century, Christopher Columbus, sponsored by the government of Spain, reached parts of the American continent. He was followed by other Spanish explorers. The Venetian John Cabot (1450–99), sailing for England, arrived on Newfoundland, in present-day Canada, in 1497. Jacques Cartier (1491–1557) of France reached the Strait of Belle Isle, off Canada's east coast, in 1534.

In the region of North America which later became the USA, the first permanent European settlement was founded in 1565 by the Spaniard Pedro Menendez de Aviles, at St Augustine in Florida. This was an area populated mainly by Seminole tribes. Sir Walter Raleigh of England attempted to set up settlements in the late 16th century, but these did not last. The first permanent English outpost was established in the 17th century.

THE IROQUOIS

By the 16th century, five Native American tribes of the Iroquoian language family, the Mohawk, Onondaga, Cayuga, Oneida, and Seneca, founded a confederacy. They dominated the region of present-day New York, and later expanded to neighboring areas. Their staple diet was corn, though they also grew pumpkin, beans, and tobacco.

1526–1531

1526 Turks defeat Hungarians at battle of Mohacs.
1527 Jakarta in Indonesia is founded.
1528–72 Christian missionaries convert native populations in Mexico.

1529 Zahir-ud-din-Muhammad Babur of India defeats the Afghans at the Battle of Ghaghra.
1530 Babur dies at the age of 48.

Course of the Maya, Aztec, and Inca empires

South and Central America saw conquests by Spain and Portugal. Civilizations that had existed for hundreds, even thousands, of years were destroyed, and new ways of life imposed. Spain occupied Maya, Inca, and Aztec lands. In the early 16th century, the Portuguese settled in Brazil.

The great Maya civilization had declined, but several distinct groups still existed until the arrival of the Spanish in 1517. As the Maya had many different centers, it took the Spanish a long time to establish control over them. The last states were conquered in 1697. Though the Maya produced a large number of books, only a few survived, as most were destroyed by the Spanish.

In 1427, the Aztec ruler Itzacoatl, with his capital at Tenochtitlan, joined with the cities of Tlacopan and Texcoco to defeat the Tapanec city of Azcapotzalco. The Aztecs now expanded into a large empire. By this time, Tenochtitlan, and its neighboring city Tlatelolco, were inhabited by more than 200,000 people. In 1502, Montezuma became Aztec emperor. The empire finally ended when Hernando Cortes (1485–1547), a Spanish soldier, reached Mexico and defeated the Aztecs in 1521.

In the first half of this period, the Inca empire continued to expand, and extended along the coast from northern Ecuador to Chile, a distance of 2,983 miles. The Incas had a state religion and a centralized administration. Priests conducted sacrificial rituals and prophesied the future. The Incas had developed an advanced system of medicine,

even conducting successful surgeries. The beautiful city of Machu Picchu, with stone buildings and terraced fields, was built between two mountain peaks in the Andes in c. 1450.

In 1532, the Spaniard Francisco Pizarro's attack brought the main empire to an end. However, a new Inca empire was created in the northwest mountainous region of Vilcabamba. It survived till 1572, before being subjugated by the Spanish.

Machu Picchu.

1530 Babur succeeded by his eldest son Humayun.
1530 Spaniard Alvarado defeats the Mayas.
• Knights Hospitaller settle on island of Malta; become known as Knights of Malta.

1530–84 Life of Ivan IV (the Terrible) of Russia.
1531 Protestant Schmalkaldic League formed against Holy Roman Emperor.

THE AGE OF DISCOVERY

Africa saw continuous changes in boundaries and dynasties, often due to conflict over natural resources or trade. Islam, initially a religion of the ruling classes and urban centers, began to be accepted by ordinary people, especially in Sudan.

The Songhai empire

Artist's impression of Askia Muhammad of Songhai.

The last and largest of the precolonial empires in West Africa, the **Songhai empire**, had its capital at Gao near the Niger River. Songhai expanded in all directions until it stretched west to the Atlantic coast and east into Niger and Nigeria. The city of Gao was established around 800, but it was only in the 11th century that it was first referred to as the capital city. **Sunni Ali Ber** was considered as the first great ruler of Songhai, responsible for conquering the cities of **Timbuktu**, **Jennen**, and **Gao**, which were great trading centers as well as places of Islamic learning. Later, during the reign of Askia Muhammad (1493–1528), with Islam becoming an important part of the empire, Sharia law was introduced. He expanded his empire and took charge over the trade around Mali. In 1591, the Moroccan army invaded and conquered the cities of Timbuktu and Gao.

Economic structure

A well-guarded economic trade existed throughout the empire, due to the 200,000 army personnel stationed in the provinces. Primary to the economic foundation of the Songhai empire were the gold fields of the Niger River. These gold fields, which were often independently operated, provided a steady supply of gold that could be purchased and bartered for salt. Salt was considered so precious a commodity in West Africa that gold was traded for equal weight in salt. Salt, gold, and the slave trade put together were the bulk of trans-Saharan trade, and the Songhai dominance in these commodities solidified Songhai's role as a leader in the system.

The julla, or merchants, formed partnerships which the state protected, and so it protected the port cities on Niger. It was a very strong and powerful trading kingdom. Also,

1534–1541

1534 Protestant Christianity established in England; the king is supreme head of Church.

1535 Wales incorporated into the English legal and government system by the Act of Union.

1536 Spanish conquest of Aztec and Inca empires complete.

1538 Ottoman Turks led by Khair ad-Din (Barbarossa) defeat combined forces of Venice,

the government was centralized by creating a large and elaborate bureaucracy to oversee the empire's interests. Weights, measures, and currency were standardized so that culture throughout the Songhai became homogenized.

Decline of the Songhai empire

Like its predecessors Ghana, Kanem, and Mali, Songhai was fraught with civil war; in the late 16th century, a situation made worse by drought and disease. The empire might have survived these challenges were it not for the wealth of the kingdom and the determination of their foes to control the gold trade. The economic dominance of the Songhai empire proved to be its downfall, as it enticed many of its competitors to use military force to stifle the

Great Mosque, built by Emperor Musa I of Mali in 1327, Timbuktu, Mali.

power of the Songhai. Most significant among the challengers to the Songhai dominion was the Morocco, which sought control of Songhai's extensive wealth. In 1591, Moroccan Sultan Ahmad I al-Mansur Saadi dispatched a strong force under Judar Pasha. (Judar Pasha was a Spaniard by birth but was captured at a young age and educated at the Moroccan court.) After a cross-Saharan march, Judar's forces razed the salt mines at Taghaza and moved on to Gao. When Askia Ishaq II met Judar at the Battle of Tondibi, the Songhai forces were routed by the Moroccan gunpowder weapons, despite their vastly superior numbers. Judar sacked Gao, Timbuktu, and Djenné, destroying the Songhai as a regional power.

However, governing a vast empire over a long distance proved too much for the Moroccans, and they soon relinquished control of the region, letting it splinter into dozens of smaller kingdoms. The final blow to the Songhai Empire was not losing to the Moroccans, but the inability of the disjointed smaller kingdoms to form a political alliance and reassert a strong central government. The Moroccan invasion also served to free many of the Songhai tributary states that had previously been plural sources of slaves for the trans-Saharan trade routes. Seizing their chance of freedom, the slave populations rose to deal the final blow to the weakened empire. The largest of these groups was the Doghorani, who played an instrumental role in the rebellion.

Holy Roman Emperor Charles V, and Pope Paul III in naval battle; control Mediterranean.
1539 Sher Shah defeats Humayun in the Battle of Chausa in India.

1540 Sher Shah defeats Humayun in the Battle of Kanauj.
1541–1614 Life of Spanish painter El Greco.

THE AGE OF DISCOVERY

Gao

The ancient city of Gao has been reconstructed from oral history and tombstone writings at the burial sites of kings. While the two sources of historical record do not always agree in detail, together they sketch the story of Gao, beginning in the seventh century CE. However, it was not considered to be the center of the Songhai Empire until early in the 11th century. The earliest records of Gao describe it as a bustling trade center that had established political autonomy.

The beautiful Tomb of Askia in Gao is a UNESCO World Heritage Site.

Capitalizing on the conditions already existing in Gao, the Songhai chose it as their capital in 1010, a move which set Gao along the road of future development and growth.

Dia Kossoi

Dia Kossoi was the first ever recorded dia or king of the Songhai empire. He was responsible for converting the empire to Islam in 1010, and naming Gao as the new capital of the kingdom. His conversion was a pragmatic measure to further relations with Berber traders, who controlled the caravans and played a major role in the economy of the empire. The existence of non-Muslim customs in the royal court even after Dia Kossoi's embrace of Islam is proof of his pragmatism.

Under Mali rule

In the early 14th century, the powerful ruler of Mali, Mansa Musa, led a series of campaigns to seize control of the trans-Saharan trade routes and gain the wealth of Gao. Although he was successful, his new territories proved to be too expansive, and Mali governance over Songhai lands only lasted about 50 years.

1542–1555

1542 Jalaluddin Muhammed Akbar born to the second Mughal Emperor Humayun and his teenaged bride Hamida Banu Begum in Sind, now in Pakistan.

1543 Copernicus dies
1545 Sher Shah of India dies.
1545–96 Life of British explorer Francis Drake.

Also, Mansa Musa and Mali are mentioned back on page 118 when he lived from 1307-1332, so I believe 15th century should be 14th. This would explain some of my confusion over dates.

But both this and the next paragraph (or the first half of it) are in the wrong chronological place.

Sunni dynasty

Around 1335, the line of Dia kings came to an end and was replaced by a new series of leaders whose title was Sunni or Shi. The second man to bear the title of Sunni, Suleiman-Mar, was responsible for gaining Songhai independence from Mali in 1375. The establishment of an independent Songhai Empire caused another period of geographic expansion, spearheaded by Sunni Ali.

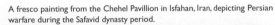

A fresco painting from the Chehel Pavillion in Isfahan, Iran, depicting Persian warfare during the Safavid dynasty period.

1546 Catholic forces defeat Schmalkaldic League in Battle of Muhlberg.

1553 Mary, Queen of England, suppresses revolt of supporters of Lady Jane Grey.

1555 Peace of Augsberg allows German states to follow their chosen Catholic or Protestant religion.

• French astrologer and physician Nostradamus writes his prophecies.

Sunni Ali, crowned around 1464, was a military leader who led by example and used war as an effective means of uniting dissenting factions. He was never defeated in battle and used his military prowess to quell Tuareg raids in the north and Mossi incursions in the south. His military campaigns provided economic benefit to the empire, as he controlled the critical trade routes and cities such as Timbuktu. Sunni Ali brought great wealth to the Songhai Empire, which at its height surpassed the wealth of the Mali.

Askia dynasty

In the late 16th century, the reigning Sunni, Muhammad Turay, or Askia the Great, of the Mandé people gained power. His rise to power was facilitated by religious strife within the Songhai empire, as previous leaders had tried to appeal to many religious groups at once, and in doing so, failed to satisfy any of them. Drawing his largest power base from Muslim urban centers, Askia the Great broke with Sunni tradition and a political system based on strict interpretations of Islamic law. His dictates were enforced by a well-trained military and were carried into the far reaches of the western Sudan under a program of expansion.

Muhammad Turay brought political reform, along with the implementation of religious ideology and revitalization. He set up a complex bureaucracy with separate departments for agriculture, the army, and the treasury, to each of which he appointed supervising officials.

The Bornu kingdom

The Bornu Empire (1396–1893) was a medieval African state, founded centuries earlier by the **Sayfawa dynasty**, which today includes the modern-day countries of **Niger, Chad, Cameroon**, and **Nigeria**. Idris Alooma (r. c. 1580–1617) was the best-known ruler of the Bornu kingdom, which existed in the Sudan region from the 8th century to the 17th century. Idris is known for his military skills, administrative reforms, and Islamic piety. Alooma introduced a number of legal and administrative reforms based on his religious beliefs and Islamic law (Sharia). His army included a camel corps, and Bornu was the only state in the region with firearms, bought from the Ottomans.

1555–1561

1555 Humayun recaptures Kandahar in india; meets accidental death after falling from the staircase of his library.

1556 Akbar the Great becomes Mughul emperor.

1556 Philip II becomes king of Spain.

• Tobacco introduced in Europe (Spain) from Central America; reaches England by **1585**.

Timbuktu

Founded probably in the 11th century, Timbuktu, north of the great bend in the Niger river, was incorporated into the kingdom of Mali by the 14th century. It developed into a renowned center of Islamic culture and learning. The city reached its height under the Songhai empire, and in the 16th century, held a population of around 40,000. It was an important center on the trans-Sahara trade network.

There are several stories concerning the derivation of the city's name. Possibly Timbuktu was named after an old woman left to oversee the camp while the Tuareg roamed the Sahara. Her name meant "mother with a large navel," possibly describing an umbilical hernia or other such physical malady.

In 1468, the city was conquered by the Songhai ruler Sonni Ali. He was generally ill-disposed toward the city's Muslim scholars, but his successor—the first ruler of the new Askia dynasty, Muhammad I Askia of Songhai (reigned 1493–1528)—used the scholarly

Timbuktu's Sankore Mosque had evolved into a great university by the time the Songhai empire was established.

1559 Peace treaty of Cateau-Cambresias ends wars between France and Spain over territory in Italy.

1560 Religious reformer John Knox establishes Presbyterian Church in Scotland.

1560 Tycho Brahe predicts a total eclipse of the Sun.

1561–1636 Life of Italian physician Sanctorius Sanctorius; initiates studies in human metabolism.

elite as legal and moral counselors. During the Askia period (1493–1591), Timbuktu was at the height of its commercial and intellectual development. After it was captured by Morocco in 1591, the city declined. European explorers reached Timbuktu in the early 19th century.

The Ottomans in Egypt

In 1517, before being conquered by the Ottoman Turks, Mamluks ruled Cairo under the protection of the Abbasid caliphs. Under the rule of Ottomans, Egypt was divided into 24 districts, each district being called an emir. The Mamluks, however, were retained in the administration, and by the 17th century they had assumed real power, while acknowledging, at the same time, the supremacy of the Ottomans.

East African city-states

Malindi, Mogadishu, and Mombasa were some of the city-states of East Africa. Each of these cities evolved from agricultural villages that produced goods on a small scale. The rulers at that time were the Arab-Africans, while the ordinary people were Bantu speakers. Swahili, as a culture and society, emerged from complex historical interactions between Africans and immigrants in a dynamic Indian Ocean world.

Great Zimbabwe

The ruins of Great Zimbabwe.

A great civilization emerged in south-central Africa, located on the Zimbabwe Plateau between the Zambezi and Limpopo rivers. Great Zimbabwe was one of the largest trading empires between 1the 11th and 15th centuries, with all its trade conducted across the coast of the Indian Ocean. The word "Zimbabwe" meant stone houses in The Bantu language. Its founders were the ancestors of the modern Shona people of Zimbabwe. Around 1100, settlements within thick stone walls were built. Trade in gold and copper crossed the Indian Ocean to China. Luxury goods were imported in return. By c. 1450, the settlement at Great Zimbabwe was at the pinnacle of its fame. Massive stone walls

1564–1571

1564 Galileo Galilei is born in Pisa, Italy.
1564–87 Life of Tintoretto, Italian artist.
1564–1616 Life of English poet and playwright William Shakespeare.

1568 Oda Nobunaga ends control of Ashikaga shoguns in Japan.
1569 Gerardus Mercator, Flemish geographer and cartographer, creates a map projection named after him.

surrounded the complex, though the houses were simple thatched structures. Other centers have been found in modern Zimbabwe and in neighboring states.

The Manchu

Emperor Kangxi.

In China, the Ming were replaced by the Qing dynasty, also known as Manchu, in 1644. Though the Chinese resented the new rulers, who were from Manchuria, they gradually came to accept them. The Manchu were familiar with Chinese ways, and did not make drastic changes in the system of government, though they retained the top posts. The Manchu also introduced the practice of wearing the hair in a pigtail. In 1661, emperor Shunzi was succeeded by his seven-year-old son Kangxi, who reigned for 61 years. He respected Chinese traditions, maintained the Chinese as high officials in the civil service, and rebuilt Beijing. Old books and manuscripts were collected, and a 5000-volume encyclopedia was produced. Confucian ideals were emphasized.

Emperor Qianlong (r. 1736–96) destroyed Mongol power in Central Asia, and brought the Xinjiang Ughyur region under Chinese control. During his reign, China had a period of peace and prosperity. Qianlong was a great patron of arts, and himself studied painting and calligraphy. China became famous for its glazed pottery, textiles, art, and learning. Trade increased and new towns emerged. Tea and porcelain were exported to the Western world.

1570 Panama, in Central America, becomes important trading post.
- Jewish rabbi and mystic Isaac ben Luria develops influential school of Kabbalah.

1571 Ottoman fleet defeated in Battle of Lepanto; Turkish control over Mediterranean ends.
- Ridolfi plots to assassinate Queen Elizabeth I and place Mary, Queen of Scots, on the throne of England fails.

WARS, COLONIES, AND NEW STATES

The Tokugawa

There was a civil war between rival claimants for power in Japan. Ieyasu, of the powerful Tokugawa feudal family, won the Battle of Sekigahara against Ishida Mitsunari, and became the shogun in 1603. The Tokugawas ruled from Edo (modern Tokyo), while the emperors lived in luxury at Kyoto. Samurai warriors kept peace in the empire; another type of warrior were the ninja, trained in martial arts and employed as spies or assassins. Distrusting foreigners, Japan isolated itself from the rest of the world, becoming insular and dated. The period of Tokugawa shoguns lasted till 1868.

SIKHISM

In India, Guru Nanak (1469–1539) founded the Sikh religion. His basic tenets—belief in one god, who has no shape or form; an emphasis on ethical behavior; meditation on the divine name—were expanded by nine gurus (spiritual teachers) following him. The fifth guru, Arjan Dev, compiled the sacred teachings in what was later known as the Guru Granth Sahib, the holy book of the Sikhs.

Guru Nanak.

Mughals: Peak and decline

In north India, the Mughal rule continued under Jahangir (r. 1605–27), Shah Jahan (1628–58), and Aurangzeb (1659–1707). Wars and conquest were pursued by all three, but Aurangzeb became entrapped in attempts to conquer the independent kingdoms of central India. He spent 25 years away from the capital, Delhi.

Art and culture were vibrant under the Mughals. Jahangir's reign is known for its fine miniature paintings, and Shah Jahan's for grand buildings, including the white-marble wonder Taj Mahal. Aurangzeb did not promote the arts, but, in his absence, Delhi became a center of learning and culture. With the devastation caused by the invasion of Nadir Shah (1739), and later by the Afghan Ahmad Shah Abdali, the center of culture moved for some time to Lucknow.

Meanwhile, the Sikhs and Marathas were also struggling for control in India. Europeans, including the Portuguese, French, Dutch, and English, were establishing

1572–1582

1572 Danish astronomer Tycho Brahe discovers supernova in Cassiopeia constellation.
1576 English explorer Martin Frobisher discovers Baffin Island in Canada.

• Spanish Carmelite monk St John of the Cross describes mystical experiences in his poems.
1577–1640 Life of Flemish painter Peter Paul Reubens.

trading centers, while battling with each other and with indigenous rulers. By 1800, the British were the dominant power on the subcontinent.

There were ongoing warfare and political instabilities during the 17th and 18th centuries in central Europe. While various European powers had begun colonizing the world, within **Europe** wars continued. Some, such as the **Seven Years' War** (1756–63), fought both within and outside Europe, were over territory and trading rights, whereas the **Thirty Years' War** was over religious differences. Other conflicts arose from challenges to the "divine right" of kings to rule.

The Taj Mahal, Agra, built by Shah Jahan in memory of his wife.

Civil war in Britain

In 1640, King Charles I (1625–49) asked parliament for funds to suppress a long-lasting Scottish revolt. In return, parliament demanded more powers, and in 1642, civil war began between the king and representatives of the people, who raised their own armies. Charles was executed in 1649, and a republic, the English Commonwealth, was established, with the anti-royalist general Oliver Cromwell appointed as its leader or Protector in 1653. He provided stable government until his death in 1658, but in 1660 the royalty was revived under Charles II.

Politically unsuccessful, Charles I was a patron of the arts, commissioning portrait-painter Anthony van Dyck (1599–1641) and the architect Inigo Jones (1573–1652).

When he became a king, he came to strongly believe in king's divine right to rule, and because of this he lost the trust of the House of Commons. His reign was marked by religious and political strife.

Charles was a High Anglican, whose ways were responsible for arousing suspicion among his Protestant countrymen. As a result of which, in the first 4 years of his rule he dissolved parliament thrice. But in 1629, the parliament was dismissed by him altogether. This greatly angered the general public as ruling alone meant raising funds by non-parliamentary means. Meanwhile, religious oppression in the kingdom forced both

1578 Mongolian ruler Altan Khan bestows title of Dalai Lama (spiritual leader) on the leader of Tibet's Gelugpa Buddhist sect.

1578–1606 Manila becomes an important trading town in the Philippines.

c. 1581 Queen Anna Nzinga, one of the great women rulers of southwestern Africa (Angola) is born.

1582 Pope Gregory XIII introduces Gregorian calendar.

WARS, COLONIES, AND NEW STATES

Puritans and Catholics to move to the North American colonies.

Rising unrest in Scotland forced Charles's reign to come to an end, and the king was forced to call parliament back into session to obtain funds for war. In November 1641, the king faced violent military uprising in Ireland. Soon after, in 1642, civil war broke out in England. Charles and his army were defeated in 1646 by a collaboration of Scots and the New Model

A Delft blue and white vase.

THE DUTCH STATE

After a long fight for independence from Spain, the Dutch Republic of the United Provinces was established in 1648. The new state became rich through trade. Dutch blue and white pottery from Delft gained worldwide fame. There was significant scientific advancement: Christian Huyghens (1629–95) discovered that light travels in waves. Antonie van Leeuwenhoek (1632–1723) described the composition of blood, and observed bacteria and protozoa with a simple microscope. In painting, Rembrandt van Rijn (1606–69) and Johannes Vermeer (1632–75) are the great names from this time.

Army. As a result of this, Charles surrendered and was handed over to parliament. In 1647, he escaped to the Isle of Wight. But the parliamentarian general Oliver Cromwell defeated his army within a year, and thus ended the Second Civil War. Charles was tried for sedition and found guilty and sentenced to death. As stated earlier, Charles I was beheaded in London, England, on January 30, 1649.

Oliver Cromwell

A soldier and statesman, Oliver Cromwell was born on April 25, 1599 in Huntingdon, England. He supported religious tolerance although he himself firmly believed in the Puritan movement which held that the Church of England was only partly reformed, and needed to be purified of Roman Catholic practices. Puritans embraced piety both in personal behavior and in public bodies.

Oliver Cromwell.

1582–1597

1582 Akbar tried to start a new state religion in India called *Din-i-ilahi*.

1584 El Escorial, palace of the kings of Spain, completed near Madrid.

1587 Mary, Queen of Scots, executed by Elizabeth I of England.

1588 English defeat Spanish Armada, near Calais.

In 1640 Cromwell was elected a member of parliament for Cambridge, a city where there was a large Puritan population. On the outbreak of the Civil Wars he became an officer in the parliamentary army, winning several small battles and rising to become second-in-command of the newly formed New Model Army in 1645. He insisted on strict discipline, but also ensured his troops were well trained and equipped, and paid on time. His military prowess played a major part in winning the first civil war, and he later led campaigns in Ireland and to suppress further Royalist uprisings.

Cromwell supported the execution of the king and in 1653 became Lord Protector of the new Commonwealth of England, Scotland, and Ireland. He worked to restore England's status as a major European power, and died on September 3, 1659 in London. His republic did not last long: The monarchy was restored in 1660.

John Dryden

John Dryden (born on August 9, 1631, in Aldwinkle, Northamptonshire) was a English poet, dramatist, and literary critic who dominated the literary world of his time, a period known as the Age of Dryden.

Dryden attended Trinity **College**, Cambridge in 1950, from where he received his BA degree in 1654. He contributed to a memorial volume for Oliver Cromwell in 1959 which gave him importance as a poet. Then, John Dryden. when Charles II was restored to the throne in May 1660, Dryden wrote a poem of welcome He wrote *To His Sacred Majesty* for the coronation of the king in 1661. Dryden's ambitions and fortunes as a writer grew with his relationship with the monarchy.

Drydenwwrote the long sonnet, *Annus Mirabilis* (1667), to celebrate the two triumphs by the **English armada** over the Dutch and the Londoners' survival of the Great Fire of 1666. He became the first poet laureate in 1668 and 2 years later was appointed royal historiographer.

Soon after his restoration to the throne in 1660, Charles II granted two patents for theatres, which had been closed by the Puritans in 1642.

Dryden was one of the greatest poets of 17th century but he also wrote almost 30 tragedies, comedies, and dramatic operas. He played a key role as a critic of that time, which made Dr. Samuel Johnson call him "the father of English Criticism."

1591 The Moroccan army invades and conquers the cities of Timbuktu and Gao.

1591 French mathematician François Viète introduces new system of algebraic notation.

1596 Kepler creates his first work *Mysterium cosmographicum*.

1597 Jacopo Peri writes *Dafne*, the first opera.

WARS, COLONIES, AND NEW STATES

The Thirty Years' War

Ferdinand II.

Beginning in Bohemia as a Protestant struggle against the Catholic Habsburg King Ferdinand II, who was also the Holy Roman Emperor, the war (1618–48) gradually involved Denmark, Norway, Sweden, France, and numerous German states, many of which were worried about Habsburg power. Ferdinand II wanted to restore Catholicism as the only religion in the Holy Roman Empire, but the conflict soon became much wider than a religious war. It developed into a power struggle for dominance in Europe. At that time the family ruled Austria, Bohemia, Hungary, Spain, and other areas. The struggle ended with the Peace of Westphalia. France emerged as the major power in Europe, while the Habsburgs and the Holy Roman Emperor were weakened. The German states were devastated, losing at least 20 per cent of their population and going into economic decline.

Wars of Succession

The **War of the Spanish Succession** (1701–14) arose after the death of the last Spanish Habsburg ruler, Charles II, as he had no children of his own and succession to the throne of Spain became disputed. This war was fought by the Habsburg Holy Roman Empire, England, Portugal, and other European powers against Philip, Duke of Anjou, who was named the heir in Charles II's will. Philip

The Battle of Blenheim (1704) during the War of the Spanish Succession.

was the grandson of Louis XIV of France, and was supported by France, Bavaria, and Hungary. The war ended with Spain under the **Bourbons of France**.

Another major conflict was the War of the Austrian Succession (1740–48), when rival claimants challenged the accession of a woman, Maria Theresa, to the Habsburg Austrian lands. Most European countries were drawn in before her claim was recognized.

1599–1610

1599 Oliver Cromwell is born.
1600 English East India Company formed.
 • William Gilbert (1544–1603), English physicist, writes *De Magnete* (Of Magnets) on magnetism.

1601 Tycho Brahe dies.
1602 Dutch East India Company formed.
1605 Akbar dies in India.
1608 English East India Company ship reaches Surat, India.

PETER I

In the 17th century, Peter the Great was a Russian czar, best known for his innovative reforms. He was one of his country's greatest statesmen, organizers, and reformers. He was born in Moscow, Russia, on June 9, 1672. Among his achievements were the creation of a strong navy, reorganization of his army according to Western standards, the introduction of new administrative and territorial divisions of the country, and secularized schools with high standards. Peter the Great reigned with his brother Ivan V from 1682, untill Ivan expired in 1696.

Peter I.

When Peter assumed the throne, he inherited a nation that was regarded underdeveloped compared to other European countries. One reason for this was that Russia had shunned modernization, while the rest of Europe was swept by the Renaissance.

SWEEPING CHANGES

Under him, there was an all-round development of science, and he employed experts to enlighten his people about scientific advances. He was so passionate to make his country "developed," that he even traveled incognito to the advanced countries of the West, under the name of Sgt. Pyotr Mikhailov, to see how they had developed. He also studied shipbuilding and worked in the yard of the Dutch East India Company at Zaandam, Holland, while the services of foreign experts were engaged for work in Russia. He also concentrated on developing the commerce and industry of his country, modernized the Russian alphabet, established the first Russian newspaper, and introduced the Julian calendar. Overall, Peter was a far-sighted diplomat who banned Russia's old-fashioned government, and introduced refreshing and ground-breaking changes in all branches of administration.

TERRITORIAL GAINS

Peter was successful in making territorial gains, in the regions of Estonia, Latvia, and Finland. He fought several wars with Turkey in the south by which he was successful in gaining access to the Black Sea. He also defeated the Swedish army. In 1712 he established the city of St. Petersburg on the Neva River and moved the capital there from its former location in Moscow. St. Petersburg was soon to become Russia's "window to Europe." Under him, Russia became a great European nation. In 1721, he proclaimed Russia an empire and was given the title of Emperor of All Russia, and "the Great." He also took the title of "Great Father of the Fatherland." Peter the Great died on February 8, 1725. He is entombed in the Cathedral of Saints Peter and Paul, located in St. Petersburg.

1609 Johannes Kepler formulates laws of planetary motion.
• Japan and Korea inaugurate period of friendship.

1609–10 Galileo Galilei confirms Copernicus' theory that the Earth and planets revolve around the Sun.
c. 1610 Christianity spreads through South America.

REVOLUTION AND LEARNING

The French Revolution

A series of events, collectively called the French Revolution, took place in France between 1789 and 1799, stimulating the development of new ideas in other parts of the world.

When Louis XVI was crowned in 1774, France was undergoing a financial crisis, which continued despite his economic reforms. So he authorized elections for the first Estates-General assembly since 1614. This body consisted of representatives from three groups: The clergy, the nobility, and the common people. Meeting at Versailles on May 5, 1789, the assembly could not reconcile the conflicting demands of the elite and the common people, and the latter formed a new National Assembly. Louis's plans to cancel this led to protests in Paris, and the storming of the Bastille, the fortress-prison, on July 14.

LOUIS XIV
The reign of Louis XIV (1643–1715) of France, known as the "Sun King," is remembered for his patronage of art and culture, and for the glorious palace he built at Versailles. Louis founded academies of painting and sculpture, science, and architecture. A national theater, the Comédie Française, was established in 1680. Playwrights Molière (1622–73) and Jean-Baptiste Racine (1639–99) thrived.

The National Assembly then assumed power and drew up a constitution that proclaimed the basic rights of man: Liberty, equality, and respect for life and property.

A new assembly, the National Convention, declared France a republic on September 21, 1792. Louis and his wife Marie Antoinette were executed and the Jacobins, a radical group in the Convention, started a "reign of terror" under Maximilien Robespierre, during which thousands accused of opposing the Revolution were executed. In 1794, Robespierre was himself executed by an rival group, and, in 1795, another government was formed.

The storming of the Bastille.

1611–1623

1611 King James Bible published in England.
1611–32 Gustavus Adolphus becomes the king of Sweden.
1612 Spanish writer Cervantes composes *Don Quixote.*

1613 English playwright John Webster writes *The Duchess of Malfi.*
1613–29 Gabor Bethlen becomes the prince of Transylvania; also the king of Hungary 1620–21.
1616 Manchurian forces invade China.

Cultural and scientific flowering

Despite the turmoil, this was an age when new ideas came to the fore, and great strides were made in the Arts and Sciences. The baroque style in painting, sculpture, architecture, and music emerged in the first half of the 17th century. In art and architecture, it was characterized by dramatic effects and contrasts of light and shadow. Baroque evolved into the lighter, more decorative rococo in the early 18th century. In music, the opera took shape. Classical styles developed between about 1750 to 1820, with great composers Joseph Haydn (1732–1809) and Wolfgang Amadeus Mozart (1756–91) of Austria, and the German Ludwig van Beethoven (1770–1827).

Wolfgang Amadeus Mozart.

Great philosophers included the Englishman John Locke (1632–1778), the Frenchmen Voltaire (1694–1778) and Jean-Jacques Rousseau (1712–78), and the British-American Thomas Paine (1735–1805). Isaac Newton (1642–1727), another Englishman, discovered the laws of gravity and motion; French chemist and physicist Antoine Lavoisier (1743–94) put forward a new combustion theory; and plants and animals were classified for the first time by Swedish botanist Carl Linnaeus (1707–78).

Jean-Jacques Rousseau.

FREDERICK THE GREAT

Prussia, one of the main states of Germany, began to expand from the time of Frederick I (r. 1701–13). Frederick II (the Great), king from 1740 to 1786, made Prussia a major power in Europe. He was a patron of culture, and was himself a prolific writer and a musician.

OCEANIA DISCOVERED

The Spanish, Portuguese, and Dutch explored the islands of Asia and Oceania. Portuguese explorer Luis Vaez de Torres reached New Guinea in 1606, while Dutch seafarers reached Tasmania, New Zealand, Tonga, and Fiji, and the northern coasts of Australia.

Jacob Roggeveen, a Dutch navigator, landed on Easter Island in 1722. Though Europeans had reached Australia, the aboriginals continued their peaceful lifestyle there.

1616 Prince Khurram annexes Ahmadnagar in India.
1619–24 The Dutch dominate Indonesian spice trade.
c. 1620 Cornelis Drebbel, Dutch inventor, designs first submersible craft; tested on river Thames.

1620 Ottoman Turks invade Poland; are driven out.
1623 Tommaso Campanella, Italian philosopher, writes utopian treatise *La Citta del Sole* (City of the Sun) when imprisoned in Naples, Italy.

Sir Isaac Newton

Sir Isaac Newton (1643–1726) was an English physicist, astronomer, mathematician, and researcher. He was one of the most influential scientists ever, who laid new laws of mechanics, gravity, and movement. His work *Principia Mathematica* heralded the Scientific Revolution of the 17th century. An extraordinary **polymath**, Newton's areas of interest also included optics, religion, and speculative chemistry.

Isaac Newton (1643–1726).

Isaac Newton was born on Christmas Day, 1643 to a family of modest gentlemen farmers in Lincolnshire, England. He attended the King's School at Grantham in Lincolnshire, but had to leave before completing his studies in order to help on the family farm. However, he later passed the exams to allow him to attend Cambridge University in 1661. When the university closed because of plague in 1665–66, he returned home and began a 2-year intensive period of scientific advances, making unprecedented discoveries in optics, mechanics, and calculus, and formulating his famous theory of gravity.

According to legend, he reached his ideas on gravity when an apple fell on his head. This is probably only a story, but certainly his observations of a falling apple led him to conclude that the same force—gravity—is what makes a humble apple fall and is what keeps the Moon in the sky, circling around the Earth rather than falling to Earth. It was a huge step forward since he presented the first coherent explanation of how the planets remain in orbit around the sun.

Newton was easily depressed by criticism and after he received one set-back, he stopped offering his ideas to the scientific community. His groundbreaking work was only published by accident when the astronomer Sir Edmund Halley (who gave his name to Halley's Comet) consulted Newton on an astronomical problem. To his surprise, he found that Newton had created a complete scientific theory, that gravity is a universal force holding together the structure of the universe. Halley paid for Newton to publish his theory in the book Philosophiae Naturalis Principia Mathematica (Mathematical Principles of Natural Philosophy), usually known just as the Principia, one of the most important books in the history of science.

1623–1631

1623 Nzinga named Governor of Luanda for the Portuguese and holds the position until 1626.

1624 Dutch settlers acquire Manhattan from local tribes and name it New Amsterdam.

1625 Plague in London kills at least 40,000 people.

1626 French colonizers settle in Madagascar.

1627 Korea invaded by Manchus; **1636** Seoul captured.

It was published in 1687, and as well as containing his theory of gravity, it put forward his three laws of motion:

- First law of motion, or law of inertia

An object at rest will stay at rest and an object in motion will remain in motion until acted upon by an external force.

- Second law of motion, or law of acceleration

A force acting upon an object will change the object's velocity in the direction of the force, directly proportional to the force applied and inversely proportional to the mass of the object.

- Third law of motion

For every action there is an equal and opposite reaction.

Newton's work underpins modern disciplines such as rocket science, and his ideas remain valid except for the comparatively new fields to do with near-light speed relativity and quantum mechanics

Principia was also influential because it laid out Newton's rigorous investigative and analytical methods. These inspired future generations of scientists to follow proper standards of research.

In 1665–66 Newton also laid the foundations for differential and integral calculus, some years before a method of calculus was independently discovered by the German polymath Gottfried Leibniz.

Newton became Lucasian Professor of Mathematics at Cambridge in 1669, but embarked on a new career as a member of parliament in 1689. In 1696 he was appointed Master of the Royal Mint, and cut out the corruption and counterfeiting that had existed there. He was elected president of the Royal Society in 1703, and was re-elected annually until his death in 1727, although in those years he made more notes about Biblical history than he did about science. In 1705 he was knighted by Queen Anne, the first Englishman to receive that honor for his scientific work. He said about his groundbreaking work: "If I have seen a little further it is by standing on ye shoulders of giants."

Isaac Newton's Telescope.

Galileo Galilei

In 1583, Galileo entered the University of Pisa to study medicine. Armed with high intelligence and talent, he soon became fascinated with many subjects, particularly mathematics and physics. While at Pisa, Galileo was exposed to the Aristotelian view of the world, then the leading scientific authority and the only one sanctioned by the Roman Catholic Church. At first, Galileo supported this view, like any other intellectual of his time, and was on track to be a university professor. However, due to financial difficulties, Galileo left the university in 1585 before earning his degree.

Galileo quickly found a new position at the University of Padua, teaching geometry, mechanics and astronomy. The appointment was fortunate, for his father had died in 1591, leaving Galileo entrusted with the care of his younger brother Michelagnolo. During his 18-year tenure at Padua, he gave entertaining lectures and attracted large crowds of followers, further increasing his fame and his sense of mission.

In 1604, Galileo published The Operations of the Geometrical and Military Compass, revealing his skills with experiments and practical technological applications. He also constructed a hydrostatic balance for measuring small objects. These developments brought him additional income and more recognition. That

Portrait Galileo Galilei.

1632–1643

1632–54 Queen Christina rules in Sweden.
1633 Italian scientist Galileo faces charges of heresy from the Inquisition for defending Copernicus' theory of heliocentrism.

1635 Zaidi imams reestablish themselves as rulers of Yemen.
1637–1709 Safavid dynasty declines; Ghalzai Afghans occupy Kandahar.

same year, Galileo refined his theories on motion and falling objects, and developed the universal law of acceleration, which all objects in the universe obeyed. Galileo began to express openly his support of the Copernican theory that the earth and planets revolved around the sun. This challenged the doctrine of Aristotle and the established order set by the Catholic Church.

In July 1609, Galileo learned about a simple telescope built by Dutch eyeglass makers, and he soon developed one of his own. In August, he demonstrated it to some Venetian merchants, who saw its value for spotting ships and gave Galileo salary to manufacture several of them. However, Galileo's ambition pushed him to go further, and in the fall of 1609 he made the fateful decision to turn his telescope toward the heavens. In March 1610, he published a small booklet, The Starry Messenger, revealing his discoveries that the moon was not flat and smooth, but a sphere with mountains and craters. He found Venus had phases like the moon, proving it rotated around the sun. He also discovered Jupiter had revolving moons, which didn't revolve around the earth.

In 1623, a friend of Galileo, Cardinal Maffeo Barberini, was selected as Pope Urban VIII. He allowed Galileo to pursue his work on astronomy and even encouraged him to publish it, on condition it be objective and not advocate Copernican theory. In 1632, Galileo published the Dialogue Concerning the Two Chief World Systems, a discussion among three people: one who supports Copernicus' heliocentric theory of the universe, one who argues against it, and one who is impartial. Though Galileo claimed Dialogues was neutral, it was clearly not. The advocate of Aristotelian belief comes across as the simpleton, getting caught in his own arguments.

In the 20th century, several popes acknowledged the great work of Galileo, and in 1992, Pope John Paul II expressed regret about how the Galileo affair was handled. Galileo's contribution to our understanding of the universe was significant not only in his discoveries, but in the methods he developed and the use of mathematics to prove them. He played a major role in the scientific revolution and, deservedly so, earned the moniker "The Father of Modern Science."

Galileo died in Arcetri, near Florence, Italy, on January 8, 1642, after suffering from a fever and heart palpitations. But in time, the Church couldn't deny the truth in science. In 1758, it lifted the ban on most works supporting Copernican theory, and by 1835 dropped its opposition to heliocentrism altogether.

1640 French mathematician Blaise Pascal invents early form of calculator.
1640 Portugal asserts independence from Spain.

1641 Tibet becomes a religious state under fifth Dalai Lama.
1642 Galileo Galilei dies.
1643 Sir Isaac Newton is born.

COLONIES AND TRADE

There were numerous kingdoms all over Africa, each with their own myths and stories, indigenous religion, arts and crafts, and forms of music and dance. European colonization began and the slave trade grew. The Portuguese, Dutch, and British established bases and settlements.

The Ottoman Empire was so large by this time that local *pashas* or governors assumed various degrees of control. Tripoli, Tunis, and Algiers in North Africa asserted their autonomy. The latter became virtually independent in 1710. In the 18th century, there was a revival of Islamic dynasties among the Fulani, Mandingo, Soso, and Tukulor people.

A busy scene from the city of Constantinople.

African kingdoms and the slave trade

African kingdoms that carried out a slave trade included Asante, Dahomey, and Benin (different from today's state of Benin). African states were constantly at war among themselves; the war prisoners were sold as slaves to the Europeans. Some of the African warlords, in fact, found capturing Africans from neighboring ethnic groups and selling them a lucrative opportunity. The natives inhabiting regions near the Niger river were taken to European trading ports and sold for firearms and goods such as cloth or alcohol. Slaves were sent to America, the Caribbean islands, Asia, and Europe, and by 1730, about 50,000 slaves were being transported every year to the Americas alone. By the 1780s, the number had risen to about 90,000.

The Asante were united in 1701 by Osei Tutu, chief of the small Asante state of Kumasi. They controlled gold mines and supplied slaves to European nations, receiving firearms in return. Kings of Yoruba origin founded three kingdoms—Allada, Abomey, and

1648–1663

1648 Treaty of Westphalia ends Thirty Years' War in Holy Roman Empire and Eighty Years' War between Spain and Netherlands.

1649 King Charles I beheaded before of England.

1650 Sultan bin Saif al Yarubi drives Portugese out of Muscat and founds Yarubid dynasty that rules Oman up to **1749**.

1652–54 First Anglo-Dutch War begins

1655 British capture Jamaica from the Spanish.

Whydah—in the early 17th century. By 1727, they were united by King Agaja of Abomey as the kingdom of Dahomey, which began supplying slaves to the Europeans. He is also known for creating a corps of women soldiers.

In the 16th and 17th centuries, Benin, in what is now Nigeria, traded in palm oil, spices, ivory, and textiles. In the 18th century, it was also a slave-trading kingdom. Benin city's wide streets had large palaces and houses with wooden pillars. It was known for ivory and bronze carvings.

THE YORUBA

The first remains at the ancient sacred city of Ife, to which the Yoruba people trace their origin, date between 12th and 15th centuries. In the 17th century, Oyo was the most important Yoruba state, controlling a large area between the Volta and Niger rivers. In the 13th and 14th centuries, Yoruba bronze casting was used in a big way, which could not be equalled in Western Africa.

Yoruba drummers.

The Yoruba, located in the southwestern part of the country, form one of the three largest ethnic groups of **Nigeria**. The Yoruba numbered more than 20 million at the turn of the 21st century. They speak a language of the Benue-Congo branch of the Niger-Congo language family. Most Yoruba men are farmers, growing yams, corn (maize), and millet as staples and plantains, peanuts (groundnuts), beans, and peas as subsidiary crops; cocoa is a major cash crop. Women do little farm work but control much of the complex market system which gives them their own status in the society.

The large and elaborate palace of the oba, or ruler, lies at the center of a traditional Yoruba town. Medieval Yoruba settlements were surrounded with massive mud walls. Traditional Yoruba buildings incorporated verandahs, and had walls made from mud and palm oil. Thatch was usually used for roofs. material comprised puddle mud and palm oil while roofing material ranged from thatches to aluminum and corrugated iron sheets.

1657 Great fire kills thousands in Edo, Japan.
1658 Aurangzeb announces himself as the emperor of India.
1659 Oliver Cromwell dies.
1660 Royal Society founded in London, England.

1662 Robert Boyle, English scientist, formulates law of the pressure-volume relationship of gas.
1663 and '65 Plague epidemics in Amsterdam and London.

COLONIES AND TRADE

Developments in Ethiopia

Although Islam was followed by some, the kingdom's main religion was Monophysite Christianity of the Orthodox Church. Jesuits tried to convert Ethiopian Christians to the Western Church, though with little success. Emperor Fasilides (r. 1632–67) established a new capital at Gondar, which became a great center of trade, art, and culture. Castles, palaces, and churches, including the Debre Berhan Selassie Church, were constructed here. Ethiopia continued to resist colonial inroads. A period of feudal anarchy persisted during 1700–1850, with several local rulers holding sway.

Fasilides's palace in Gondar.

1665–1685

1665–67 Second Anglo-Dutch War.
1666 Great fire destroys London.
1668 John Dryden becomes England's first poet laureate.
1669 Hanseatic League comes to an end.

• Famine kills three million in Bengal, India.
1676 Observatory established at Greenwich, England.
1679 Habeas Corpus Act passed in England; no imprisonment allowed without court appearance.

QUEEN NZINGA

Queen Anna Nzinga (c. 1581–1663), also known as Ana de Sousa Nzinga Mbande, is one of the great women rulers of southwestern Africa-Angola. In the 17th century, Ndola Nzinga fought against the slave trade and European influence. She successfully kept Angola safe from European powers; however, after her death at the age of 82, weak rulers were unable to prevent the Portuguese from regaining control. In the late 16th and early 17th centuries, when the Portuguese required slaves for their new colony in Brazil, Europeans were negotiating interests in the African slave trade. The Portuguese moved their slave-trading activities to the south which today is known by the name of Congo and Angola. In 1623, Nzinga was named governor of Luanda for the Portuguese and held the position until 1626.

Queen Nzinga Mbande's sculpture outside the Angola Pavilion.

A year after the treaty was signed, the Portuguese resumed the slave trade against the terms of the treaty. She developed an effective anti-Portuguese coalition that virtually held the Europeans at bay for 30 years. Mbandi, her brother, was an ineffective leader. Desperate to act, Nzinga poisoned her brother and succeeded him as queen of the Ndongo kingdom in 1623. Nzinga proved to be a capable leader despite the limitations of her gender. Iron-willed, intelligent, and brave, Nzinga fought for freedom and to bring peace to her people.

It seems that Queen Nzinga enjoyed fighting and sometimes dressed like a man. She has been called the greatest military strategist ever to confront the armed forces of Portugal. Nzinga handpicked her sister, Dona Barbara, to succeed her as queen and married her to the general of the army; however, a succession struggle ensued after Nzinga's death.

1680–92 Pueblos of New Mexico revolt against Spanish colonists.
1681 Pennsylvania founded in North America.
• Languedoc canal constructed in France; connects Atlantic Ocean and Mediterranean Sea.

1683 Formosa (Taiwan) taken over by China.
1684 English East India Company establishes first trading post in Canton, China.
1685–1750 Life of Johann Sebastian Bach, German musician.

A NEW WORLD ORDER

European Rivalry for Positions and Trade along the Atlantic Coast of Africa

In the 1580s – after Spain's Habsburg king, Philip II, expanded his rule to Portugal – exclusive right to trade along the Gambia River was sold to English merchants, confirmed by letters of patent from Queen Elizabeth. The Dutch were at war with Philip, and in 1593, soon after they had declared independence from Habsburg rule, they launched attacks against Philip's Portuguese shipping. The world's most successful merchant mariners, the Dutch from 1593 to 1607 sent about 200 ships to trade along Africa's Atlantic coast, and in each of the years 1610 and 1611 they sent twenty ships. The Dutch were able to ship more goods and lower prices, giving them an edge in trading in their competition with the English, French and Portuguese.

The Europeans competed for forts along Africa's Atlantic coast. The English drove the French from the mouth of the Senegal River. In 1631, the English built a fort on what was called the Gold Coast – a stretch of coastline that included Portuguese positions at Elmina and Axim. The Dutch established a fortified position at the mouth of the Zaire (Congo) River and at points on the shore along the coast, including the capture of Portugal positions at Elmina and Axim.

The Dutch had taken Brazil from the Portuguese – who were again independent of Spanish rule. And the Dutch wanted slaves for their new colony. The Dutch also took from the Portuguese the island of São Tomé. In August 1641, an armada of 21 Dutch ships appeared off the coast of Angola. The Dutch captured Luanda and Benguela, and the Portuguese retreated inland where they held off assaults by the Dutch and by Jaga tribesmen.

The French in 1645 established a hold at the mouth of the Senegal River, where they traded for gum and slaves. The French increased their trading on the Ivory Coast, and Swedes, Danes, and Germans from Brandenburg came and built forts on the coast. And it was standard among them to pay rent for the forts to local kings.

The Kingdoms of Oyo, Dahomey and Asante

From the 1640s, four inland states near the Gulf of Guinea were growing in wealth and power from the slave trade. The kingdom of Oyo, around 300 kilometers (190 miles) inland, was the most successful of these kingdoms. It benefited from terrain sufficiently

1685–1705

1685–1759 Life of Georg Friedrich Handel, German musician.

1687 Venice gains Athens from Ottoman Turks.

1689 Russia and China sign Treaty of Nerchinsk whereby Russia cedes some territory to China, but retains other important areas.

1694 Bank of England established in London.

1697 After 11 years' fighting, France loses War of the League of Augsburg to European coalition.

1697–1718 Charles XII rules in Sweden.

1698 London Stock Exchange established.

deforested and free of the tsetse fly and other disease-carrying insects to allow for the breeding of horses. The Oyo kingdom used cavalry effectively in expanding southward where savanna split coastal forest. Oyo forced the coastal kingdom of Allada to pay it tribute, and it gained direct access to trade with Europeans. Oyo was a slave state, and its king used slave labor on his vast farmlands. In wars, Oyo took more slaves than it needed for the royal farms, and it traded them to the Europeans for guns, cloth, metal goods and cowry shells. It traded also with Africans to its north for horses and for more captives for the slave trade. And the kingdom acquired wealth by taxing trade that crossed its territory to and from Hausaland.

Another power in the region was the kingdom of Abomey, which was founded in the early 1600s by the brother of the king of Allada, a coastal kingdom that had grown wealthy from the slave trade. The brother, Do-Aklin, cut off village chiefs from having any say in selecting his successor. Rule in Abomey passed to his grandson, Wegbaja, who consolidated his power – while both Allada and Abomey were paying tribute to the more powerful kingdom of Oyo. In Abomey, human sacrifices were used to honor the king's ancestors – the sacrifices usually captives from warfare.

West of Abomey were the Ashanti (Asanti), who were dominated by the Denkera to their southwest, to whom the Ashanti paid tribute. The primary political unit among the Ashanti had been the village, governed by clan elders. In the 1660s, an Ashanti warrior named Osei Tutu grouped clan chiefs around him and formed an alliance with the leading Ashanti religious figure, Anokye. They created a golden stool, representing power and spiritual unity, on which the ruler of the Ashanti was to sit, and they sanctified the golden stool with sacrifices.

Osei Tutu and Anokye extended their power across Ashanti chiefdoms, unifying the Ashanti. And with the power that accrued from this unity, the Ashanti defeated the Denkera and absorbed some of their subject states. These victories gave the Ashanti contact with the Europeans, to whom they sold slaves. And the Ashanti began an expansion inland for more slaves and for gold.

Meanwhile, Oyo cavalry invaded the Abomey four times, but Abomey retained enough power to expand against Allada on the coast. The king of Abomey, Agaja, was interested in buying arms from the Europeans. Conquering Allada in the 1720s gave him access to European trading. The enlarged rule of Agaja became known as Dahomey, and it began to prosper from the sale of slaves to the Europeans.

- First steam engine made by English engineer Thomas Savery; used to pump water from coal mines.
- **1699** Sikh leader Guru Gobind Singh founds the Khalsa, order of baptized Sikhs, in India.
- Habsburgs acquire most of Hungary by Treaty of Karlowitz.

1702–14 Anne is queen of England and Scotland.
1703 Peter the Great founds city of St. Petersburg in Russia.
1704 First newspaper of North America, *The Boston News-Letter*, published.
1705–11 Joseph I is Holy Roman Emperor.

COLONIES AND TRADE

Colonization of North America

The Boston Tea Party.

Europeans began to extend their settlements in America. The French, English, Swedish, and Dutch were in North America, while the Spanish and Portuguese were prominent in South and Central America.

The first permanent English settlement was founded in 1607 at Jamestown, and, in 1624 the British crown took control of the area. As the economy expanded through the cultivation of tobacco, the importation of African slaves to serve as cheap labor began. In 1620, a dissident religious group of English Protestants, later known as the Pilgrim Fathers, landed in Massachusetts. They composed a self-governing agreement known as the Mayflower Compact (named after their ship, the *Mayflower*). It is considered the first constitution of America. More colonies emerged in this region, which came to be known as New England. A small college founded here in 1636 developed into Harvard University by 1780.

The French gained control over the fur trade in Canada and in 1604 established their first settlements. In 1627, the colony of New France was founded along the St. Lawrence river. Expansion continued into the Mississippi valley area and the territory known as Louisiana. By the Treaty of Paris in 1763 after the Seven Years' War, New France came under the British. Deeply in debt after the series of wars, the British tried to gain revenue in its American colonies by taxes and duties. These were resisted by the colonists, and, finally, only a tax on tea was retained.

After a monopoly on the tea trade was granted to the English East India Company in 1773, the colonists destroyed boxes of tea landing at Boston—an event later known as the Boston Tea Party. The British reacted with repression.

Spanish and Portuguese in South America

In 1717, Spain founded the viceroyalty of New Granada, made up of the present-day states of Panama, Ecuador, Colombia, and Venezuela. Spain later expanded its empire into Mexico and Peru, while the Portuguese controlled Brazil. Native Americans and African slaves worked under poor conditions in Peruvian and Mexican silver mines and in gold and diamond mines in Brazil.

1707–1727

1707 Mughal emperor Aurangzeb dies in India.
1707 Aurangzeb's eldest son Bahadur Shah Zafar II dies.
1707 By Act of Union, England and Scotland join to create Great Britain.
1708–09 King Charles XII of Sweden invades Russia; is defeated in Battle of Poltava.

1711 North American tribes fight against North Carolina planters in the Tuscarora Indian War.
1712 British inventor Thomas Newcomen (1663–1729) makes steam engine using atmospheric pressure.

American Independence

Representatives from the American colonies formed the First Continental Congress in 1774, and sent a petition containing their grievances to king George III of Britain. As this had no effect, a second Continental Congress was held in 1775, when the Americans declared independence. The Revolutionary War began the same year, with colonists fighting against British troops. On July 4, 1776, the colonies adopted the Declaration of

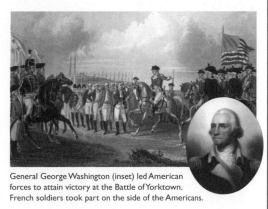

General George Washington (inset) led American forces to attain victory at the Battle of Yorktown. French soldiers took part on the side of the Americans.

Independence, and the United States of America, comprising 13 states, came into existence. Fighting continued for 5 years until the British surrendered at Yorktown, Virginia. In 1783, by the Treaty of Paris, the USA was recognized as a separate nation.

State delegates drew up a constitution for the new nation in 1787, and in 1789 George Washington became the first president of the United States.

AMERICAN COLONIAL ART AND ARCHITECTURE

In the 17th and 18th centuries, Europeans in North America developed art styles based on those in Europe. There were Spanish influences in the west, and British, Dutch, and French styles in the east. Native American styles also contributed. Early buildings in New Mexico were made of adobe (sundried mud), whereas the English used wood, first of all for log cabins, then as boards for larger

houses. Cities laid out on grid plans were built from the 18th century. Portrait painting was predominant, while religious art was also common.

Palladian-style home of Thomas Jefferson, third president of the USA, in Virginia, built between 1768 and 1826.

1713–14 Treaties of Utrecht end War of the Spanish Succession and Queen Anne's War.
1714 Gabriel Fahrenheit, German physicist, makes first mercury-filled thermometer and develops scale for measurement of temperature.
1714–27 George I is first Hanoverian king of Great Britain.

1717 Tibet comes under Chinese rule.
• In India, Mughal emperor Farrukhsiyar allows East India Company to trade in Bengal.
1723–90 Life of Scottish economist Adam Smith.
1727 Coffee first planted in Brazil.
1727–88 Life of English landscape artist Thomas Gainsborough.

COLONIES AND TRADE

Napoleon Bonaparte

Born in Corsica in 1769, Napoleon made his mark as a general in the French army. Returning to France in 1799 after the Egyptian campaign, he began to take control of the government; then, in 1804, declared himself emperor and began a series of wars against other nations to further French power. The Napoleonic Code of civil law instituted by him laid emphasis on written law and influenced the legal codes of many other countries.

In Europe, the first 15 years of the 19th century were dominated by the Napoleonic wars between French forces and various other countries. Finally, Napoleon was decisively defeated in 1815 at the Battle of Waterloo and exiled to St Helena.

He died in exile in 1821 but his legend lived on. His life caught the imagination of writers, artists, and musicians. Historians believe his reforms were more important than his conquests, and had long-lasting effects. At the Congress of Vienna (1814–15), French territories acquired by Napoleon were distributed among other European nations. The Congress also condemned the slave trade, and provided for free navigation of rivers across different European nations.

In the year 1799, France was facing political, economic, and social crises. When Napoleon came into power, he tried to correct problems like unemployment, inflation, financial and religious crises. During his reign he introduced many reforms in France, including the introduction of higher education, the establishment also the before centralized of centralized government bank of France, a tax code, construction of roads, building of a well-developed sewer system, and so on

The Battle of Austerlitz (1805), at which Napoleon defeated the combined forces of Russia and Austria was one of his greatest victories.

repetition. To honor military and civil achievements, he founded the order of merit, the Legion of Honor.

1739–1758

1739 John Wesley founds Methodist Society.

c. 1740 Hasidism, Jewish movement, founded by Baal Shem Tov.

1740 Maria Theresa becomes archduchess of Austria.

1741–62 Elizabeth Petrovna, daughter of Peter the Great, is empress of Russia.

1742 Swedish astronomer Anders Celsius creates centigrade thermometer.

1744 Islamic Wahhabi creed established in Dariya, Arabian Peninsula.

1748 War of the Austrian Succession ends with Treaty of Aix-la-Chapelle.

MAJOR REFORMS BY NAPOLEON BONAPARTE

Concordat of 1801: In 1801, Napoleon signed this agreement with Pope Pius VII. Catholicism was recognized as the majority religion in France, but freedom of worship was guaranteed. Napoleon would appoint and pay the clergy, but they had to swear an oath of allegiance to the state.

Ownership of property and land: The French revolutionary government began some reforms in the area of land and property ownership by removing the last vestiges of feudalism. Napoleon's civil code confirmed the inviolabily of property rights and arranged for equal inheritance. Napoleon also confirmed that lands confiscated from the church or aristocrats would not be returned.

New administrative system: Napoleon reorganized the government by establishing a centralized state. He created different government departments, headed by men he appointed, who were chosen partly for their honesty. His administration successfully removed problems such as corruption, embezzlement, and inefficiency.

Commerce and industry: Before the arrival of Napoleon, the two sectors of commerce and industry were known as "the laughing stock of Europe," as they had so many problems. They were crumbling from corruption, restrictive taxes on trade, and lack of government support. Napoleon's new central Bank of France, founded in 1800, organized loans to traders and manufacturers. He introduced fairer taxes, and unemployment began to fall.

Developments in agriculture: Napoleon's government began to spend money on this sector. He drained swamps and reclaimed land in order to increase the amount of cultivable land, and introduced modern farming methods. Food production increased and the fear of famine receded.

Reforms in financial system: Napoleon established the Bank of France in 1800 which was assigned the duty of giving loans and circulating money for regulation of a smooth economy in the country. He also tried to stabilize the money on the gold standard system. Conquered states were made to pay taxes to help the French economy become stable.

Formation of laws: In the late 18th century there was no clear-cut set of laws in France. There were Royal decrees, regional codes, old Roman laws, and local customs. Napoleon replaced them all with one clearly written civil code, the Code Napoléon. The code offered some civil rights, and was to equally to everyone.

Modernizing the army: Napoleon forged his army into one of the best in the world. He mixed experienced soldiers with raw recruits, offered military training, and promised promotion on merit alone. Although the primary purpose of his army was to win more territory, soldiers were also used to maintain law and order within France.

A NEW WORLD ORDER

Revolutions of 1848 and nationalism

The inequalities and economic hardships created by the Industrial Revolution, demand for social reform, and nationalist movements, all led to a series of revolutions across Europe. Prince Klemens Wenzel von Metternich (1773-1859), the powerful chancellor of Austria, was forced to abdicate, and, in France, the Second Republic was established, though it did not last long.

Prussian Chancellor Otto von Bismarck.

Nationalist ideals continued to gather momentum. The movement for the unification of Italian states, driven by the endeavors of Giuseppe Mazzini (1805-72), Giuseppe Garibaldi (1807-82), and Count Cavour (1810-61), achieved its objective in 1870. Similar efforts by Otto von Bismarck (1815-98), prime minister of Prussia, brought about the unification of the various states of Germany in 1871.

The revolutions of 1848 occurred because of the bad governments, a rise in food prices due to poor harvests, widespread unemployment and economic depression across Europe.

Countries like France, Germany, Prussia, the Austrian Empire, various Italian states, Moldavia, and Wallachia were directly affected by revolutions in 1848.

The **Revolutions of 1848** were also known in some countries as the **Spring of Nations, People's Spring, Springtime of the Peoples**, or the **Year of Revolution**. These were a series of widespread political upheavals throughout Europe. The revolutions were essentially democratic in nature, independent national states. The wave began in France and spread to most of Europe. Some of the major contributing factors were widespread dissatisfaction with political leadership, demands for more participation in government and democracy, demands for freedom of press, other demands made by the working class, the upsurge of nationalism, and the regrouping of established governmental forces.

Tens of thousands of people were killed, and many more forced into exile. The revolutions arose from such a wide variety of causes. Technology was also revolutionizing life of the common people. Another factor were the serious crop failures, particularly those of 1846, which caused great hardship to peasants and the working urban poor.

The middle and working classes shared a desire for reform, and agreed on many of the specific aims. Their participations in the revolutions, however, differed. It was the middle classes and the lower classes which carried through the revolutions. The revolts first erupted in the cities and soon engulfed entire countires.

1761–1775

1761 Afghans defeat Marathas in Third Battle of Panipat, India.

1762–96 Catherine the Great is the empress of Russia.

1764 Scottish inventor James Watt designs first steam engine; improved model in 1782.

1767 English inventor James Hargreaves develops spinning jenny, a hand-operated spinning machine: Important development in early Industrial Revolution.

1767–1847 Life of Indian musician Tyagaraja.

1768 Royal Academy of Arts founded in Britain.

A painting by Claude Monet in the Impressionist style.

TRENDS IN ART, LITERATURE, AND MUSIC

In Europe and America the 1800–1850 period is considered the era of Romanticism, typified by an imaginative and emotional intensity, and freedom of thought and approach. In music, Beethoven's and Franz Schubert's (1797–1828) compositions helped build a bridge between classical and Romantic styles. Other great Romantic musicians were Robert Schumann (1810–56), Hector Berlioz (1803–69) and Frederic Chopin (1810–49). William Blake (1757–1827), Eugene Delacroix (1798–1863), and John Constable (1776–1837) were some of the Romantic artists.

Impressionist art developed in the latter half of the 19th century, inspired by French artist Edouard Manet (1832–83). Impressionist paintings rejected classical formalism and Romanticism, while placing importance on capturing the effects of light. Realism was another artistic trend. In post-Impressionistic styles, the use of color was similar to that of the Impressionists, but the paintings were freer and not accurate representations of reality. Major artists of this late 19th-century genre were Vincent van Gogh (1853–90), Paul Gauguin (1848–1903), and Henri de Toulouse-Lautrec (1864–1901).

A poster by Henri de Toulouse-Lautrec.

1768–74 Russo-Turkish War; Russia gains navigation rights on Black Sea.

1769 Napoleon born in Corsica.

1769 Richard Arkwright invents "water frame" for spinning cotton yarn.

• Nicholas-Joseph Cugnot, French engineer, invents steam-powered tricycle, which can draw carriages.

• Major famine in Bengal, India.

1770–1850 Life of William Wordsworth, English poet.

1774 Warren Hastings becomes first British governor-general in India.

1775 French philospher and scholar Denis Diderot completes his *Encyclopedia*.

A NEW WORLD ORDER

Memorial to the revolt of 1857–58 in Delhi.

Spurred on by the Industrial Revolution, European powers raced to carve out spheres of influence and control in Asia. Towards the end of this period nationalist movements for independence began.

British ascendancy in India

Two major battles were fought in India which turned the course of history. In the year 1757, the Battle of Plassey was fought between the British and the Nawab of Bengal, Siraj ud-Daulah, who was defeated by the British. In the year 1764, the Battle of Buxar was fought in which the Mughal emperor Shah Alam, the Nawab of Awadh, and the Nawab of Bengal were pitched against the British army, but they were defeated.

In north India, Mughal emperors retained their hegemony only in name, as British control over the subcontinent strengthened. In 1857–58, a widespread revolt, beginning as a mutiny in the army, broke out, proclaiming Bahadur Shah Zafar, the titular Mughal emperor, as the ruler of India. The British emerged victorious. Delhi was destroyed. Bahadur Shah's sons were killed, and he was exiled to Rangoon (Yangon), where, in 1862, he died a lonely death.

Also known as the Sepoy Mutiny, the 1857 revolt spread thoughout India and involved many of the country's ruling families. But, it was not a united effort and hence was suppressed by the British.

As a result of the revolt, the English East India Company, which had so far managed affairs in India, was abolished, and India came directly under the British crown.

India's First War of Independence, the revolt of 1857.

The arrest of Bahadur Shah.

1775–1802

1775–83 American Revolution began.
1780–84 Fourth Anglo-Dutch War, over secret Dutch trade with American colonies.
1781 William Herschel, German-born British astronomer, discovers the planet Uranus.
1782–1840 Life of Italian composer and violin player Nicolo Paganini.

1789 French Revolution began.
1792–1822 Life of English poet, Percy Bysshe Shelley.
1794 English writer Ann Radcliffe writes *The Mysteries of Udolpho*; develops genre of Gothic novel.
1796–1869 Life of Mirza Ghalib, Indian Urdu poet.

The Great Game

Central Asia was the battleground for the "Great Game," a shadowy war between Britain and Russia for control of the area that took place from about 1839 to the early 20th century. The British fought wars in Afghanistan, and gained control of its foreign relations, while the Russians advanced into Khiva and Turkistan. In Iran, Russian influence pervaded in the north, whereas the British dominated in the south.

Dost Mohammad, emir of Afghanistan (1826–1863), during the Great Game.

THE BAHÁ'Í RELIGION

Babism emerged in Iran as a religious offshoot of Islam in 1843, and, in 1863 developed into a separate religion founded by Mirza Husain Ali, known as Bahá'u'lláh (Glory of God). The Bahá'ís believe in one God, whose divine messengers or prophets, including Abraham, Moses, Jesus, and Muhammad, proclaimed the truth through the ages. God's final message, to unite everyone through universal love, was revealed through Bahá'u'lláh.

Opium Wars

China admitted foreign traders but confined them to the ports of Canton (Guangzhou) and Macao, mainly to stop the opium trade carried out by the British. After the Chinese burned a consignment of the drug at Canton, two "Opium Wars" (1839-42 and 1856-60) were fought with Britain, who had the support of other foreign nations. China was forced to provide more trade concessions and to grant Hong Kong to the British.

Numerous ports were then opened in China for the purpose of foreign trade. Trade in tea and silk rose and started to flourish in foreign countries.

The Chinese copper currency began to lose its value, partly because of a shortage of copper, and partly because of poor administration in China. In 1853, new paper money was printed in China.

Chinese junks destroyed by British warships in the Battle of Anson's Bay (1841), during the First Opium War.

BOXER REBELLION

At the end of the 19th century, China suffered humiliating defeats by Japan and Western countries, who then gained a commercial foothold in China and forced unequal commercial terms on China. The economic problems this caused led to growing resentment amongst poor people, culminating in a violent uprising in 1899, the Boxer Rebellion.

At first the anger was directed at the Chinese government, but Empress Cixi diverted the rebels' hatred toward foreigners. Led by a secret society known as the Society of Righteous Fists, or Boxers, the rebels attacked foreigners and Chinese Christians, and destroyed railroads and foreign-owned property.

Eight nations allied to defeat the Boxers, and in 1901 China was forced to grant more humiliating concessions and make reparations.

Taiping rebellion

From 1850, Hong Xiuquan, a schoolteacher and religious visionary, organized an uprising against the Manchu rulers of China. The Taiping rebellion, as it was known, extended to 15 provinces and led to the deaths of 20 million people. In return for helping the Manchu rulers crush the rebellion, European powers were given trade facilities. Despite the unrest, Chinese arts thrived, and a type of Chinese opera, known as Beijing opera, developed in the late 18th century.

Hong Xiuquan.

The Meiji restoration

In Japan, opposition to the shoguns led to the restoration of the rule of the emperor in 1868. Japan developed a nationalist ideology, with a revival of the traditional Shinto religion, and new industry and railways were promoted.

1802–1817

1802–20 Emperor Gia-long unifies Vietnam.

1803 USA buys Louisiana, a large territory in North America, from France.

1804–30 Black War fought in Tasmania; Europeans kill aborigines.

1805 Japanese doctor Hanaoka Seishu uses anesthetics in surgery.

1809 Finland brought under Russian rule.

1809–82 Life of Charles Darwin, British naturalist; wrote *On the Origin of Species*, seminal book on evolutionary biology.

1810 Mexico revolts against Spanish rule.

• Hawaiian islands united by king Kamehameha I.

KATSUSHIKA HOKUSAI

Japanese arts flourished in the 19th century. Hokusai (1760–1849) was a painter and a master of woodcut print-making, whose series, Thirty-six Views of Mount Fuji (1826–33), is considered the highest development of landscape printing.

The print *Red Fuji*, from Hokusai's series on the mountain.

This was a period of great change. There were far-reaching developments in industry and technology, accompanied by political change. Colonialism expanded.

Agricultural revolution

By the year 1800, Europe witnessed more than one revolution— the Agricultural Revolution and the Industrial Revolution. It started in Britain. This increased Britain's agricultural productivity more than any other nation in Europe. An act was passed in Britain called the Enclosure Act, according to which wealthy lords could purchase large estates. This led many small-scale laborers to search for jobs and wages in cities. These people provided the labor force for the industries and gave rise to Industrial Revolution.

The Agricultural Revolution in Britain.

1811–18 Muhammad Ali of Egypt overruns much of Arabia; first Saudi empire ends.

1811–32 Evariste Galois, French mathematician, develops group theory.

1812–15 War between the U.S. and Britain happens.

• Jacob and Wilhelm Grimm publish their collection of folk tales, *Grimm's Fairy Tales*, in German.

1812–70 Life of British author Charles Dickens.

1813 English novelist Jane Austen writes *Pride and Prejudice*.

1815 British restore Java to the Dutch.

1817 James Monroe becomes the fifth US president.

• German philosopher GWF Hegel composes his *Encyclopedia of the Philosophical Sciences*.

A NEW WORLD ORDER

Mainland Southeast Asia

Over the course of the nineteenth century, Southeast Asia was colonized by Britain, France, and Holland. In 1799, the Dutch government took over the Dutch East India Company's rule of parts of the Indonesian archipelago. Over the next hundred years, it controlled the entire archipelago, including Sumatra and Bali. The modern boundaries of Indonesia were established during this time. In 1824, Britain fought to control Burma, finally incorporating it into its Indian empire in 1886. It

Ritual seat found in Indonesia, Sumatra, Gomo and Tae River region.

gradually took over peninsular Malaya as well, and, by 1874, effectively ruled the area that would become modern-day Malaysia. By strengthening central authority over local chiefs and opening trade routes to Europe, Thailand remained free under a stable and strong monarchy. But France colonized Vietnam, Laos, and Cambodia to proclaim the French Indochina Union in 1887.

Colonization had an enormous impact on the populations and economies of the region. The British favored Indian and Chinese immigrants for skilled positions in Malaysia, and dismissed the general Malaysian population as peasantry. Education policies deepened ethnic divides. In Cambodia, the French favored the Vietnamese over the local population, while the British encouraged widespread immigration of Indians and Chinese into Burma, a policy that lead to political divisions which were carried through till modern times. The Burmese economy, long based on subsistence farming, shifted drastically to an export economy. A policy called Cultuurstelsel, applied in Indonesia, forcing farmers to grow export crops. Though successful in some ways, the policy caused famine and impoverishment. The desire to sell European goods in colonial markets eroded the traditional crafts, such as the production of batik and ikat textiles in Indonesia. Regular wars waged to gain control further damaged the region.

Under colonial domination, however, ancient monuments and texts were closely studied, preserved, and restored. Angkor Wat, for instance, was rediscovered in the mid-nineteenth century, and the monuments of Cham, in Vietnam, come to public attention

1817–1835

1817–18 First Seminole War between the Seminole tribe of Florida and US troops.

1818 Florida transferred to the USA from France.

1819 Pomare II establishes first legal code on Society Islands, in the South Pacific.

1820 Missouri Compromise in the USA establishes balance between free and slave states.

• George IV rebuilds Windsor Castle, UK.

1821 Scottish philosopher and economist James Mill writes *Elements of Political Economy*.

1821 Napoleon dies in exile.

in 1885. Photography helped in the documentation of these monuments: Angkor Wat was photographed for the first time in 1866. From the mid-nineteenth century onward, colonial governments began to open museums and found archaeological surveys.

Many traditions continued to thrive in the nineteenth century. Religious imagery continued to be conservative and relatively immune to Westernization. Many indigenous courts patronized craftsmanship in textiles, metalwork, jewelry, and ceramics. Manuscript paintings remained largely traditional, though some reveal European influenced the Company School paintings of India. During the early nineteenth century, China became a dominant cultural influence in mainland Southeast Asia. However, elite culture becomes increasingly Westernized as colonial powers expand their control. In Burma, for instance, European pictorial conventions dominated the frescoes at the Kyauk-Taw-Gyi Temple (1849 -50), while the Altumashi Monastery in Mandalay (1857) was a mix of European and indigenous architectural structures and motifs. The Javanese painter Raden Saleh (ca. 1807 -1880), considered the "father" of Indonesian modern art, traveled to Europe to study painting in 1829. Western art made an impression much later in Vietnam, beginning with a few painters like Le Van Mien (1873 -1943) who worked in oils in the late nineteenth century. Despite Thailand's independence, the passion for things Western were in demand by the elite during that time as well. The architecture of King Mongkut (r. 1851 -68) incorporated Greek orders and Chinese ceramics into the Thai style. Over the next half century and well into the early twentieth, photography and naturalistic painting and sculpture dominate Thai court art.

While the great majority of the population in this period are Muslim, Buddhist, or Christian, Southeast Asia was also home to a diversity of indigenous peoples, who shared aspects of their language, art, and culture with the Polynesians, Micronesians, and other Pacific Island groups. Often living in isolated enclaves separated by hundreds, even thousands, of miles, the region's indigenous peoples nonetheless exhibited remarkable similarities in their art and cultures, indicating that these groups shared a common ancestry. One of the most striking similarities was in their conception of the human form, which is typically depicted in a seated or crouching position with the legs drawn close to the body and the hands or forearms resting on the knees.

Crown from Indonesia, Sulawesi.

A NEW WORLD ORDER

Age of machinery begins

The term Industrial Revolution describes the major changes brought about by a host of inventions and discoveries enabling the development of new technology, machinery, and modes of production. Machinery was used to complement or substitute human labor. For example, wind, water, human, and animal power were replaced to some extent by the use of steam power. Steam generation

The Crystal Palace in Hyde Park, London, built for the Great Exhibition of 1851.

needed coal, leading to a massive increase in demand. The harnessing of electricity was another important stride. Machine tools and parts were standardized, and factories became the centers of production. The railways ushered in a transport transformation, linking cities and distant areas. New methods of making iron, glass, and steel were developed. Pride in technology was displayed as in the Great Exhibition held in London in 1851.

The Industrial Revolution, which began in Great Britain in the 18th century, spread by the end of the 19th century to other countries in Europe, the United States of America, and Japan. The enormous potential of the new modes of production induced a shift from the focus on agriculture toward the accumulation of capital. Skills such as marketing and management emerged, along with new practices in banking and insurance.

With an unprecedented capacity for mass production, industries now needed large quantities of raw materials as well as markets to sell the finished goods. These two factors helped drive the acquisition of colonies by European powers. In the 19th century, capitalist economics were best analyzed by Karl Marx, in his voluminous work, *Das Kapital*.

The smoking chimneys of Manchester as seen from Kensal Moore.

1836–1840

1836 Texas gains independence from Mexico.
1837 German educationist Friedrich Froebel establishes first kindergarten, an educational system of activity and play.
• Victoria becomes the queen of England.

1837–39 Working class Chartist movement in Britain.
1839 Ottomans start modernization program in Turkey.
1839–42 *Amistad* revolt, a shipboard uprising on the coast of Cuba, leads to debates on slavery.

In the 1800s, new biomedical devices and instruments were developed by scientist and doctors. In the year 1816, French doctor Rene Laennec invented a device called stethoscope. In 1895, Wilhem Roentgen, a German physicist, discovered X-rays.

New techniques and information were introduced to farmers for better yield and production.

Karl Marx.

Child labor

By the early 19th century, machines had largely replaced manual laborers. Factories spread everywhere, and factory owners began to use children as workers. Power-driven machines did not have to be operated by adults: Children were strong enough to do the job and they were cheaper than adults. In 1810 around 2 million children were working 50–70 hours a week in the USA, for very low wages.

Teachers, churches, and workers' groups all spoke out against the evils of child labor. Charles Dickens' novel *Oliver Twist* highlighted the horrors that could be found.

Britain was the first to take steps against child labor. From 1802 onwards, a series of laws raised the age at which children were allowed to work, shortened their working hourse, and generally improved conditions.

Child labor.

The working class

A new class emerged: Industrial workers, including children, who toiled for long hours, often in terrible conditions, for low pay. In protest against this and against the machines themselves, groups such as the British Luddite Movement (1811–12)

- First Anglo-Afghan War; British troops massacred.
- **1839–1906** Life of French painter Paul Cézanne.
- **1840** Treaty of Waitangi signed in New Zealand.
- Kamehameha III introduces a constitutional monarchy in Hawaii.

- Postage stamp introduced in Britain; soon becomes widespread.
- **1840–89** Pedro II rules Brazil; introduces reforms.
- **1840–1917** Life of French sculptor Auguste Rodin.

A NEW WORLD ORDER

smashed machinery. Gradually, workers united into unions, which bargained for fewer working hours and better pay.

As people flocked to cities for work, new ideas emerged along with new social relationships. Robert Owen (1771–1858) envisaged a cooperative society, while Karl Marx (1818–83) and Friedrich Engels (1820–95) analyzed class struggle in *The Communist Manifesto*.

SOME 19TH-CENTURY INVENTIONS AND INNOVATIONS

Davy's safety lamp.

1800 Alessandro Volta (1745–1827), Italian. Early form of electric battery or cell.

1804 Joseph Marie Jacquard (1752–1834), French. Jacquard loom, to weave textiles with elaborate patterns.

1810 First tin cans.

1814 George Stephenson (1781–1841), British. Railway locomotive.

1815 Humphry Davy (1778–1829), British. Miner's safety lamp.

1829–30 Barthelemy Thimonnier (1793–1857), French. Sewing machine.

1832 William Sturgeon (1783–1850), British. Electric motor.

1836–37 Samuel Morse (1791–1872), American; Charles Wheatstone (1802–75), British. Telegraph/ Morse code.

1849 Walter Hunt (1796–1859), American. Safety pin.

1855 Robert Bunsen (1811–99), German. Spectroscope, spectrum analysis, gas burner.

Alexander Graham Bell.

1876 Alexander Graham Bell (1847–1922), Scottish-American. Telephone.

1879 Karl Benz (1844–1929), German. Car engine (two-cylinder).

1883 Thomas Alva Edison (1847–1931), American. Light bulb.

1893 Rudolf Diesel (1858-1913), German. Diesel engine.

1895 Guglielmo Marchese Marconi (1874–1937), Italian. Wireless telegraph.

Thomas Alva Edison.

1843–1850

1843–72 Maoris and British battle in New Zealand.

1844–1926 Life of Italian physician Camillo Golgi; identifies two types of nerve cells.

1845–49 The British annexes Punjab in India.

• Catastrophic famine in Ireland after failure of potato crop.

1845–1918 Life of German mathematician George Cantor; develops set theory.

1846 Planet Neptune discovered by German astronomer Johann Galle.

1846–48 USA–Mexican War; the USA gains territory.

1847 Briton Charlotte Bronte writes *Jane Eyre*.

The Sokoto caliphate

The Fulani, originally pastoral nomads, started expanding from north Nigeria in 1804, and established a number of kingdoms between Senegal and Cameroon. Osman bin Fodio led the Fulani jihad (1804–8), which integrated the Hausa states of this area into a political and religious entity: The Sokoto caliphate that is sometimes called the Fulani empire. The Sokoto were defeated by the British by 1903.

Emir Sokoto palace in Northern Nigeria.

The British accepted the Sokoto sultan as a ceremonial ruler. He proved his loyalty to the British in 1906 when, an uprising inspired by religious fanaticism took place. The revolt was aimed at driving the white man out of the country. The Sultan willingly disowned the leader of the uprising. The leader was sentenced to death in the Sultan's and was executed in the market place of Sokoto.

The modern Sokoto State was created on 3 February 1976 as part of Nigeria.. Sokoto City is the modern-day capital of the Sokoto State. Being the center of the former Sokoto Caliphate, Sokoto city is predominantly inhabited by Muslims and an important center of Islamic learning in Nigeria.

Events in various states

Seku Ahmadu, a Muslim, founded a state in 1818 in Macina (the region of modern Mali). In 1862, al-Haji Umar, an Islamic scholar and mystic, conquered Macina and created the Tukolor empire, which was annexed by the French at the end of the century.

Algeria was wrested by the French from the indirect rule of the Turks in 1834. The Sufi Abd al-Qadir (1808–83) organized a revolt against the French. Although he did not succeed, he remains a heroic figure in Algerian history.

- William Makepeace Thackeray writes *Vanity Fair*, a novel depicting English society.
- **1848** Karl Marx and Friederich Engels publish the *Communist Manifesto*.
- **1848–1916** Rule of Francis Joseph I, last Habsburg emperor of Austria, the king of Hungary (from **1867**).

1850 Four Australian colonies gain some powers from the British.
- English poet Lord Alfred Tennyson composes *In Memoriam*.
- **c. 1850s** Black African journalism and secular literature emerge.

A NEW WORLD ORDER

Ethiopia saw a revival in stature under three powerful emperors: Tewodros II (r. 1855–68), Yohannes IV (r. 1872–89), and Menelik II (r. 1889–1913). In 1840, Omani sultan Sa'id Sayyid ibn Sultan shifted the sultanate to the island of Zanzibar. This was done with the aim of consolidating Omani control over the Swahili coast. This helped restore trade relations with Western powers. This ultimately resulted in the United States, France, and Britain opening consulates on the island.

In 1875, the Free Church of Scotland established the Livingstonia Mission at Cape Maclear. The aim of the mission was to teach Western agricultural and manufacturing techniques. Merchants and artisans from the United Kingdom were employed for this purpose.

In 1878, King Leopold II of Belgium sponsored the exploration of the Congo River basin. In 1880, France gained control over the northern Congo region. In 1884, the Berlin conference resulted in the division of Africa.

Bamako in Mali.

1851–1866

1851 Mongkut becomes the king of Thailand; brings in reforms.
1852 Louis Napoleon of France becomes Emperor Napoleon III.
1853–78 King Mindon reigns in Burma.
1854 British mathematician George Boole develops Boolean algebra.

• Florence Nightingale organizes nursing during Crimean War.
1855 English novelist Elizabeth Gaskell writes *North and South* showing conditions in factories.
1858 Fenian movement for Irish independence founded.
1861 Serfdom abolished in Russia.

The Mahdi war

The Mahdi War.

Egypt under Muhammad Ali, viceroy of Oman, asserted its independence, and extended its sway over Sudan (1819) and parts of the Middle East. During Egyptian rule over Sudan, high rates of taxation were imposed. Young men were enslaved. Egypt gained absolute control over all Sudanese trade which shattered livelihoods and hampered indigenous practices. Many Sudanese men and boys died on their long march from the Sudanese hinterlands to Aswan, during military enlistment. Ali's tenure as Egyptian governor ended in 1848, but the suffering of the Sudanese people under Egyptian rule did not. However, Sudan rejected Egyptian dominance, and in the 1870s, Muhammad Ahmad proclaimed himself the mahdi (the "guided one," an Islamic messiah), and instigated a revolt against Egypt and Britain. The Mahdists managed to gain control after a long struggle, but were ousted by the British in 1898. In June 1885, Muhammad Ahmad died. The result was that the Mahdist movement dissolved due to internal rivalry among claimants. This inspired the British to return to Sudan in 1896 with Horatio Kitchener as the commander of the Anglo-Egyptian army. In the final battle, Ahmad's successor was killed, putting an end to the Mahdist state.

1861–65 American Civil War leads to end of slavery in the USA.
1862 French encroach on Indochina.
1864–70 Paraguay fights war against Argentina, Brazil, and Uruguay.
1865 Wellington becomes the capital of New Zealand.

- Lewis Carroll writes *Alice's Adventures in Wonderland.*
- British surgeon Joseph Lister discovers antiseptics.
- US president Abraham Lincoln assassinated.
1866 Seven-Weeks' War between Prussia and Austria.

A NEW WORLD ORDER

The Scramble for Africa

As their explorers ventured deeper into Africa, European nations struggled for control of the continent. Britain acquired Cape Colony in 1814. The Dutch Boers in the Cape moved away from British control, and clashed with the Zulus and other Bantu people. They first settled in Natal, and established the Republic of Transvaal (1852) and Orange Free State (1854).

Cecil Rhodes (1853–1902) expanded British power beyond Cape Colony, while King Leopold II (1835–1909) of Belgium acquired Congo (Zaire). Around 1880, what is known as the "Scramble for Africa" began. At the Conference of Berlin (1884-85), European powers decided their spheres of influence on the continent. Following the Anglo–Boer War of 1899–1902, the British appropriated Boer territories, but gave them certain concessions. By the end of the 19th century, most of Africa was parceled between various European nations. Only Ethiopia and Liberia were independent.

SLAVE TRADE: ABOLITION

In 1822, the American Colonization Society established the African colony of Liberia for freed slaves. Gradually, through the 19th century, Western nations banned the practice.

1794 Abolished by France's National Convention; 1848 final abolition.

1807 British ships prohibited from engaging in the trade; Slavery after 1833 abolished in Britain.

1808 The USA prohibits importation of slaves; 1865 slavery abolished.

1814 William I of Netherlands forbids his subjects to engage in slavery.

The USA expands

In 1800, the USA consisted of 13 colonies. Three years later, the new nation bought the vast territory known as Louisiana, extending west from the Mississippi river to the Rocky mountains, from France. Gradually, the USA gained more territories and new settlers moved westward. The southern states, who wished to continue with slave labor, seceded from the USA, causing a civil war (1861–65) in which the southern Confederacy was defeated. By 1900, the country consisted of 45 states.

1867–1879

1867 Alaska purchased by the USA from Russia.

• Swedish chemist Alfred Nobel invents dynamite.

1868–1910 Rama V modernizes Thailand.

1869 Suez Canal opened.

1869 Mohandas Karamchand Gandhi is born.

1870 Frenchman Jules Verne writes *Twenty Thousand Leagues Under the Sea*; considered originator of modern Science fiction.

1870–71 Franco-Prussian War happens.

1870s Zulu wars against Britain.

1870–88 Antonio Guzman rules Venezuela; introduces reforms.

Uprooting of Native Americans

The herds of buffalo that had been the mainstay of the Native American way of life on the Great Plains were wiped out. Many people died of diseases brought in by European settlers, and the Indian Removal Act of 1830 forced the tribes to move to the west onto reservations; thousands died along the way. The Sioux formed the main Native American opposition, defeating American forces under George Custer at the battle of the Little Bighorn in 1876. Native American resistance ended after the massacre at Wounded Knee (South Dakota) in 1890, where 200 unarmed men, women, and children were killed by US troops.

The Sioux Ghost Dance.

Art and literature

Winslow Homer (1836–1910) and Thomas Eakins (1844–1916) were some of the great American painters, and literary figures included Mark Twain (1835–1910), Herman Melville (1819–91), Harriet Beecher Stowe (1811–96), Nathaniel Hawthorne (1804–64), and the poets Walt Whitman (1819–92) and Henry Wadsworth Longfellow (1807–82).

JOHN JAMES AUDUBON

In 1838, the artist and natural historian John James Audubon (1785–1851) produced Birds of America, *with 435 hand-colored plates. Between 1831 and 1839, he wrote* The Ornithological Biography, *on the characteristics of birds, with the Scottish naturalist William MacGillivray.*

Right: White gerfalcons drawn by Audobon.

1871–1940 Third Republic in France.
1872 Yellowstone, America's first National Park, founded.
1874 Benjamin Disraeli is prime minister of England for the second time.
1874–91 Prince David Kalakaua rules Hawaii.

1876 German musician Johann Brahms composes *Symphony No I*, first of his great orchestral works.
• Alexander Graham Bell invents the telephone.
1877–78 Russo-Turkish War; some Balkan states gain freedom.
1879–84 Chile, Peru, and Bolivia involved in the War of the Pacific.

A NEW WORLD ORDER

Canadian consolidation

Meanwhile, Canada resisted US incursions, and became a self-governing dominion of the British empire in 1867. At this time, it was a federation of Nova Scotia, New Brunswick, Québec (Lower Canada), and Ontario (Upper Canada). The opening of the transcontinental Canadian Pacific Railway helped to expand settlement and unite the vast area.

The Canadian Pacific Railway.

Liberation of South American states

By 1830, the Spanish and Portuguese yoke had been thrown off, and most states had gained independence. Prominent revolutionary leaders included José de San Martin (1778–1850) in Chile, Argentina, and Peru, and Simon Bolivar (1783–1830), founder of Bolivia, in Venezuela. Revolutions, conflicts, and border disputes continued.

Simon Bolivar.

Europeans colonize Australia, New Zealand

Convicts were transported to Australia from Britain until 1868, and wealthy settlers also emigrated there. Sheep breeding began, and between 1809 and 1821 governor Lachlan Macquarie improved the economy. By the end of the century, Australia consisted of six colonies, which agreed to join together in a federation.

In New Zealand, British colonists established settlements in 1840, and founded the town of Wellington. A treaty made with the native Maori leaders, offering them land rights and British citizenship, was not honored, and resulted in war.

1880–1888

1880 France annexes Tahiti.
1881 Mustafa Kemal Ataturk is born.
1882 Tsar Alexander II of Russia assassinated.
• Triple Alliance between Germany, Austria, Italy.
1883 Peter Carl Fabergé, Russian jeweler and goldsmith, creates elaborate art objects.

• *The Story of an African Farm,* a novel by Olive Sriner, a white South African, explores race and gender relations.
• Eruption of Krakatoa volcano; thousands die in Java and Sumatra.
1884–85 The Berlin Conference; European powers and the USA define spheres of influence in Africa; no African state is invited.

Contemporary cartoon expressing the nervousness of the great European powers with the volatile state of affairs in the Balkans in 1912-13.

The early 20th century saw increasing development, with the USA becoming highly industrialized, more so than any country in Europe. Within Europe, Germany had become a leading industrial nation, overtaking Britain in the production of pig-iron and steel. In Asia, Japan had become a major power, defeating Russia in a 1904–05 war. Despite the rapid changes that were taking place, Europe continued to dominate world affairs, and World War I, beginning in Europe, involved practically the whole world.

Prior to World War I, there were several other wars in Europe. The huge Ottoman empire faced internal problems, with the rise of the Young Turks and the growth of nationalism in its subject countries. The Italo-Turkish War of 1911–12 ended in victory for Italy, who occupied three Ottoman provinces that later became Libya. The Ottoman defeat inspired two Balkan Wars that took place in 1912 and 1913. In the first, Bulgaria, Greece, Montenegro, and Serbia (the Balkan League) attacked the Ottoman empire gaining some victories, while in the second, Bulgaria attacked Serbia and Greece. Montenegro, Romania, and the Ottoman empire later joined in against Bulgaria. Albania gained independence from the Ottomans, and Serbia emerged as a stronger state.

The Balkan Wars did not directly lead to World War I, but created a volatile situation within Europe.

SCIENCE AND TECHNOLOGY

During this period, science and technology continued to develop. Max Planck's quantum theory (1900), Albert Einstein's special theory of relativity (1905), and Niels Bohr's theory of atomic structure (1913–15) were among the most notable scientific advances. The first airplane flight took place, and mass production of cars began. Sigmund Freud introduced theories of the subconscious and of psychoanalysis, publishing The Interpretation of Dreams *in 1899–1900.*

Albert Einstein.

Sigmund Freud.

Niels Bohr.

1885 Indian National Congress founded; spearheads movement for independence.
- Canadian Pacific Railway completed.

1886 American Federation of Labor formed.
- German philosopher Friedrich Nietzsche writes *Beyond Good and Evil*, rejecting traditional Christian morality.

1886–1900 Neo-Impressionist movement in French art.

1887 Ferdinand of Coburg becomes king of Bulgaria.

1888 August Strindberg (1849–1912), prominent Swedish literary figure, writes realist plays, including *Froken Julie* (Miss Julie).

1888–1918 William II rules Germany.

WAR AND THE WORLD

NOBEL PRIZE HISTORY

Alfred Bernhard Nobel, a Swedish inventor and industrialist, was the founder of the Nobel Prizes. These awards are widely regarded as the most prestigious awards given for intellectual achievement in the world. After Nobel's death, the Nobel Foundation was set up to carry out the provisions of his will and to administer his funds.

Nobel arranged for five annual prizes "to those who, during the preceding year, shall have conferred the greatest benefit on mankind." The prizes that were established are the Nobel Prize for Physics, the Nobel Prize for Chemistry, the Nobel Prize for Physiology or Medicine, the Nobel Prize for Literature, and the Nobel Prize for Peace. The distribution of the prizes started from December 10, 1901, which was the fifth anniversary of Nobel's death.

A Nobel Prize medal.

Nobel's will named the institutions which should award the prizes. From Stockholm, the Royal Swedish Academy of Sciences confers the prizes for physics, chemistry, and economics; the Karolinska Institute confers the prize for physiology or medicine; and the Swedish Academy confers the prize for literature. The Norwegian Nobel Committee based in Oslo confers the prize for peace. The Nobel Foundation owns the legal rights and functional administration of the funds, but the decisions regarding the award relies on the four institutions.

ALBERT EINSTEIN

Albert Einstein was a German-born theoretical physicist. As a young medical student, Einstein was influenced by his friend Max Talmud, who introduced him to higher mathematics and philosophy. At the age of 16, Einstein was intrigued by a children's science series by Aaron Bernstein, *Naturwissenschaftliche Volksbucher* (1867–68; *Popular Books on Physical Science*), in which the author imagined riding alongside electricity that was traveling inside a telegraph wire. This thought lingered in his mind for next 10 years: What would a light beam look like if you could run alongside it? If light were a wave, then the light beam should appear stationary, like a frozen wave. Even as a child, he knew that light beams were not stationary, so it was paradoxical. Einstein wrote his first "scientific paper" at the age of 16—*The Investigation of the State of Aether in Magnetic Fields.* The year 1905 is often called the Einstein's "miracle year" which altered the course of modern physics as he wrote four major papers. He developed the Theory of Relativity, one of the two pillars of modern physics. His most famous equation is the mass–energy equivalence formula $E = mc^2$. The physics community ignored Einstein's papers until he received the attention of none other than Max Planck himself, the most influential physicist of his generation

1890–1901

1890 First election in Japan.

1893 New Zealand is the first country to grant voting rights to women.

• Czech musician Antonin Dvorak composes *Symphony From the New World (No 9)*, using Native American themes.

1894 Tower Bridge completed in London.

1894 Timbuktu captured by the French.

1894–95 Japan-China War; Japan occupies Korea.

1895 Bulgarian prime minister Stefan Nikolov Stambolov assassinated.

1896 Ethiopians defeat Italians at Battle of Aduwa.

• First modern Olympics happens in Greece.

and founder of the quantum theory. In 1921, Einstein received the Nobel Prize for Physics, but for his contribution to the photoelectric effect rather than for his relativity theories. During his acceptance speech, Einstein chose to speak about relativity theories instead of the photoelectric effect. There were two pillars of physics in the 19th century: Newton's laws of motion and Maxwell's theory of light. Einstein was alone in realizing that they were in contradiction and that one of them must be wrong. After World War I, two expeditions were sent to test Einstein's prediction of deflected starlight near the Sun. One set sail for the island of Principe, off the coast of West Africa, and the other to Sobral in northern Brazil in order to observe the solar eclipse of May 29, 1919. On November 6, the results were announced in London at a joint meeting of the Royal Society and the Royal Astronomical Society, proving Einstein right. Almost immediately, Einstein became a world-renowned physicist, the successor to Isaac Newton. He is still arguably the most influential physicist of the 20th century.

SIGMUND FREUD

Sigmund Freud, an Austrian neurologist, was the founder of psychoanalysis, which includes a clinical method of treatment where a dialogue between a patient and a psychoanalyst is required for exploring psychopathology. In 1873, Freud chose medicine as a career after a public reading of an essay by Goethe on nature, and graduated from the Sperl Gymnasium. *The Interpretation of Dreams* is known as his predominant work in which he presented his findings.

Based on his own dreams and those recounted by his patients, Freud concluded that dreams are essential to understand the psyche. According to Freud, all dreams, including nightmares, provide a kind of wish fulfillment for an individual, of things that might be unattainable in reality. When the desires are in conflict with social prohibitions, dreams provide a relief to the psyche by realizing those desires which are otherwise out of one's reach. Dreams, therefore, have to be decoded to be understood, and not merely because they are actually forbidden desires experienced in a distorted manner. In 1904, Freud published *Zur Psychopathologie des Alltagslebens* (*The Psychopathology of Everyday Life*), in which he explored seemingly insignificant errors such as slips of the tongue or pen (later colloquially called Freudian slips), misreading, or forgetting of names. These errors too, according to Freud, were symptoms of psychic condition and thus subject to interpretation, even though, unlike dreams, they are manifestations of conscious emotions rather than repressed.

NIELS BOHR

A Danish theoretical physicist, Niels Bohr was born in Copenhagen in 1885. His investigations of atomic structure and the radiation emitted by atoms contributed towards the modern understanding

1898 The USA wins Spanish-American War; gains territories in the Caribbean and Pacific.
• Cuban independence.
• The USA annexes Hawaii.
1900 Boxer rebellion in China.
• Manchuria occupied by Russia (up to 1904).

• New Zealand appropriates Cook Islands (formal annexation in 1901).
1900 Max Planck came out with quantum theory.
1901 Commonwealth of Australia established.
• Nobel Prizes awarded for the first time.
• Asante in west Africa annexed by Britain.
• The USA takes over Philippines.

of quantum theory. He was one of a small group of physicists whose work in the early 20th century revolutionized scientific understanding of the nature of matter and reality.

Electrons were only discovered in 1897, and Ernest Rutherford (1871–1937) soon showed that they carry a negative charge while whirling in a cloud around the positively charged nucleus of an atom. Yet since opposite charges attract, there was no explanation for why electrons did not collapse onto the nucleus, particularly when they lose energy.

Bohr suggested that electrons lie in rings or orbits around the nucleus according to how much energy they contain. He also "quantized" the atom, that is he applied Max Planck's theory of small quanta of energy, and theorized that if an electron receives a quantum of energy, it jumps to an outer orbit, and, when it drops down to a lower orbit, it loses a quantum, but it can never fall beyond the innermost orbit.

While they are moving about, Bohr established that electrons themselves radiate a quantum of electromagnetic energy in the form of light. His proposal that they start at different orbits or energy levels, also explains why the light they emit has different frequencies.

In 1937 Bohr produced the founding theory for nuclear energy and nuclear bombs when he suggested that the nucleus of an atom is not one single particle, but is a compound structure, held together only by energy, that might therefore be split or undergo fission.

While in Nazi-occupied Denmark during World War II, Bohr passed on to the Allies news that the Germans were seeking to split the atom. This spurred on the USA to develop its own atomic bomb. Bohr and his family were rescued from Denmark and he joined the Manhattan Project that was building the bomb, though he always campaigned for the peaceful use of nuclear energy.

He died in Copenhagen in 1962.

World War I begins

The main underlying cause of World War I (1914–18) was competition for land and resources, both in Europe and elsewhere. Europe was already divided into two groups of protective alliances. The Triple Entente comprised the UK, France, and Russia, with Japan, the USA, and Spain becoming affiliated to this group. On the other side was the Triple Alliance of Germany, Austria–Hungary, and Italy, although Italy later switched sides. The

Austrian archduke Franz Ferdinand and his wife Sophie.

1901–1905

EARLY 1900s British mathematician Karl Pearson (1857–1936) contributes to theories of statistics.

1901–71 Life of American jazz musician Louis Armstrong.

1902 Irish Nationalist Party Sinn Fein founded.

- Influential French novelist André Gide writes *L'Immoraliste* (The Immoralist), exploring individual freedom.
- **1903** Britain takes over Sokoto caliphate in Africa.
- First airplane flight by Orville and Wilbur Wright.
- First crayons created from charcoal and oil.
- Alexander, king of Serbia, assassinated.

trigger for war was a conflict between Austria and Serbia, originating in the rise of Serbian nationalism. Serbia wanted to unite the Serbs and Croats and create a separate nation of Yugoslavia, encompassing Bosnia, which was part of Austria. On a visit to Sarajevo in Bosnia, the Austrian archduke Franz Ferdinand was shot dead by a Serbian terrorist group on June 28, 1914.

The foreign minister, Leopold, Graf von Berchtold, of Austria-Hungary viewed the crime as an opportunity to humiliate Serbia which could ultimately lead to enhancing Austria-Hungary's prestige in the Balkans. The German Kaiser Wilhelm II had already assured him of Germany's support in case Austria-Hungary started a war against Serbia.

On July 19, 1914, the Austrians presented Serbia with an ultimatum. They were relying on Germany to stop Russia from intervening. But, on July 24, Russia affirmed that Austria-Hungary would not be allowed to crush Serbia.

Serbia accepted all the demands except for two. In spite of the fact that Serbia offered to submit the issue to international arbitration, Austria-Hungary instantly severed diplomatic relations and ordered partial mobilization. In the meanwhile, the German foreign office kept on encouraging von Berchtold and ultimately he persuaded the Austrian emperor Franz Josef to authorize war against Serbia. The result was that war was declared on July 28. Austro-Hungarian artillery began to bombard Belgrade the next day.

THEODORE ROOSEVELT

Theodore Roosevelt was one of the most famous heroes of the Spanish-American war. During the war, he was a lieutenant colonel in the Rough Riders regiment.

Senator Tom Platt, who needed a hero to draw attention away from scandals in New York State, accepted Roosevelt as the Republican candidate for governor in 1898. Roosevelt won and served with distinction.

Theodore Roosevelt became president of the USA in 1901. His policies favored small businesses rather than large monopolies, and he referred to his actions as aiming for a "square deal" between labor

1904–09 Ismael Montes is the president of Bolivia; brings in reforms.

1904–1990 Life of B.F. Skinner, exponent of behavioral school of psychology.

1905 Alberta and Saskatchewan provinces formed in Canada.

• In Russia, revolt against tsar Nicholas II leads to grant of constitutional reforms.

1905 Special theory of relativity of Albert Einstein.

1905–06 British New Guinea comes under Australia; renamed Territory of Papua.

WAR AND THE WORLD

and business. He made this a slogan for his 1904 election campaign, and after his reelection he extended the term Square Deal to refer to other programs that would help ordinary citizens. He also expanded forest reserves and national parks. In 1906, he won the Nobel Peace Prize for helping end the Russo–Japanese war of 1904–05. Roosevelt remained president until March 1909.

As president, Roosevelt believed that the ideal government is one that acts as an ultimate arbitrator of the differing economic forces in the nation, preferably between capital and labor. He believed that government should guarantee justice to everyone and offer favors to none.

World War I

After Austria's declaration of war on Serbia, Russia ordered a troop mobilization to support the latter, and Germany declared war on Russia (August 1, 1914) and France (August 3, 1914). Germany invaded Belgium and besieged Liège, on the way to France. This caused Britain to enter the war, and other powers soon joined the fray. European countries also pulled in native troops from their colonies. Machine guns, tanks, aerial bombing, and poison gas were used in the war. Casualties were higher than in any war

A 1914 war vessel.

1905–1908

1905–07 Maji Maji revolt against German colonial rule in East Africa.
c. 1906 Bakelite, the first synthetic resin, invented.
1906 Protestant Pentecostal movement begins in the USA.
• Cuba occupied by the USA.

• Simplon railway tunnel built through Alps linking Switzerland to Italy; 12 miles long, it was longest railway tunnel till the English Channel tunnel was opened in 1993.
1906 France and Spain gain control in Morocco.
1907 New Zealand becomes a separate dominion.

before: around 10 million soldiers died, 21 million were wounded, and about eight million were taken prisoner or went missing. Civilian deaths amounted to about 10 million.

The 4-year war ended in a crushing defeat of the Central Powers (Germany, Austria–Hungary, Turkey, Bulgaria). An armistice was agreed on November 11, 1918, and a series of peace treaties were signed. Though the objective was to bring about a lasting peace, the humiliation suffered by Germany led to the growth of militarism and nationalism in that country. Another result of the war was the transfer of European colonies in Africa from German or Italian control to France or Britain. Some of the Asian colonies such as India were expected to be given more rights to self-governance, as had been promised during the course of the war.

One positive aspect of World War I was the creation of the League of Nations, the first organization created in an attempt to maintain peace in the world.

At the outbreak of the war, the Allied powers possessed greater overall demographic, industrial, and military resources than the Central Powers. They were able to have easy access to the oceans for trade with neutral countries, especially with the United States.

Internal communication sources of Germany and Austria enabled them to move their forces to important points on the battlefronts by the shortest possible route.

Due to Germany's efficient railway network, it could move eight divisions of its army concurrently from the Western Front to the Eastern Front in four and a half days.

The invention of new weapons and the improvement of existing ones played a vital role in the planning and conduct of war. Some crucial developments took place in the field of machine guns plural and the rapid-fire field artillery gun in the period

The front-page headlines from a newspaper in 1914.

- Hans Kuzel adapts the existing technology to create tungsten filament lamps.
- Maria Montessori develops Montessori method of education for young children.
- French physicist Pierre-Ernest Weiss develops theory of ferromagnetism.

- International Peace Conference with 44 participants held at The Hague, Netherlands.
1908 Austria annexes Bosnia-Herzegovina.
- Belgium occupies Congo in Africa.
- First Model T car produced by Henry Ford.
- Oil discovered first in the Middle East.
- Young Turk revolution in Turkey.

WAR AND THE WORLD

leading up to the war. A machine gun could fire 600 bullets per minute with a range of more than 900 yards. The period saw the introduction of improved breech-loading mechanisms and brakes. Machine guns, when used in combination with rapid-firing artillery, gave a definite advantage to the defence.

The initial clashes between the French and German armies along the Franco-German and Franco-Belgian frontiers are collectively known as the Battle of the Frontiers. The battle lasted from August 14 until the beginning of the First Battle of the Marne on September 6 and was the biggest battle of the war. More than two million troops were involved in this battle.

One of the greatest successes of German wartime diplomacy was the entry of Turkey into the war as a

The first large scale use of chemical weapons was during World War I.

German ally. Germany had skilfully gained a dominating influence over Turkey which had been under the control of the Young Turks since 1909. German military trainers

pervaded the Turkish army, and Enver Paşa, the leader of the Young Turks, looked at alliance with Germany as the best way of serving Turkey's interests, especially for protection against the Russian threat. He encouraged the grand vizier, Said Halim Paşa, to make a secret treaty. Under the treaty, Turkey pledged to be on the side of Germany in case Germany had to take Austria–Hungary's side against Russia.

World War I ends on November 11, 1918.

1909–1911

1909 American explorer Robert Peary reaches North Pole.
• Russian-born mathematician Hermann Minkowski develops concept of space–time.
1910 Union of South Africa formed.
• German Ferdinand Graf von Zeppelin develops the first airship.

• Revolution in Portugal.
• Sri Aurobindo, spiritualist, philosopher, nationalist, sets up ashram in Puducherry, India.
• Wilhelm Ostwald, German physical chemist, wins the Nobel Prize for chemistry; had developed method of producing nitric acid.

ART, LITERATURE, AND MUSIC

At this time, the modern period of individualistic styles, based on the artist's own vision, began. Expressionism, Futurism, Fauvism, and Cubism were some of the new trends. Dadaism emerged out of a rejection of the War and sought new themes and methods that aimed to shock and scandalize. Constructivism developed in the USSR, with three dimensional and "dynamic" constructions.

In literature, the stream-of-consciousness style was introduced by Marcel Proust, and taken forward by James Joyce. T.S. Eliot, Ezra Pound, W.B. Yeats, and Rainer Maria Rilke were great names in poetry, and poets Wilfred Owen and Siegfried Sassoon were directly inspired by the war. Jazz music, a fusion of different traditions but primarily African American, began to develop in America.

Many war artists offered harsh but realistic visual depictions of the death and destruction that resulted from combat. For example, when we look at C.R.W. Nevinson's stark painting, Paths of Glory, irony comes to the forefront. Paul Nash's 1917 work, The Menin Road, depicts a ruined Belgian landscape.

First World War literature also presents a range of perspectives. Rupert Brooke's patriotic "1914" sonnet sequence became hugely popular in the early years of the war. At the outset of the war, many people in Britain were moved by the heroic sentiments of the poems, especially, "The Soldier."

During the years leading up to the war, writers and authors broke free of traditional parameters of form and imagery and brought the very materials of their crafts to the forefront.

Women artists and writers played a significant role in documenting civilian and service experiences. Vera Brittain, who volunteered as a nurse, recorded her impressions of work and loss in her memoir, Testament of Youth. Women artists documented other civilian realities such as female workers in factories, doing jobs vacated by men in the military, who had become crucial for war-related production.

To recognize individual sacrifices, the British government issued memorial bronze plaques and paper scrolls to the family of each service person who died as a result of the war. And, on November 11, 1920, a solemn ceremony dedicated two of Britain's most famous public war monuments, Edward Lutyens's Whitehall Cenotaph and the Unknown Warrior, buried in Westminster Abbey.

A portrait in the Cubist style (1912) by the artist Juan Gris (1887–1927).

1910 Igor Stravinsky composed The Firebird.
1910–13 Bertrand Russell (1872–1970) and Alfred North Whitehead (1861–1947) complete the three-volume Principia Mathematica on logic and mathematics.
1911 Igor Stravinsky composed Petrushka.

1911 Chinese Revolution.
• First Hollywood studio founded.
• Norwegian Roald Amundsen reaches South Pole.
• Morocco becomes French protectorate; France cedes territory to Germany in French Congo.

WAR AND THE WORLD

WORLD WAR I: MAJOR BATTLE SITES

Arras, France September–October, 1914, and July, 1915, France vs Germany; April–May, 1917, Britain and Canadian and Australian troops vs Germany; March, 1918, Britain vs Germany; August–September, 1918, Britain; and Canadian troops vs Germany.

Ardennes, France August, 1914, France vs Germany.

Heligoland Bight, Frisian Islands August, 1914, Britain vs Germany (naval battle).

Marne, France September, 1914, France, Britain vs Germany; July–August, 1918, Germany vs France.

Ypres, Belgium October–November, 1914, Britain, France, Belgium vs Germany; April–May, 1915, Belgium, France, Britain, Canada vs Germany; July–November, 1917, Britain vs Germany (also known as Battle of Passendale or Passchendaele).

Gallipoli campaign 1915–16, British empire forces, France vs Ottomans, Germany.

Verdun, France February–December, 1916, France vs Germany. The Battle of Verdun was the longest and costliest battle of World War I. It began in February 1916 with a German attack on the fortified French town of Verdun, where fighting continued for most of the year.

Jutland, Denmark May–June 1916; Britain vs Germany (naval battle). The Battle of Jutland was the largest naval battle of World War I. It was the only time that the British and German fleets actually came to blows.

Jutland was a chaotic and bloodstained action ground involving 250 ships and around 100,000 men. Initial encounters resulted in the loss of several ships. The Germans damaged Allied flagship HMS *Lion*. HMS *Indefatigable* and HMS *Queen Mary* blew up when German shells penetrated their ammunition magazines.

Somme, France July–November, 1916, Britain, France

A British trench during the Battle of the Somme.

1912–1916

1912 New Mexico and Arizona become US states.
1912 African National Congress founded in Union of South Africa to promote civil rights.
• British ocean liner *Titanic* sinks; about 1500 die.
• Polish-born American biochemist Casimir Funk identifies the function of vitamins in the body.

1912–13 Balkan Wars.
1913 Igor Stravinsky composed *The Rite of Spring*.
1913 Young Turks organize coup in Turkey.
• South Africa reserves 87 percent land for whites.
• Rabindranath Tagore of India wins the Nobel Prize for Literature.
1913–15 Niels Bohr's theory of atomic structure.

and Allies vs Germany. Intending to achieve a decisive victory over the Germans on the Western Front, British and French forces launched a joint operation near the river Somme. The resulting battle remains the most painful memory of First World War for many in Britain.

Caporetto, Austria October–December, 1917, Germany, Austria–Hungary vs Italy.

Argonne, France September–November, 1918, France, USA vs Germany.

Brusilov Offensive 4 June–20 September 1916. Named after the Russian commander Aleksei Brusilov who led it, the Brusilov Offensive was the most successful Russian offensive and one of the most successful breakthrough operations of World War I. Brusilov used a short, sharp artillery bombardment and shock troops to exploit weak points, helping to return an element of surprise to the attack.

The offensive was part of the effort to relieve pressure not only on the French at Verdun, but also on the Western Front as a whole. The Russian attack drew Austro-Hungarian forces away from the Italian front and put increased pressure on the already strained and increasingly demoralised Austro-Hungarian Army.

ANZAC DAY: GALLIPOLI CAMPAIGN

The Gallipoli campaign was intended to allow Allied ships to pass through the Dardanelles, capture Constantinople and ultimately knock Turkey out of the war. But the Turks proved to be more resistant than the Allies had expected. Australia sent over 330,000 volunteers to fight in the war. Their worst losses were at Gallipoli, where the Australian and New Zealand Army Corps (Anzac) landed on April 25, 1915, and fought against Turkish troops. General Sir Ian Hamilton placed the British 29th Division at Cape Helles and the Anzac at the north of Gaba Tepe in an area later dubbed Anzac Cove. Both landings were quickly contained by determined Ottoman troops and neither the British nor the Anzacs were able to advance. Anzac Day (April 25) remains a national holiday in Australia and New Zealand, commemorating the losses in this and other wars.

1913–21 Woodrow Wilson is the President of the USA.

1914–18 World War I.

1914 Germany declares war on Russia.

1914 Britain and France occupy German colonies in West Africa.

- Panama Canal opens.

1915 Italy, Bulgaria join World War I.

1916 The 5175-mile-long Trans-Siberian railway, from Moscow to Vladivostok, completed.

- Husain ibn Ali of Mecca declares himself king of the Hejaz and caliph of all Muslims.

- Romania joins World War I.

REVOLUTION

While the World War was taking place, revolutions and struggles for independence continued across the world. Perhaps the most drastic changes took place in China and Russia.

Sun Yat-sen

Ruled by the Manchu Qing dynasty, China was conservative and resistant to change. Sun Yat-sen was among many who believed that the Manchu government needed to be overthrown and a republic established.

In 1905, he founded the Tongmenghui (United Revolutionary League) in Tokyo, based on three principles: Nationalism, democracy, and the well-being of the people. A revolution took place in 1911, and the Republic of China came into being on 1 January, 1912. Sun Yat-sen was made provisional president. In March, he was replaced by Yuan Shikai, the former military governor. Though the monarchy ended, China was not politically united.

Sun Yat-sen.

Sun was born to a family of poor farmers in Xiangshan, in the South China province of Guangdong. Sun first came into contact with Western influences in Honolulu as a student at a British missionary school for 3 years and at an American school, Oahu College, for another year.

Sun's political doctrines are summarized in his three principles of the nationalism, democracy, and people's livelihood. The principle of people's livelihood included the regulation of private capital and equalizing land rights. His Plan for National Reconstruction explained basic parliamentary procedures. Sun did not believe in the traditional Chinese saying that to know is easier than to do. He put forth an impressive plan for China's industrialization. The plan was laid down by Sun without much help from engineers or economists.

Although approved by his followers, Sun's doctrine was not his only attraction. All contemporary sources regard him as a charismatic personality. He had a great capacity for tolerating the weaknesses of others. His dedication towards pursuit of power was immense. He had unmatched knowledge of the West as compared to that of his political rivals. He is regarded as the symbol of Chinese modernization.

1917–1920

- **1917** Ras Tafari (Haile Selassie) is regent of Ethiopia.
- Russian Revolution.
- Balfour Declaration promises homeland to Jews.
- **1918** Oilfields opened in Venezuela.
- Salote becomes the queen of Tonga.
- Women over 30 years of age granted conditional vote in Britain.
- **1919** Kloet volcano erupts in Java, killing 16,000.
- First airplane crosses the Atlantic Ocean.
- Jallianwala Bagh massacre in India.

RUSSIAN ARTS AND CULTURE

This was a particularly productive period of artistic endeavor, much of it inspired by the Russian Revolution. Aleksandr Aleksandrovitch Blok (1880–1921) composed one of his greatest poems, *The Twelve*, an account of a Red Army patrol that was actually led by Jesus Christ. Ivan Alexseyvitch Bunin (1870–1953) wrote realistic stories and novels based on Russian life, and was the first Russian to win the Nobel Prize for Literature, in 1933, although Maxim Gorky (1868–1936) is perhaps the best known writer of this time. Vladimir Mayakovsky (1893–1930) explored new styles in poetry. Sergei Diaghilev (1872–1929) encouraged and revived ballet, and established the Ballets Russes (1909–29) company, with dancers such as Vaslav Nijinsky (1890–1950) and Anna Pavlova (1881–1931). The musician Igor Stravinsky (1882–1971) created ballets especially for Diaghilev, apart from other compositions.

Vaslav Nijinsky.

Aleksandr Scriabin, Sergey Rachmaninoff, and Igor Stravinsky were the three major Russian musicians that emerged in the early 20th century. Scriabin, a piano expert, permeated his music with mysticism and developed a futuristic expression with the help of which he created a musical equal to the Symbolist literature of the period. Rachmaninoff was also a pianist. He is best known for his concerti and for his *Rhapsody on a Theme of Paganini* (1954) for piano and orchestra. Stravinsky, a pupil of Rimsky-Korsakov, Stravinksy, wrote *The Firebird* (1910), *Petrushka* (1911), and *The Rite of Spring* (1913) for the Ballets Russes. that were premiered in Paris:

- Worldwide flu epidemic kills millions.
1919–1923 Weimar Republic in Germany.
1920 Women in the USA granted the vote.
- In India, Mahatma Gandhi (1869–1948) leads Non-Cooperation Movement against the British.

- First radio station begins broadcasting from Pittsburg, Pennsylvania, USA.
- Right-wing Kapp Putsch (revolt) in Germany.
1920–33 Prohibition in the USA.

REVOLUTION

The Russian Revolution

During 1894–1917, Russia was ruled by the autocratic tsar Nicholas I. Peter Stolypin, prime minister during 1906–11, tried to improve the conditions of peasants and workers, but widespread unrest and a desire for change persisted and intensified. Russia's participation in World War I created further economic problems. Meanwhile, the power of the revolutionary parties was growing. The Bolsheviks and Mensheviks were the two main ones. Both believed in Marxist ideas and revolution, but the Bolsheviks (meaning the majority), led by Vladimir Lenin, insisted that peasants and workers should be involved, whereas the Mensheviks (the minority) believed in cooperation with the middle-classes.

The bond between the tsar and most of the Russian people had been broken by 1917. Governmental. Two revolutions took place in March and November 1917 (February and October, according to the Julian calendar followed in Russia at that time). Nicholas I abdicated and the Russian monarchy came to an end. A provisional government was set up, but it was overthrown by the Bolsheviks in November. This made Russia the first communist state in the world. After the Revolution, four socialist republics were established on Russian territory: the Russian, Transcaucasian, Ukrainian, and Belorussian. However, for the Bolsheviks or Communist Party to establish control over the whole of Russia was not simple, as there were several contending forces.

Lenin speaking at the Second Soviet Congress on October 26, 1917.

1921–1923

1921 Albert Einstein receives the Nobel Prize for physics.
- Swiss psychiatrist Carl Jung writes *Psychological Types*; founds analytical school of psychology.
- Treaty of Nystadt; Sweden cedes Baltic provinces to Russia.

1921–28 New Economic Policy introduces a period of economic liberalization in the USSR; policy ended by Stalin.

1922 Fuad becomes the king of Egypt with nominal independence under the British protectorate.

Russia withdrew from the World War I and by the Treaty of Brest Litovsk (March, 1918) lost a number of her western territories, including Poland, Georgia, and Finland. Civil war followed between the Bolsheviks and a mixed group known as the Whites, who included the Mensheviks. Foreign troops aided the Mensheviks, but by the end of 1920 the Bolsheviks had established power. The building of a new country began. The four newly formed socialist republics came together to form the Union of Soviet Socialist Republics (USSR) in 1922, to which other republics were later added. Vladimir Lenin headed the party and the country until his death in 1924.

Corruption and inefficiency were widespread. The tsar's conservative policies that included the occasional dissolution of the Russian parliament had spread dissatisfaction even to moderate elements. The Russian Empire's many ethnic minorities grew increasingly agitated under the Russian domination.

The government's inefficiency to deal with the challenges of World War I was the most important cause of dissatisfaction among Russian people. Ill-equipped and poorly led, Russian armies suffered catastrophic losses in campaign after campaign against German armies. The war made revolution important in two ways. It showed that Russia was no longer a match to the military capabilities of central and Western Europe. The second reason was that the war terribly disrupted the economy.

The Russian Revolution of 1917 was an event of international significance. The Revolution exposed the values of western culture to a difficult challenge. The fundamental principles of trade and industry were equally challenged. The well-established systems of government were put to the test. The revolution brought to light the limitations of social, economic, and political institutions. The entire world was drawn to re-examine the western values of democracy.

The revolution alarmed the capitalists as it made a tempting appeal to the working class. The revolution claimed that working men have nothing to lose but slavery. The revolution united the working men of all countries against the capitalist class. It led to the declaration of war against dictatorship and democratic socialism. The most important aspect of this revolution put forward the importance of Marxism.

The revolution had a major influence on people in colonized countries around the world, giving them a new realization of their political rights and inspiring the growth of self-determination movements.

- First radio broadcast by the British Broadcasting Corporation.
- Irish Free State formed.
- Literary classic *Ulysses* written by Irish writer James Joyce.

- Poet T.S. Eliot completes *The Wasteland*.
- **1923** Earthquake at Kwanto, Japan, destroys Yokohama and Kyoto; about 140,000 dead.
- Three-light traffic signals invented by American Garett Morgan.

THE INTERMEDIATE YEARS

Franklin Delano Roosevelt (1882–1945).

The War had ended, peace treaties had been signed, but the world was still reeling from its debilitating effects. European countries had to come to terms with the tragic loss of people and destruction of property. Industries that had grown to meet war needs were in decline. Unemployment rose as soldiers returned to civilian life. Inflation soared. It was a period of turbulence and transition. The Russian Revolution had provided hope to millions who struggled with economic hardships. Perhaps because of this, communist movements and trade union activities were on the rise. General strikes took place, and unrest was widespread. European colonies in Asia and Africa were seeking independence and change.

A road-building program, part of the New Deal.

Huge sums of money borrowed by the Allies during the war were owed to the USA. The USA itself was relatively unaffected by the war, and remained prosperous till 1929, when the Great Depression, a severe economic crisis, took place. The Depression's effects soon spread to other parts of the world. In 1933, president Franklin Roosevelt introduced policies known as the New Deal, which helped to revitalize the US economy. Among various measures introduced were the temporary takeover of banks by the government, and acts to help farmers and to stimulate industry.

Of the European countries already facing an economic crisis before 1929, Germany had to make massive reparations, leading to a collapse of its economy. In 1923, inflation rose to such an extent that the German mark became totally worthless. A search for strong leadership, and a desire to reassert German power, led to the rise of Adolf Hitler, leader of the fascist Nazi Party.

France was exhausted by the war and remained economically backward, while political instability caused a rapid change in governments.

On the whole, Great Britain weathered the changes with her democracy intact, though there were several internal problems, including unrest in Ireland, the decline of industry, a general strike in 1926, and unemployment during the Great Depression. However, what

1924–1927

- Adolf Hitler leads Beer Hall Putsch, a revolt that fails, in Munich.
- **1924** Ramsay Macdonald leads the first Labour government in Britain.

- German novelist Thomas Mann's major work, *The Magic Mountain*, published.
- **1925** F Scott Fitzgerald, one of the greatest American novelists, writes *The Great Gatsby*.

was notable was the rise of the Labour Party, which was able, for the first time, to form two governments during this period.

Spain was a constitutional monarchy ruled by Alfonso XIII from 1885, but general Primo de Rivera seized power as a dictator in 1923. Also affected by the economic crisis, Spain was beset by unemployment. It was a weak and unstable country with deep divisions between radical groups such as socialists and communists, and conservative factions such as the Catholic church, the military, and business owners. Alfonso abdicated in 1931, and a republic was proclaimed. However, a fierce civil war was fought

Adolf Hitler and Benito Mussolini in Venice, 1934.

between 1936 and 1939, ending in a victory for the right-wing nationalists—it was a war between fascists and loyalists. The fascists were led by General Francisco Franco. Other fascist countries like Germany and Italy sent soldiers, money, and equipment to help the Spanish fascists. The Soviet Union sent money and supplies to help the loyalists. Democratic countries like the USA, France and Britain and the League of Nations did nothing to support the Spanish Republican government. The fascists won the war in 1939 leading to the end of the Spanish Republic. General Franco then took control of the government. Friendly to Hitler and Mussolini, Franco established a dictatorship in Spain.

Italy's economy had been strained during the war and she had not benefited from the post-war treaties. The difficult circumstances caused five governments to rise and fall between 1919 and 1922. Meanwhile, in 1919, Benito Mussolini formed the Italian Fascist Party. In 1922, Italian king Victor Emmanuel III invited Mussolini to form the government, and he gradually assumed dictatorial powers.

Munich Marienplatz during the failed Beer Hall Putsch.

1926 John Logie Baird invents system for television in Britain.

- Erwin Schrödinger, Austrian physicist, develops mathematical theory of wave mechanics.

- Gertrude Ederle, American Olympic swimmer, becomes first woman to swim the English Channel.

1927 Canberra is made the federal capital of Australia.

THE INTERMEDIATE YEARS

In Germany, veterans from World War I formed the National Socialist German Workers Party (Nazi Party). Hitler joined the party and soon became its leader. In 1923, after attempting a coup in Munich that has become known as the Beer Hall Putsch, he was arrested and sent to prison for 9 months.

While in prison he wrote Mein Kampf (My Struggle), which outlined the goals of the Nazi Party. During the period from1923 to 1930 the party had little impact, but as the Great Depression hit Germany, the Nazis rose to power. In 1933 the Nazis won most votes in parliamentary elections, and Hitler became chancellor of Germany.

Hitler blamed the country's economic problems on Jews, communists, and the harsh measures forced on Germany as reparation for World War I. When he stopped making reparation payments in 1933, and started to build up the military in violation of the Treaty of Versailles, his following increased dramatically.

That year a fire at the Reichstag (parliament building) gave the Nazis the opportunity to tighten their grip on the country. Blaming the fire on communists, Hitler imposed "emergency measures" that took away personal rights and freedoms. Persecution of Jewish people began, and in 1934 Hitler took dictatorial powers as Führer or "leader" of what he called the Third Reich, or third German empire.

Art and design

I n 1920s, the International Style of architecture through the innovative work of several architects who were to gain great influence in their field. Walter Gropius (1883– 1969) was one of them. Others included J.J.P. Oud in the Netherlands and Le Corbusier in France. Gropius was best known for his

Walter Gropius's *Monument to the March Dead* (1921) dedicated to the memory of nine workers who died in Weimar resisting the Kapp Putsch (a revolt).

1928–1929

- American Charles Lindbergh makes non-stop flight across Atlantic in his monoplane.
- *The Jazz Singer*, first feature-length film integrating sound, made.
- **1928** Briton Alexander Fleming discovers penicillin.

- First version of Oxford English Dictionary completed in 10 volumes.
- President of Albania, Ahmed Zogu, crowns himself as the king; known as Zog I.
- All women in Britain above the age of 21 gain voting rights.

structures of glass curtain walls spanning steel girders that form the skeleton of the building.

The Bauhaus school founded in Weimar, Germany, by Walter Gropius in 1919 pioneered new trends in architecture and interior design. Important examples of Gropius's other works are the Fagus Works in Alfeld-an-der-Leine, Germany (constructed in 1911), and the Graduate Center at Harvard University in Cambridge, Massachusetts (constructed in the year 1949–50). All of these works show Gropius's concern for uncluttered interior spaces.

Oud helped to bring more rounded and flowing geometric shapes to the movement. Le Corbusier, too, was interested in the freer treatment of reinforced concrete, but added the concept of modular proportion in order to maintain a human scale in his work. Among his well-known works in the International Style is the Villa Savoye in Poissy, France, constructed in 1929–31.

Industrial design, commercial printing, graphics, and innovative furniture also began to develop. In the 1920s, surrealism rejected traditional art forms and looked to symbolism and the subconscious for inspiration. The Art Deco style used stylized and decorative natural and geometric forms. In the 1930s and '40s the International Style spread from its base in Germany and France to North and South America, Scandinavia, Britain, and Japan.

The Bauhaus building in Dessau, Germany.

The Art Deco spire of the Chrysler building in New York, built in 1928–30.

THE INTERMEDIATE YEARS

Joseph Stalin.

The war had benefited Japan economically as it supplied the Allies and countries in Asia with various products. However, after 1921, European production began to recover, and Japan's exports suffered. The country experienced an economic crisis from 1929 and, in 1932, the powerful army virtually took over.

Following the death of Lenin in 1924, Joseph Stalin assumed power in Russia in 1929. He ruled as an absolute despot. Key Communist Party members became the new rich elite in the USSR. Thousands who had participated in the 1917 Revolution were killed.

China was engaged in a struggle between the Kuomintang, the Nationalist People's Party, and the communists.

In Turkey, Mustafa Kemal Atatürk, a young general, denounced the Treaty of Sevres signed after the war, by which his country suffered huge losses. He negotiated the more favorable Treaty of Lausanne (1923). The last Ottoman sultan abdicated, and Kemal became first president of the Turkish Republic, modernizing the country and curbing the social and legal role of Islam.

Mustafa Kemal Atatürk

"Everything we see in the world is the creative work of women."

–Mustafa Kemal Atatürk

Mustafa Kemal Atatürk was a Turkish nationalist and the founder of the modern republic of Turkey.

1930–1934

1930 Civil Disobedience movement led by Mahatma Gandhi in India.
- Gerulio Vargas becomes president of Brazil; rules as dictator from 1937.

1931 102-story Empire State Building inaugurated in New York.
- Trans-African railway from Angola to Mozambique completed.

Mustafa, the son of Ali Riza, was born in Salonika in the Ottoman empire (now Thessaloniki in Greece) early in 1881. He was given the additional name Kemal, meaning "The Perfect One" by a teacher, supposedly because of his ability in mathematics. When he was 12 he chose a military career, attending a military high school followed by a military academy, and graduated into the Ottoman army as a captain in 1905.

Mustafa Kemal Atatürk.

Mustafa Kemal joined the Young Turks movement, a group seeking to overturn the absolute monarchy of the Ottoman sultan and to restore the suspended constitution. In 1908 the Young Turks revolution overthrew Sultan Abdul Hamid II in favour of his brother Mehmed V, who ruled as the nominal head of the Ottomans' first multi-party constitutional government.

Taking part in the First and Second Balkan Wars in 1912 and 1913, Mustafa Kemal became a national hero in World War I, which the ailing Ottoman empire entered on the side of the Central Powers. He led the Ottoman defences at Gallipoli, repulsing the Allied landings.

But after Germany, Austro-Hungary and the Ottomans lost World War I in 1918, the Allies began to break up the Ottoman empire. The following year, on May 1919, Mustafa arrived to take command of the army in Anatolia. There, he and others began a nationalist revolution. His movement defeated Greek attempts to encroach on Turkey, and he was able to renegotiate the terms of the post-World War I peace settlement, securing mainland Turkey as an intact state.

1932 American Amelia Earhart becomes the first woman pilot to fly across the Atlantic.
1932–35 Chaco War fought between Bolivia and Paraguay.

1933 Franklin D. Roosevelt becomes the President of the USA.
1934 Oil pipeline from Kirkuk, Iraq, to Tripoli, Syria, opened.

THE INTERMEDIATE YEARS

In 1921 Mustafa set up a provisional government in Ankara, and the following year the Ottoman sultanate formally came to an end. The republic of Turkey was founded in 1923 with Mustafa Kemal as its president. Established as a secular democracy, Turkey under Mustafa Kemal was modernized and reformed.

Some of his most important changes were the emancipation of women; the introduction of the Latin alphabet, the Western calendar, and a legal code based on Western European codes; industrialization, and the abolition of religious government institutions. In 1935, surnames were introduced in Turkey, and he took the name Atatürk, meaning "Father of the Turks." Mustafa Kemal Atatürk died in Turkey on November 10, 1938. His mausoleum overlooks Ankara.

Positive results of the war

Welfare schemes were expanded, and more groups were granted the right to vote. Many women had started working in the war years, and their social and economic position improved. The telephone and telegraph spread through the world. Production of cars increased and commercial flights started. Consumer goods, such as washing machines, became widespread in Europe.

The Citroën Traction Avant car that began production in the 1930s.

1936–1940

1936–39 Civil war in Spain.
• *Falling water*, a residence and an icon of modern architecture, is built by Frank Lloyd Wright.
1937–45 Sino-Japanese conflict.
1938 Hungarian George Biro invents ball-point pen.

1938 Atatürk, "Father of the Turks," passes away due to cirrhosis of the liver.
1939 American novelist John Steinbeck writes *Grapes of Wrath*.
1939 Robert Menzies becomes the Prime Minister of Australia.

The colonies

Britain, with the most territories, as well as the dominions of Canada, Australia, New Zealand, and South Africa, promised that independence would gradually be granted to her colonies. Meanwhile, southern Ireland gained dominion status (1922), Egypt semi-independence (1922), and Iraq independence (1931). France, with the second largest possessions, as well as most of the other colonizers, suppressed nationalist movements.

The media

A poster for the movie *Battleship Potemkin*.

The 1930s saw literature from other languages translated into English. Paperback books were introduced and more newspapers were published. But the greatest media revolutions were in radio and cinema. Radio became widespread in developed nations. Its reach enabled music of different regions to be accessible to the world. News broadcasts, however, gained popularity only during World War II.

Both art films and popular cinema were produced. Of the former, the Soviet director Sergei Eisenstein's (1898–1948) *Battleship Potemkin* (1925) is considered a masterpiece, while Charlie Chaplin (1889–1977), an Englishman settled in the USA, was one of the greatest personalities of avant-garde films.

THE LEAGUE OF NATIONS

Created on January 10, 1920, the League aimed to maintain peace in the world, and encourage international cooperation. There were some successes in the 1920s as the League settled several conflicts. The dispute between Finland and Sweden over the Aaland Islands (1921) was resolved. So were conflicts in Upper Silesia (1921); over the port of Memel (renamed Klaipėda) in Lithuania (1923), and between Bulgaria and Greece (1925). However, the League was unable to resolve the crises of the 1930s. For instance, it could not prevent the Japanese invasion of Manchuria (1931), or the Italian invasion of Abyssinia (1935). Finally, it was unable to prevent World War II. The League was dissolved in 1946, but had laid the foundation for its successor organization, the United Nations.

1939 World War II: Australia, Belgium, Canada, New Zealand, and South Africa are among many countries that declare war on Germany following its initial outbreak.

1940 Radar developed by British scientists.
- Winston Churchill becomes the British Prime Minister.
- World War II: British and French forces are evacuated from Dunkirk, France.

World War II

The seeds of World War II were sown in the peace treaties following World War I and in the economic crisis that then hit almost all the world. The immediate cause was the policies followed by Germany, under Adolf Hitler's (1889–1945) Nationalist Socialist German Workers (Nazi) Party. In 1933, Hitler was appointed chancellor, and, in 1934, he became Führer, the leader of Germany. Hitler gained popularity as he restored national pride, rebuilding Germany's economy and the army. However, he focused on the so-called "Aryan" racial superiority, and blamed Jews for the country's ills.

Preceding events

Hitler signed defensive pacts, while at the same time convincing European powers of his peaceful aims. In 1936, Germany and Italy formalized a pact known as the Rome–Berlin Axis, giving rise to the name "Axis powers" for Germany and her allies. In 1936, Germany and Japan signed the Anti-Comintern pact. Hitler's troops took possession of the

The "big three" Allied leaders: (from left) Churchill of Britain, Roosevelt of the USA, and Stalin of the USSR.

Rhineland, the demilitarized zone on the German border near France, in 1936. In March 1938, he united Austria with Germany. Following this, in September 1938, he was allowed by Britain and France to occupy Czechoslovakia's Sudetenland. Keen to avoid a war, the Allied powers (Britain and France) did little to oppose German expansion in Czechoslovakia and Lithuania—this policy of "appeasement" is considered a major factor responsible for the war.

Germany and the USSR agreed to divide the territory of Poland between them. Then, on September 1, 1939, German armies invaded Poland. In defense of Poland, France and Britain declared war on Germany on September 3. World War II had begun.

The city of Wieluń, in Poland, burning on September 1, 1939, the first day of World War II.

1941–1943

- American writer Ernest Hemingway writes *For Whom the Bell Tolls*.
- **1941** American chemist Glenn Seaborg discovers plutonium; **1951** wins Nobel Prize.

- World War II: German General Erwin Rommel attacks British forces in Africa. German battleship *Bismarck* sunk in the Atlantic Ocean.
- Ethiopia regains independence.
- **1941–79** Muhammad Reza Pahlavi is the Shah of Iran.

The course

Allied ships near the Normandy coast on D-day (June 6, 1944), the invasion of German-occupied France.

The war lasted for 6 years. The turning point came when Hitler invaded the USSR (June, 1941), breaking his pact with them, and Japan bombed Pearl Harbor (December, 1941), an American naval base, leading to the USA's entry into the war. From mid-1942, Axis powers began to suffer defeats. Hitler committed suicide in April 1945, Germany surrendered in May, and Japan followed suit in August of the same year.

The cost

Prisoners in Mauthausen labor camp, in Austria, liberated on May 5, 1945 by the US army.

Sixty-one countries participated in World War II. At least 110 million people were mobilized for military service. Huge amounts of money were spent on the military: $341 billion by the USA alone. A total of 19 million military personnel from both sides died in Europe. Japanese killed around 5,964,000 people. In addition, Allied civilian losses are estimated at 44 million, and Axis at 11 million. Another 21 million were displaced.

During the war, Jews were 6 subject to a planned extermination campaign. They were shot, gassed, and murdered in concentration camps or held in sub-human conditions. By the end of the war, six million Jews had been killed.

BOMBING OF HIROSHIMA AND NAGASAKI

The war ended with the use of the latest and most horrific weapon of the time: The atomic bomb. On August 6 and 9, 1945, U.S. aircraft dropped one bomb each on the Japanese cities of Hiroshima and Nagasaki, killing around 84,000 and 40,000 people respectively. An equal number were injured, and those exposed to radiation suffered serious health problems. The USA justified it as a means to end the conflict, but it remains the most controversial action of the war.

The most famous image of the Hiroshima mushroom cloud, taken minutes after the Enola Gay, a B-29 bomber aircraft, dropped the atomic bomb.

1942 In India, Quit India Movement against British.
• World War II: The USA forces bomb Tokyo. Germany defeated at Battle of El Alamein, Egypt.
• Indian National Army founded.

• Russian Dmitri Shostakovich composes *Leningrad* symphony during the German siege of that city.
1943 French writer Jean Paul Sartre writes his philosophical work *Being and Nothingness*.

INDEPENDENT NATIONS

European countries were exhausted by World War II. Germany and Italy had been crushed, and the center of power had shifted to the USA. Economically and militarily depleted, Britain did not feel strong enough to hold on to her colonies, which were at the same time clamoring for independence. In addition, world ideology was shifting towards the belief that nations had the right to govern themselves.

France, the Netherlands, Spain, and Portugal gradually gave up their possessions. During the war, Japan had wrested territories such as Burma, Malaya, Singapore, the Dutch East Indies, and Indochina from European colonial powers. These had seen the myth of European supremacy destroyed, and had no wish to return to colonial rule.

In the East, India, Israel, and Vietnam typified different problems faced by newly independent nations.

Jawaharlal Nehru (1889-1964) and Mahatma Gandhi (1869–1948) led India's struggle for independence.

India and Pakistan

In 1947, the British agreed to grant independence to India, dividing the country into two states, India and Pakistan, based on religious differences. Pakistan was fragmented, its western and eastern halves separated by Indian territory, and overall the partition resulted in savage riots, between Hindus and Sikhs on one side, and Muslims on the other. Around one million were killed, and 10 million displaced, as refugees frantically attempted to cross the borders in order to reach safety. The two new nations were hostile to each other from the beginning of their creation.

POST-COLONIAL IDEOLOGY

New ways of writing history, fiction, and films emerged, expressing themes of independence and struggle, division and strife.

Edward Said (1935–2003), a key intellectual who re-examined Western approaches to history, particularly of the Middle East.

1944–1946

- World War II: Allies take Tripoli in Africa from Italy. Soviet forces win Battle of Kursk. Mussolini resigns.
- **1944** World War II: Allied troops begin reconquest of Europe and Asia. Anglo-American forces enter Rome. French Resistance helps liberate Paris.

- Synthesis of quinine marks breakthrough in treatment of malaria.
- Ukrainian-born American biochemist Selman Waksman discovers streptomycin.
- First nuclear reactors built.

Mahatma Gandhi

"An eye for an eye only ends up making the whole world blind."

—Mahatma Gandhi

Mohandas Karamchand Gandhi, more commonly known as Mahatma Gandhi, one of the primary leaders of India's independence movement, was born on October 2, 1869, in Porbandar in pre-independent India. He was a believer of nonviolence, and led civil disobedience actions that influenced people all around the world. He was a lawyer, who worked for the civil rights of Indians, both at home under British rule and in South Africa. He was assassinated by a fanatic in 1948.

His father, Karamchand Gandhi, served as a chief minister in Porbandar and other states in western India. His mother, Putlibai, was a deeply religious woman who fasted regularly. Though Gandhi grew up worshiping the Hindu god Vishnu, he later followed Jainism, an ancient Indian religion that advocates nonviolence, fasting, meditation, and vegetarianism.

As a child, Gandhi was shy and timid, an average student. At the age of 13, he was married to Kasturba Makanji, a merchant's daughter.

In 1885, his father died. In 1888, Gandhi left for London to study law. In England, he struggled with this shift to Western comma not semicolon during the 3 years he spent in London, he became a vegetarian, joined the executive committee of the London Vegetarian Society, and read a variety of sacred texts to learn more about world religions.

In 1891, when he came back to India, Gandhi found that his mother had died. He

Gandhi with his wife Kasturba Gandhi, 1922.

1945 World War II: US army enters Germany.
- World Zionist Conference held.
- Benito Mussolini killed.
- United Nations established with 51 member states.

1945–81 Life of Bob Marley, Jamaican reggae singer and song writer.
1946 First electronic computer invented by John Mauchly and John Eckert.

INDEPENDENT NATIONS

tried to start a legal practice, but in his first court case, an apprehensive Gandhi lost his nerve when the time came to interview a witness. He instantly fled the court in the wake of repaying his customer for his lawful expenses. In attempt to look for some kind of employment in India, Gandhi got a 1-year contract to in South Africa. After the birth of his second child, he left for Durban in South Africa in April 1893.

Kasturba Gandhi wife of Mahatma Gandhi with her four sons in South Africa 1902.

As soon as he reached South Africa, he was shocked to see the prejudice and racial isolation suffered by Indians at the hands of British.

Upon his first appearance in a Durban court, Gandhi was requested to remove his turban, which he refused to do, and left the court. He was even called "an unwelcomed guest" by the *Natal Advertiser*.

A fundamental moment in Gandhi's life occurred on June 7, 1893. While going to Pretoria, a white man questioned his presence in the first class train carriage, despite him

In 1894 Gandhi helped found the Natal Indian Congress in South Africa, to unify local population.

having a ticket. This experience stirred in him a desire to give himself up to battling the "profound infection of shading preference." From that night onward, the little, unassuming man developed into a very strong force for social liberties.

Gandhi founded the Natal Indian Congress in 1894 to battle segregation. When his year-long contract was about to end, he arranged to go back to India. However, on learning of a bill before the Natal Legislative Assembly that

1947–1948

- Juan Peron becomes the president of Argentina.
- Republic established in Italy.
- The USA tests new types of atomic bombs at Bikini Atoll, on Marshall Islands.
- Felix Bloch, Swiss-born U.S. physicist, develops analytical technique of nuclear magnetic

resonance, used in medical diagnostics (magnetic resonance imagery, or MRI).

1947 Edwin Herbert Land, an American physicist, develops Polaroid camera.

would deny Indians the right to vote, he was persuaded to stay and lead the battle against the act. Though Gandhi failed to he attracted worldwide sympathy.

After a short excursion to India in late 1896 and mid-1897, Gandhi came back to South Africa with his wife and two sons. Gandhi's law practice flourished. Gandhi continued to focus on world religions during his years in South Africa. In 1906, Gandhi composed his philosophy of nonviolent, noncompliance protest, which he called "Satyagraha" (truth and immovability), in response to the Transvaal government's new limitations on the rights of Indians. He and many other Indians were detained in 1913 because of their protests.

In 1915 Gandhi returned to India, joined the Indian National Congress

Gandhi (center) with his secretary, Miss Sonia Schlesin, and his colleague Mr. Polak in front of his Law Office, Johannesburg, South Africa, 1905.

(the main organization campaigning for Indian independence), and began to lead non-violent protests against the British administration. Tensions between the independence movement and the British increased in 1919 with the passing of the Rowlett Act, which allowed the police to arrest and hold for two years without trial anyone suspected of subversion. Gandhi organized a satyagraha protest against the Act, but in some areas the peaceful protests turned violent, culminating in the Amritsar massacre in the Punjab. There, unarmed protestors and religious pilgrims were fired upon by troops of the British Indian Army.

At least 379 Indians were killed, and over 1,000 people were wounded. The massacre led to a new British policy of "minimum force," but it was too late. The anger felt by Indian nationalists resulted in Gandhi's Non-cooperation Movement of 1920–22. Gandhi became leader of the Indian National Congress in 1920, and called for mass, nonviolent resistance. Protesters were urged to withdraw from anything to do with the British

- Russian Mikhail Kalashnikov designs AK-47 assault rifle.
- By the Truman Doctrine, the USA promises aid to any country resisting communism.
- USA's Marshall Plan offers economic help to countries in need.

- Transistor invented.
- General Agreement on Tariffs and Trade (GATT) signed by 23 countries.

1948 Mahatma Gandhi, Indian leader, assassinated.

INDEPENDENT NATIONS

administration, such as the police, civil service, law courts or schools, and were asked to boycott British goods, especially cloth, in favor of locally manufactured materials.

The movement was a huge success, but ended when violence once more broke out and 22 police officers were killed.

Gandhi's next protest was the most significant yet. In the 19th century, British administrators had

Gandhi seen leading the famous Salt March.

imposed a high tax on Indian salt in order to encourage sales of British salt. The Salt Act also made it illegal to take salt from the sea. Taxes were increased in the 1920s, so Gandhi organized the Salt March in 1930, walking with his followers 240 miles from Ahmedabad to the coast of Gujarat. Over the 24 days of the March they were joined by thousands of people as well as the international media. On arrival at the coast, Ghandi broke the law by producing salt from seawater.

The nonviolent protest drew thousands into the movement against the British, and gained Gandhi a worldwide audience; he was named Time magazine's Man of the Year for 1930. He was arrested before he could begin a satyagraha protest outside a saltworks, and overall at least 60,000 people were arrested breaking the salt laws.

Released in 1931, in 1934 he left the Congress to focus on social issues such as improving education and alleviating poverty. He was succeeded as head of the Congress by Jawaharlal Nehru.

During World War II, Gandhi campaigned for the Quit India movement, and finally, after the war was over, in 1945 Britain began to negotiate terms for Indian independence. Gandhi was firmly opposed to a division of the country along religious lines, but was unable to prevent Muslim Pakistan being separated from Hindu India.

On January 30, 1948, the 78-year-old Gandhi was assassinated by Hindu fanatic Nathuram Godse, who was angered by what he saw as Gandhi's support for Muslims. Gandhi's method of peaceful protest has inspired civil rights activists around the world, including Martin Luther King, Jr in the USA and Nelson Mandela in South Africa.

1948–1952

1948 Burma (now Myanmar), Ceylon (now Sri Lanka), gain independence from Britain.
- The state of Israel formed; thousands of Palestinians displaced.

1949 East Indies (now Indonesia) gains independence from the Netherlands.
- Konrad Adenauer becomes the first chancellor of West Germany, after the establishment of the country following World War II.

Vietnam

Indochina (Laos, Cambodia, and Vietnam) was under French rule before the Japanese occupied the region during World War II. Ho Chih Minh (1890–1969), a communist, organized a revolutionary organization and declared Vietnam independent in 1945. War with France began, and the French were decisively defeated at Dien Bien Phu (May 1954). Laos and Cambodia gained independence, but the USA, determined to prevent the spread of communism, became the decision-maker in Vietnam. The country was divided into two halves, with Ho Chih Minh's communists in the North, while South Vietnam had a separate government. A civil war started in South Vietnam, with the Viet Cong, guerrillas supported by North Vietnam, trying to unite the North and South. Pouring in troops and weapons, the USA became involved in fighting the Viet Cong. The land was devastated and thousands of civilians killed. Finally, public opinion forced American withdrawal, and Vietnam was officially united in 1976.

A burning Viet Cong camp in Vietnam (1968).

Ho Chih Minh (1890–1969).

ISRAEL

Israeli state, as proposed by UN, November, 1947.

Land conquered by Israel, 1948–49.

Land occupied by Israel after Six-Day War, June, 1967.

Beirut
LEBANON
Damascus
SYRIA
Akko
Haifa · Tiberias
Sea of Galilee
Golan Heights
Tel Aviv
Ramallah
Jerusalem · Jericho · Amman
Bethlehem
Gaza
Dead Sea
Beersheba
JORDAN
Mediterranean Sea
EGYPT
Sinai Peninsula
Eilat · Aqaba

Israel

From 1917, there was a move to create a state for Jews, who had suffered persecution for centuries. Palestine, their ancient homeland, was an Arab state under a British mandate, but Jews had begun settling there. After World War II, it was decided that Palestine be divided between Arabs and Jews. When the British left on May 15, 1948, the first Arab–Israeli War broke out immediately. Several other wars were fought in succeeding years, and hostilities continue to this day.

- Independent state of Irish Republic declared.
- The USSR tests its first nuclear bomb.
- **1951** European Economic Community or Common Market formed.
- Libya gains independence from Italy.

- Japan, the USA, and 48 other countries sign peace treaty.
- American author J.D. Salinger wins acclaim with his book *The Catcher in the Rye*.
- **1952** Elizabeth II crowned queen of UK.

Independence brought a number of problems. Colonial boundaries had cut across territories of different ethnic groups, so as colonial powers withdrew, people's loyalties veered towards their own tribes and groups regardless of national boundaries. Although some states were able to provide good government and a sound economic system, military coups and civil wars occurred in others. After independence, there was such widespread resentment towards immigrants that thousands of Asians had to leave Africa in the late 1960s. In Rhodesia and South Africa, which had a large number of white settlers, there was resistance to granting independence to blacks.

Zimbabwe born

Robert Mugabe.

Northern Rhodesia won independence as Zambia in 1964, but Southern Rhodesia, led by Ian Smith's white-minority government, declared independence from Britain in 1965. After a long civil war, it became independent in 1980 as Zimbabwe, led by Robert Mugabe. Internal problems and conflicts between political and ethnic groups continued.

POST-COLONIAL AFRICAN LITERATURE

With 53 different countries in Africa, literature is extremely diverse, with authors writing in English, French, and Portuguese, as well as African languages. The Nigerian Wole Soyinka (b.1934) was the first African to win the Nobel Prize for Literature. Books were also written by white settlers: J.M. Coetzee (b.1940), originally from South Africa, and now an Australian citizen, received the Nobel Prize for Literature in 2003.

Wole Soyinka.

1953–1959

1953 Edmund Hillary of New Zealand and Tenzing Norgay of Nepal are first to summit Mt. Everest.
- DNA discovered.
- Egypt declared a republic; gains freedom from British influence.

1955 Argentine president Juan Peron overthrown.
1956 Egyptian government takes over Suez Canal.
- Morocco and Spanish Morocco, gain independence from France and Spain.

Apartheid in South Africa

The Union of South Africa became virtually independent from Britain in 1931. Its white population was divided into Afrikaners and English speakers. In 1948, the National Party came to power and followed a policy of apartheid: Complete political and social separation of blacks and whites, with the latter dominating. The government tried to move blacks into separate "homelands," and in 1961, though South Africa became a republic, apartheid continued. Nelson Mandela led a movement for black rights which ultimately resulted in the African National Congress coming to power through multi-racial elections in 1994.

NELSON MANDELA

Born in 1918 in Transkei, South Africa, Mandela became involved in politics when a student. In 1943, he joined the black rights group the African National Congress, and in 1944 was one of the founder members of its Youth League. As a leading spokesman for black rights, Mandela was imprisoned for almost 27 years. He received the Nobel Peace Prize in 1993, along with F.W. de Klerk, South Africa's last white president. From 1994 to 1999, Mandela was the president of South Africa.

A signboard from South Africa's apartheid days.

F.W. de Klerk (b. 1936).

- Tunisia gets independence from France.
- Sudan achieves independence from Britain.
1957 Malaysia, and Gold Coast (Ghana), win independence from Britain.
- First satellite, *Sputnik I*, sent into space by the USSR.

1958 French West Africa (Guinea) attains independence.
- First Grammy awards presented in the USA.
1959 Fidel Castro takes control in Cuba.
- Dalai Lama of Tibet flees to India with his followers.

PEACE AND WAR

After the devastation caused by World War II, there were efforts to sustain peace so that a similar war would not take place again, particularly as a catastrophic nuclear war was a frightening new possibility. Some degree of stability was maintained, though there were still numerous wars: Perhaps 19–20 million were killed in over 100 wars and military actions in the developing world between 1945 and 1983.

Communist states, and power blocs

The Cold War, a period of hostility and suspicion, dominated the world during 1945–85. Its major players, the USA and the USSR, did not actually fight a war with each other, but took opposing sides on various issues. Communism, with the USSR as the dominant power, was spreading. Between 1945 and 1948, the East European countries Poland, Hungary, Romania, Bulgaria, Yugoslavia, Albania, and Czechoslovakia became communist states. After World War II, Germany was initially divided among the Allied powers into four occupation zones, but in 1949 it was split into two: The Federal Republic of Germany (West Germany) and the communist German Democratic Republic (East Germany). In Asia, communist governments were established in North Korea (1948), China (1949) under Mao Zedong, and North Vietnam (1954).

Two major defensive alliances were formed: In 1949, Britain, France, Belgium, Holland, Luxembourg, the USA, Canada, Portugal, Denmark, Ireland, Italy, and Norway formed the North Atlantic Treaty Organization (NATO), joined by West Germany in 1955. The Soviets responded with the Warsaw Pact in 1955, consisting of their satellite communist states in Europe.

The USA, quick to take action against potential communist states, became involved in wars in Korea (1950–53) and in Vietnam (1965–75). The USSR wanted her satellites in East Europe to follow policies chalked out by her. This led to an invasion of Czechoslovakia in 1968.

A section of the Berlin Wall that separated East and West Berlin.

1960–1962

- **1960** Cameroon wins independence from France and Britain.
- Nigeria and Cyprus achieve independence from Britain.
- Congo gains independence from Belgium.
- French West Africa (Mali and Senegal) acquires independence.

- Pop music group, The Beatles, become famous.
- **1961** Tanganyika gets independent from Britain; **1963** Zanzibar; **1964** unite as Tanzania.
- John F. Kennedy is the 35th president of the USA.
- The USA invades Bay of Pigs in Cuba.

Thaw, détente, and the end of the USSR

With the death of Stalin in 1953, there was some reduction in hostilities. But tensions revived in the late 1950s, and in 1961 the Berlin Wall was erected by East Germany, cutting off the West German half of the city. In 1962, the USSR placed nuclear missiles in Cuba within striking distance of the USA, sparking off the Cuban Missile Crisis that almost led to a nuclear war. From 1969, the USSR and USA attempted to limit weapons stockpiles through the Strategic Arms Limitation Talks (SALT) and a period of détente began. However, the Soviet invasion of Afghanistan in 1979–80 heightened tensions once again.

Mikhail Gorbachev (b. 1931).

Mikhail Gorbachev became leader of the Soviet Union in 1985 and attempted to transform the country through a more democratic structure and a move toward a market economy. Elections in 1989 and 1990 brought in some democracy and reduced the power of the Communist Party, and in 1988–89 the USSR withdrew from Afghanistan. Gorbachev also gave autonomy to the USSR's East European satellite countries. Relations with the USA and the West improved dramatically, and change swept through the region. The Berlin Wall was opened in 1989, and East and West Germany were reunified the next year. By the end of 1991, the USSR had dissolved, replaced by the Commonwealth of Independent States (CIS), which consisted of many of its former republics.

LITERATURE OF THE COLD WAR

The Cold War spawned a vast number of books and films. Ian Fleming (1908–64) created the British secret service agent James Bond, while John le Carré (pseudonym of David John Moore Cornwell, b. 1931) wrote fiction on the dark world of espionage. The problems of Germany and the Soviet era were the other topics.

Gunter Grass, awarded the Nobel Prize for Literature in 1999, wrote both fiction and non-fiction on themes including German reunification.

- Yuri Gagarin of Russia is the first man to travel in space.
- **1962** China invades India.
- Rolling Stones, the British rock music group, formed.
- Algeria obtains independence from France.
- Uganda achieves independence from Britain.

- Ruanda–Urundi (Rwanda and Burundi) gains independence from Belgium.
- **1962** American John Steinbeck wins Nobel Prize for Literature.
- First communications satellite, *Telstar*, launched in space.
- Cuban Missile Crisis.

PEACE AND WAR

As the world recovered from World War II, many different international organizations were formed with the aim of preserving peace and increasing cooperation among countries. Some groupings were regional but the most ambitious, the UN, embraced every country on Earth.

The United Nations

The name United Nations was coined on January 1942 by the U.S. president Franklin D. Roosevelt, and it was first used in the Declaration by United Nations of January 1942. This was at the time of World War II when the governments from 26 nations pledged to continue fighting against the Axis Power.

Founded on October 24, 1945, the UN, though not always successful, has played a major role in world affairs, providing peace-keeping forces, helping new nations emerge from colonialism, encouraging disarmament,

Eleanor Roosevelt holding the Spanish version of the Universal Declaration of Human Rights.

and keeping a check on nuclear proliferation. The headquarters of the UN is situated in Manhattan, New York City. One of the UN's primary purposes is "promoting and encouraging respect for human rights and for fundamental freedoms for all without distinction as to race, sex, language, or religion", and member states pledge to undertake "joint and separate action" to protect these rights. It has several secondary organizations, such

as its Development Programme and Children's Fund. Its role in the world was recognized by the award of the Nobel Peace Prize in 2001. However, the permanent members of its Security Council (the USA, Russia, Great Britain, France, and China) have the power to veto its decisions, leading to some imbalance and inequality among its members.

United Nations headquarters in New York, USA.

1963–1967

- **1963** Kenya gains independence from Britain.
- Thirty African nations join together to form Organization of African Unity.
- John F. Kennedy assassinated.
- **1964** The USA passes Civil Rights Act to end discrimination based on race, color, or religion.

- Malta, Nyasaland (Malawi), Northern Rhodesia (Zambia), British Guiana (Guyana), win independence from Britain.
- Martin Luther King awarded the Nobel Peace Prize.
- Palestine Liberation Organization formed to represent the rights of Palestinian Arabs.
- **1964–91** Kenneth Kaunda is the first president of Zambia.

1947–49 Persuades Dutch to grant independence to Indonesia.

1956

• USSR sends troops into Hungary; Security Council's call to withdraw is vetoed by USSR.

• Asks Israel to withdraw from Egypt; vetoed by France and Britain.

1960–64 Sends 10,000 troops to help stabilize recently independent Belgian Congo.

1966–80 Imposes economic sanctions on Rhodesia due to its apartheid policy.

1974 Maintains peace in Cyprus between Greek and Turkish Cypriots.

1979–88 The USSR occupies Afghanistan; vetoes Security Council resolution asking it to withdraw.

2003 Security Council backs US-led administration in Iraq.

The Commonwealth of Nations

The British Commonwealth was established in 1931 as a group of nations that owed allegiance to the British Empire. Later, the word "British" was dropped as more colonies became independent. The Commonwealth promotes cooperation and friendship among member nations, and encourages human rights and good government. In 1965, the Commonwealth Secretariat was established in London to organize and coordinate Commonwealth activities. The Commonwealth differs from other international bodies. It has no formal constitution or bylaws. The members have no legal or formal obligation to one another; they are held together by shared traditions, institutions, and experiences as well as by economic self-interest.

COMMONWEALTH EVENTS

1961 South Africa withdraws from the Commonwealth after being criticized for apartheid policies; **1994** rejoins.

1971 First Commonwealth Heads of Government Meeting (CHOGM); Singapore Declaration of shared principles adopted; includes peace and cooperation, liberty, freedom from racism. **1991** democracy, good government, human rights added.

1977 Gleneagles Agreement reinforces commitment to oppose racism.

1989 Malaysia Declaration on environmental sustainability.

1995 Commitment to deal with violators of shared principles.

1965 Gambia obtains independence from Britain.
• Big Bang theory of the universe developed.
• Minimalist and Conceptual American artist Sol LeWitt begins his "open cube" sculptures.
1966 Basutoland (Lesotho) and Bechuanaland (Botswana) achieve independence from Britain.
• Cultural Revolution begins in China.

• American surgeon Michael DeBakey develops artificial heart.
1967 Six-Day War between Israel and Arab states.
• Aden (S. Yemen) gets independent from Britain.
• Pulsars (pulsating radio stars) discovered by British astronomers Jocelyn Bell Burnell and Antony Hewish.

PEACE AND WAR

Non-aligned Movement

The Non-aligned Movement (**NAM**) **is an** international organization dedicated to representation of the interests and aspirations of developing countries. The Non-Aligned Movement counts more than 100 member states, whose combined population amounts to more than half of the world's population. Many Asian and African countries refused to join either of the two Cold War blocs. This Non-Aligned Movement (NAM) was formed in 1961 with 25 members. The key leaders were Jawaharlal Nehru of India, Josip Broz Tito (Yugoslavia), Gamal Abdel Nasser (Egypt), Kwame Nkrumah (Ghana), Sekou Toure (Guinea), and Sukarno of Indonesia, though Yugoslavia was part of the Warsaw Pact. The general aim of NAM was to take decisions independently, without any pressure from the Cold War powers. After the end of the Cold War, NAM redefined its aims to reflect modern needs. One of the challenges faced by the Non-Aligned Movement in the 21st century has been the reassessment of its identity and purpose in the post-Cold War era. The movement has continued to advocate international cooperation, multilateralism, and national self-determination, but it has also been increasingly vocal against the inequities of the world economic order.

The founding members of the Non-Aligned Movement.
From left to right—Jawaharlal Nehru (India), Kwame Nkrumah (Ghana), Gamal Abdel Nasser (Egypt), Sukarno (Indonesia) and Josip Broz Tito (Yugoslavia),.

1967–1972

- British engineer Godfrey Hounsfield develops computerized axial tomography (CT scanning).
- **1967–70** Civil war in Nigeria.
- **1968** French mathematician Rene Thom develops catastrophe theory, showing how gradual changes can trigger a catastrophic change.
- **1968** Mauritius and Swaziland acquire independence from Britain.
- Spanish Guinea (Equatorial Guinea) gains independence.

JAWAHARLAL NEHRU

Jawaharlal Nehru was born in Allahabad, India in 1889. In 1919, Nehru heard British Brigadier-General Reginald Dyer boasting about the Jallianwala Bagh slaughter. The slaughter, called the Massacre of Amritsar, was an episode in which 379 individuals were killed and no less than 1200 were injured when the British military personnel led by Dyer opened fire non-stop for about 10 minutes on a large group of unarmed Indians (including women and children), who were trapped within a high-walled garden called Jallianwala Bagh. After hearing Dyer's words, Nehru decided to fight the British. The episode changed the course of his life.

Nehru joined the Indian National Congress, and was elected as head of the Congress in 1928. He was greatly influenced by Mahatma Gandhi. After independence from the British in August 15, 1947, Nehru became the first prime minister of India.

Jawaharlal Nehru.

JOSIP BROZ TITO

Marshal Tito became the President of Yugoslavia in 1953. He was a great administrator who rebuilt Yugoslavia post World War II. Till his death in 1980, he brought the essence of unity in his country.

Marshal Tito became president of Yugoslavia in 1953. He was a great administrator and managed to keep peace between the different ethnic groups in the Yugoslavian federation.

He was born Josip Broz on May 25, 1892 near Zagreb, Croatia, which was then part of the Austro-Hungarian empire.

Captured by Russian forces during World War I, he was sent to a prisoner-of-war camp in Russia where he became a communist. Back in Yugoslavia, he adopted the name Tito as an alias when communism was banned.

Josip Broz Tito.

- British rock group Led Zeppelin formed.
- Martin Luther King assassinated.
- **1969** Woodstock music and art fair held in Bethel, USA; attended by 60,000 people.

- US astronauts Neil Armstrong and Edwin Aldrin are the first men to reach the moon.
- **1972** The USA passes the Equal Opportunity Act.
- Sheikh Mujibur Rahman is first Prime Minister of Bangladesh.

DEVELOPMENT AND GROWTH: ECONOMY

He contined to work underground for the communist party, and during World War II he led the Partisans, the communist groups that resisted the German occupation of Yugoslavia. He was elected prime minister in 1945.

After Stalin's death, Tito endeavored to built a group of "nonaligned" countries. Under hisleadership, Yugoslavia maintained friendly ties with the Arab states and was a very active member of the United Nations (UN).

European Union

European Union (**EU**) comprises 28 European countries and governs common economic, social, and security policies. Originally confined to Western Europe, the EU undertook a robust expansion into central and Eastern Europe in the early 21st century. Various European organizations merged in 1965 (formally 1967) to create the European Economic Community (EEC), an association aiming to strengthen economic cooperation. In 1993, it was renamed the European Union. The Euro, a common unit of currency for many of its member states, was introduced.

A map showing European Union member states, new member states of the European Union since 2004, 2007, and 2013, member states of European Free Trade Association, and the location of country capitals and major European cities.

On March 22, 2016, the Prime Minister of the United Kingdom, Theresa May invoked Article 50, by which it notified the European Council of its intention to leave. She sent a letter to Donald Tusk, the President of the European Council, which heralded the beginning of the legal process for Britain's withdrawal from the EU.

1972–1976

1972 Managua, capital of Nicaragua, destroyed by earthquake; thousands killed.

1973 110-story Sears Tower opened in Chicago, USA; it is the tallest building of the time.

- Salvador Allende, president of Chile, assassinated.

1974 Guinea (Guinea-Bissau) wins independence from Portugal.

- Watergate scandal leads to resignation of president Nixon of the USA.

1975 Mozambique and Angola gain independence from Portugal.

I n general, capitalist countries experienced a "golden age" in 1950–73. The numbers of homeless and unemployed also increased, though welfare and social security systems provided some support for them.

The U.S. economy

American students take to the streets in protest against the Vietnam war in 1968.

The USA had not suffered economically during the war, as defense production revitalized industry and created new jobs. The aircraft and shipping sectors were booming. Moreover, the war inspired technological and scientific innovations, which led to lifestyle improvements. By 1945, the USA accounted for almost two-thirds of the world's industrial production, and had a gross domestic product greater than any other country. The U.S. Marshall Plan facilitated 13,000 million dollars of aid to western Europe over 4 years from April 1948, helping to revitalize that region.

President Truman attempted to introduce welfare schemes, but Congress only approved social security benefits and an increase in the minimum wage. The USA had to deal with civil rights problems and opposition to the Vietnam war, as well as economic problems aggravated by the war. Periods of recession during 1973–75, 1981–82, and 1990–91 were followed by a long period of growth and development in the 1990s.

Martin Luther King, Jr. (1929-68), African American civil rights leader.

US President Harry Truman.

- Khmer Rouge communists take over Cambodia; their leader Pol Pot is the Prime Minister.
- Bill Gates and Paul G. Allen found Microsoft Corporation.
- The USA, Canada, and 35 European countries sign Helsinki Accords; recognize World War II boundaries and promise to maintain friendly relations.

1976 American writer Alex Haley explores the black experience through his family saga, *Roots*.
- Supersonic jet Concorde makes its first flight from London to Bahrain.

DEVELOPMENT AND GROWTH: ECONOMY

The British economy

The Labour government began state direction of the economy and nationalization of industries in order to recover from the effects of World War II. Decolonization added to economic problems, and though economic growth was slow, welfare policies were put in place. The Thatcher era (1979–90) saw privatization of major sectors, with a reduction in the role of the state. During the 1980s, Britain experienced a boom, but along with this, there was increasing social conflict and unemployment.

Margaret Thatcher (1925-2013).

Russian reforms

Russia rebuilt itself rapidly through a planned economy. As growth slowed down, Mikhail Gorbachev began to introduce economic reforms in the mid-1980s. With the dissolution of the USSR in 1991, the economy declined sharply. Real GDP dropped by 40 percent between 1990–96, and inflation and unemployment rose. In the late 1990s, the economy began to stabilize.

WORLD ECONOMIC SYSTEMS

The complexities of the post-war world required new means of cooperation.

Even before World War II ended, a method of monetary management was put in place, which came into operation in 1945. Known as the Bretton Woods system, it set up rules and regulations for the functioning of the international monetary system. All currencies were linked to the U.S. dollar, which in turn was linked to gold, and thus there was a fixed exchange rate regime. The International Monetary Fund and the World Bank were also created at this time. In 1971, the link between the dollar and gold was cut, and the world moved toward a floating exchange system.

Among other important organizations, the World Trade Organization, an international entity to oversee and liberalize world trade, came into being on January 1, 1995.

The Organization of the Petroleum Exporting Countries (OPEC) was founded in 1960. It was once able to manipulate world oil prices, but with oil now found in many other places, it has less influence. However, its 12 member countries—from the Middle East, Asia, Africa, and South America—account for two-thirds of world oil reserves, so OPEC still has a major role in the oil economy.

1977–1981

1977 British biochemist Frederick Sanger, with Paul Berg and Walter Gilbert, develops DNA sequencing technique; 1980 they are awarded Nobel Prize for chemistry.

1978 Louise Brown, first "test-tube" baby, born.

- Camp David Accords, a peace settlement, signed between Israel and Egypt.

1979 Ayatollah Khomeini overthrows the Shah; establishes Islamic republic in Iran.

- Saddam Hussein is the President of Iraq.

Shinzuku, in Tokyo, is one of Japan's most important commercial centers, where some of its biggest corporations have their headquarters.

As a communist nation, China was influenced by Russia, but soon embarked on her own path. Agricultural productivity was increased by land redistribution, cooperative farms, and communes. After Mao's death in 1976, a gradual introduction of market reforms began. By 2000, China was a major economic power, with one of the fastest growing economies in the world.

US funds helped restore Japan's economy, which had been ruined by the war, and Japan soon became the second largest economy in the world. Hong Kong, Singapore, South Korea, and Taiwan were among the fastest growing economies between the 1960s and 1990s, known as the Four Asian Tigers. Thailand, Malaysia, Indonesia, and India after the 1990s were other rapidly expanding Asian economies. However, an Asian crisis in 1997 spread from Thailand to South Korea to Japan, and had an impact across the world.

In 1945, Latin America (South and Central America and some Caribbean islands) was underdeveloped. Many economies were dependent on a small range of products, while population growth and unstable governments also created problems. Foreign ownership of industry and agriculture drained money out of many countries. However, with new initiatives, the situation began to improve. For instance, Venezuela nationalized its oil industry in 1976 and created a huge refining and marketing system. During the 1980s, a debt crisis affected much of Latin America. Good growth began to be registered from the 1990s, but inequalities continued to be rampant in the region.

Wars and coups in Africa hampered growth. The discovery of oil in some countries, such as Equatorial Guinea, in 1996, led to high growth rates, but these did not translate into overall human development.

FOOD

On the whole, world food production began to increase. Calories available per capita showed an increase of 24 percent from 1961 to 2000, with individual countries showing huge growth rates: The highest were in China (73 percent), Indonesia (69 percent), South Korea (44 percent), the USA (32 percent), Thailand (27 percent), Italy (26 percent), and India (20 percent). However, the consumption of the richest fifth of the population was 16 times that of the poorest fifth. Eight-hundred and forty million people continued to be malnourished.

- SALT II treaty signed.
- Zulfiqar Ali Bhutto, President and Prime Minister of Pakistan (1971–77), is executed.
- Smallpox eliminated from the world.
1980 Iraq declares war on Iran.

- In Poland, Solidarity trade union formed under Lech Walesa.
1981 First personal computer, the IBM PC, launched.
- AIDS disease detected in New York and California, USA.

DEVELOPMENT AND GROWTH: TECHNOLOGY

INEQUALITIES PERSIST

In 1997, 1.3 billion people in the world were living on less than 1 dollar a day. Although there was an increase in global wealth and income, as well as an improvement in health, education, and standards of nutrition, these had not reached the world's poor. The richest fifth of the world had a total income 74 times that of the poorest fifth. Vast inequalities permeated all areas of life.

Top right: A slum in Mumbai, India. Although India's economic growth from the 1990s onward was one of the fastest in the world, in 1999–2000, 26 percent of the population was estimated to be below the poverty line. In contrast, Luxembourg (above) is one of the richest countries in the world in terms of per capita income.
Left: Valéry Giscard d'Estaing, the President of France (1974–81), hosted the first G8 (then G6) summit, in Rambouillet.

WORLD GROUPS

There are numerous international groups. G77 was established in 1964 by 77 developing countries to promote their common economic interests. The G8 is a group of industrially advanced countries. The Group was founded as G6 in 1975, joined by Canada in 1976 and Russia in 1997. The G8 represent about 14 percent of the world population but 60 percent of the Gross World Product. G20, founded in 1999, consists of a group of finance ministers and central bank governors of 19 countries, plus the EU. There are several other regional groupings, such as ASEAN (Association of South East Asian Nations), established in 1967.

1982–1986

1982 Peruvian writer Mario Vargas Llosa writes his classic *La Guerre del Fin del Mundo* (The War of the End of the World), on the history of Brazil.

• First operation to implant an artificial heart in a human being in Utah, USA.

• Audio compact discs first introduced commercially; later adapted to hold electronic data.

1983 First modern cellular phone introduced in Chicago.

1984 Indira Gandhi, prime minister of India, assassinated.

A radical revolution swept people's lives through vast strides in science and technology. Yet, unequal distribution of resources and lack of access to basic facilities did not allow the benefits to percolate down to the entire spectrum of humanity.

Production processes

A gricultural productivity grew, mainly due to better machinery and fertilizers and the development of new plant varieties, including genetically modified crops.
Industrial output increased through Henry Ford's factory system—breaking down manufacturing into separate stages—but eventually work forces needed more skills and adaptability. The batch production system, where each worker has a larger share in the final product, allowed for greater diversity. Companies also took an international view, using factories in countries where labor was cheaper, and outsourcing service industries. Flexible working hours and home-working were introduced.

Surge in electronics

C olor televisions, personal computers, laptops, mobile phones, Internet, email, video conferencing, microwave ovens… Consumer demand for electronic goods rose quickly. Between 1980 and 1995 the number of televisions per 1000 people worldwide nearly doubled, from 121 to 225. Videos began to be used in teaching. Computerization revolutionized transport, finance and banking, stock markets, credit card shopping, and the control of machine tools in industry. In 1970, only 50,000 computers existed in the world; by 2000, there were over 500 million. In 1995, 50 million people used the Internet; by 2000, this had risen to 450 million. However, 91 percent of Internet users belonged to developed countries.

NEW MATERIALS

Nano technology, the development of extremely small devices, led to micro-chips. New high-strength materials were manufactured. Concrete, wood, and glass were reinvented in new forms such as fibre optics. Bionics or biomimetics was another emerging field, exploring aspects of the natural world, such as the strength of certain sea-shells, and attempting to recreate them in material form.

1985 Microsoft Corporation introduces Windows Operating System software.
1986 US unmanned spacecraft *Voyager 2* is the first to fly past Uranus; **1989** past Neptune.
- *Mir*, Russian space station and laboratory, launched.

- President Ferdinand Marcos of Philippines overthrown; replaced by Corazon Aquino.
- Accident at Chernobyl nuclear power plant in the Ukraine kills 32, contaminates thousands with radiation.

DEVELOPMENT AND GROWTH: TECHNOLOGY

Aviation

In 1945, aircraft capable of carrying 400 passengers were unheard of. Twenty-five years later, the Boeing 747 "jumbo jet" had that capacity, and by 1976, supersonic aircraft such as Concorde reached 1450 mph. However, supersonic passenger jets were not economical and were later discontinued, so average cruising speeds for passenger planes were 540–570 mph. Humanity landed on the moon in 1969 and space exploration continued.

The Boeing 747 passenger jet was certified for commercial service in 1969.

Medicine

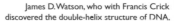

In the last 50 years, genetic research has revealed that all heritable characteristics are carried by chemicals known as deoxyribonucleic acid (DNA). From the 1990s, there were breakthroughs in genetic engineering, and brain-mapping is another area that has helped in health care.

James D. Watson, who with Francis Crick discovered the double-helix structure of DNA.

NOBEL PRIZE WINNERS IN THE FIELD OF MEDICINE SINCE 2000

2000 Arvid Carlsson, Paul Greengard, Eric Kandel (Sweden, USA, Austria): Discoveries concerning signal transduction in the nervous system.

2001 Leland Hartwell, Tim Hunt, and Paul Nurse (USA, UK): Discovery of key regulators of the cell cycle.

2002 Sydney Brenner, H. Robert Horvitz, and John E. Sulstan (USA, UK): Discoveries concerning genetic regulation of organ development and programed cell death.

2003 Paul C. Lautebur and Peter Mansfield (USA, UK): Discoveries concerning magnetic resonance imaging.

1988–1996

- The USA bombs government and military bases in Libya.
- 1988 Timbuktu designated a UNESCO World Heritage site.
- 1993 Middle-East peace accord between Yitzhak Rabin of Israel and Yasser Arafat, chairman of PLO.

- 1994 Zapatista uprising in Mexico.
- Civil war in Rwanda; 800,000 estimated killed.
- Channel Tunnel under English Channel connects England and France.
- First multi-racial elections in South Africa.

2004 Richard Axel and Linda B. Buck (USA): Discoveries of odorant receptors and organization of the olfactory system.

2005 Barry J. Marshall and J. Robin Warren (Australia): Discovery of the bacterium Hlicobacter pylori and its role in gastritis and peptic ulcer disease.

2006 Andrew Z. Fire and Craig C. Mello (USA): Discovery of RNA interference—gene silencing by double—stranded DNA.

2007 Mario R. Capecchi, Oliver Smithies, and Martin J. Eans (USA, UK): Discoveries of principles for introducing specific gene modifications in mice by the use of embryonic stem cells.

2008 Harald zur Hausen (Germany): Discovery of human papilloma viruses causing cervical cancer.

Françoise Barré-Sinoussi and Luc Montagnier (France): Discovery of human immunodeficiency virus.

2009 Elizabeth H. Blackburn, Carol W. Greider, and Jack W. Szostak (USA): Discovery of the protection of chromosomes by telomeres and the enzyme telomerase.

2010 Robert G. Edwards (UK): Development of in vitro fertilization.

2011 Bruce A. Beutler, Jules A. Hoffmann, and Ralph M. Steinman (USA, Luxembourg, Canada): For their discoveries concerning the activation of innate immunity and for discovery of the dendritic cell and its role in adaptive immunity.

2012 John B. Gurdon and Shinya Yamanaka (UK, Japan): For the discovery that mature cells can be reprogrammed to become pluripotent.

2013 James E. Rothman, Randy W. Schekman, and Thomas C. Südhof (USA, Germany): For their discoveries of machinery regulating vesicle traffic, a major transport system in our cells.

2014 John O'Keefe, May-Britt Moser, and Edvard I. Moser (USA, Norway): For their discoveries of cells that constitute a positioning system in the brain.

2015 William C. Campbell, Satoshi Ōmura, and Youyou Tu (Ireland/USA, Japan, China): For their discoveries concerning a novel therapy against infections caused by roundworm parasites and for a novel therapy against Malaria.

2016 Yoshinori Ohsumi (Japan): For his discoveries of mechanisms for autophagy.

1995 Global Positioning System (GPS) becomes fully operational.

1995 Dayton Peace Accord ends Bosnian-Croatian-Serbian war (began 1991).

• Bose—Einstein condensation, a state of matter predicted to arise at low temperatures, observed for the first time by physicists in the USA.

• Sub-atomic particle known as top quark discovered.

1996 First cloned animal, Dolly the sheep, born.

SOME MEDICAL BREAKTHROUGHS

- Severe intestinal nerve disorders have been researched and recreated with the help of human pluripotent stem cells.
- Scientists at Rockefeller University have identified which genes in a microbe's genome ought to produce antibiotic compounds and then synthesized those compounds to discover two promising new antibiotics.
- Scientists can now grow 3D models of lungs from stem cells, creating new ways to study respiratory diseases.
- Scientists at Rockefeller University have used a technique called "light sculpting" to see the neurons of a mouse brain firing in real time in three dimensions.
- The region of the Americas is the first in the world to have officially eliminated measles, a viral disease that can cause severe health problems including pneumonia, brain swelling, and even death. This achievement culminates a 22-year effort involving mass vaccination against measles, mumps, and rubella throughout the Americas.
- The U.S. Food and Drug Administration approved, the world's first artificial pancreas for type 1 diabetes.
- The U.S. Department of Veterans Affairs found strong evidence of a link between high blood pressure and past exposure to herbicides in Vietnam-era veterans. The Department of Veterans Affairs developed a light-emitting nanoparticle that promises to help in the diagnosis and treatment of bladder cancer.
- Scientists at the Scripps Research Institute have created the first stable semi-synthetic organism. This can hold two artificial bases, x and y, in its genetic code indefinitely. It could lead to entirely new forms of life with synthetic DNA, with many potential uses in medicine.

1997–1999

- Taliban, an Islamic political group, captures Kabul.

1997 Hong Kong returned by Britain to China.

- Labour Party led by Tony Blair wins elections in Britain.

- US spacecraft *Mars Pathfinder* lands on Mars.
- Kyoto Protocol agreement to reduce industrial emissions that lead to global warming.

New ultrasound scanning technique: a breakthrough in treating Alzheimer's disease

In 2015, research by the University of Queensland Brain Institute (QBI) has shown that ultrasound scanning techniques plural can reduce and remove amyloid beta plaques from the brains of mice with Alzheimer's disease. It is speculated that the new treatment could revolutionize Alzheimer's disease treatments by restoring memory. Although the same procedure could be replicated in human beings, it needs considerable modification before being tested in humans.

More breakthroughs in medicine

Scientists Peek Into Mind With Functional MRI: Functional MRI, called fMRI, traces the working of brain cells by observing changes in the oxygen levels and blood flow to the brain. The more brain activity in one area, the more oxygen will be used and the more blood will flow to that area. When the patient is asked to perform a simple task, the fMRI tracks the areas of the brain that are activated by tracing the speed at which the cells metabolize the glucose. Using this technique, researchers are obtaining valuable information about diseases such as depression, brain cancer, autism, memory disorders, and many more.

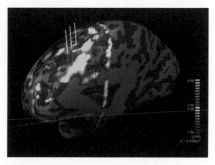

A functional MRI image, where the areas shaded yellow to red represent the highest brain activity and the areas shaded blue to green, the lowest brain activity.

The Reducation of Public Smoking: Countries across the world and many American states introduced bans on smoking in public.

these bans have resulted in a decrease in second-hand smoking, which, in turn, has decreased the rate of heart attacks and death from heart disease.

Heart Disease Deaths Drop by 40 Percent: In recent years, new drugs have been developed that are now used frequently to slow the progression of atherosclerosis—to slow

---

the build-up of the hard, waxy substance called plaque that narrows arteries. Also, there has been a breakthrough in heart bypass techniques.

Stem Cell Research: European researchers were successful in genetically manipulating bone marrow cells from two 7-year-old boys and then transplanting the altered cells back into the boys. Owing to this, the progress of a fatal brain disease called adrenoleukodystropy or ALD was halted.

Such cases give a boost to stem cell research, be it embryonic or adult stem cells. As people age, "replacement parts" become more and more indispensable. Today, it is possible to make embryonic-like stem cells directly from skin cells. In addition, new drugs based on stem cells are being developed. Limbal stem cells have been registered as a product for eye burns in Europe, and mesenchymal stem cells have been approved for pediatric graft versus host disease in Canada and New Zealand.

New Therapies for Cancer: In the late 1990s, some drugs were invented that influenced cancer treatment forever. Trastuzumab (Herceptin) is a drug that targets a type of breast cancer that is characterized by a specific cancer gene—an oncogene—called HER-2. Almost 25 percent of affected women are expected to benefit from Herceptin.

The invention of Lapatinib (TyKerb) prevents breast cancers from recurring and has significantly improved survival rate. Gleevec is another drug for cancer that retards a genetic mutation that causes cancer cells to grow and multiply in patients with a variety of cancers.

Combination Drug Therapy Extends **HIV Survival:** The highly active antiretroviral therapy or HAART has changed the deadly disease HIV/AIDS into a serious, but chronic disease, with survival rates stretching into decades.

The same effective therapy has been used to treat other diseases ranging from lung cancer to heart disease.

Robotic Techniques Revolutionize Surgery: Earlier, a patient undergoing a kidney removal operation would be left with a 10-inch long scar. But in 2007, the surgeons at the Cleveland Clinic began removing kidneys through a single incision in the patient's navel scar, with advantages of shorter and less painful recovery time. Robotic surgery also has been used increasingly in a number of centers in the USA.

2000–2001

- Western nations, led by NATO, intervene in Kosovo, in southwest Serbia.
- Complete sequencing of a human chromosome completed for the first time.

2000 Scientists announce first draft mapping of the entire human genome.

2001 Laurent Kabila, the president of the Democratic Republic of Congo, shot dead; replaced by his son, Joseph Kabila.

Major breakthroughs in Science and Technology since 2000

We have become dependent on science and technology for almost everything. Man's quest for knowledge has benefitted every sphere of life. Religion, ethics and culture takes a backseat in comparison to science.

- In 2000 Dean Kamen invented the first self-balancing, electric-powered transportation machine known as the Segway Human Transporter. Launched in the year 2001, the Segway human transporter uses dynamic stabilization to enable the transporter to balance itself with the help of tilt sensors, gyroscopes and a built-in computer. The transporter adjusts to the body movement at a rate of 100 movements per second. The first model did not consist of any brakes and traveled at a speed of 12 miles per hour, and the speed and direction could be controlled by manual mechanisms. An improvised model released in 2006 allowed users to adjust the speed and direction through computer assistance too.

- Along with the famous iPod invented by Apple Inc. in the year 2001, another remarkable invention of this year was the bio-artificial liver. Dr. Kenneth Matsumura and Alin Foundation invented the artificial liver by designing a device that utilizes animal liver cells. Instead of sticking with the age-old idea of using mechanical devices used to replace organs, this breakthrough technology included a mechanical device as well as biological elements. The animal cells are trapped behind a membrane (thin parting inside) in the bio-artificial liver. Therefore, while the cells can perform all the common functions of the liver such as filtering the blood, and eliminating toxins, the cells do not merge with human blood causing no reactions or harm to the person.

- The birth control patch, the Braille Glove, and the Nano-tex fabric were all scientific inventions of the year 2002.

Self-balancing, electric-powered transportation machine known as the Segway Human Transporter.

- Ariel Sharon becomes the prime minister in Israel.
- Albanians organize rebellion in Macedonia; peace signed in August after 6 months of fighting.
- George W. Bush becomes the 43rd US president.

- Abandoned Russian space station *Mir* crashes down to Earth.
- Netherlands becomes the first country to legalize same-sex marriages. Later, Belgium **2003**; Spain **2005**; Canada **2005**; South Africa **2006**;

2000 onward WORLD

Toyota's Hybrid Car was the invention for the year 2003.

Using leather Golf gloves, Ryan Patterson, invented a device that can identify the wearer's hand movements and transmit them wirelessly to a hand-held monitor as words. Although not very famous, the Braille Glove has enough importance in the world of impaired people. The Nano-tex fabric was another invention that went slightly unnoticed by the common people. The Nano-tex fabric goes through chemical treatment that gives them around a million tiny fibers which are one hundred thousand of an inch long, which for their basic use repel spills. The birth control patch invented by Ortho McNeil Pharmaceuticals known as the Ortho Eva patch was the first birth control patch that could be changed once a week and had the same effects as the contraceptive pills.

- Toyota's Hybrid Car was the invention for the year 2003. Getting its popular share of publicity the Hybrid car is known for its self parking attributes. The gas-electric powered automobile has a feature that lets it park itself! This happens with the help of a rear mounted camera, power steering and software called Intelligent Parking Assist, designed to direct the car into a parking space. The user does not even have to touch, talk or provide any input throughout the process.

- The two inventions that grabbed popular attention in the year 2004 were the Sono Prep, and the Adidas 1 shoes. The Adidas 1 shoes with built-in microprocessor think for themselves, deciding what kind of foot support the wearer needs. Sono Prep invented by Robert Langer, was an advancement in the field of biotechnology that

Adidas 1 shoes can think for themselves to decide what kind of foot support the wearer needs.

2002–2003

Norway, Sweden **2009**; also legal in four U.S. states.
- In Nepal, King Birendra and four members of his family are massacred.

- The USA is target of a deadly terror attack through hijacked aircraft; known as 9/11.
- V.S. Naipaul wins the Nobel Prize for Literature.
- Temporary government headed by Hamid Karzai established in Afghanistan.

can administer medications through sound waves rather than conventional methods such as injections. The device is said to direct low frequency ultrasonic waves to the skin for 15 seconds that opens up the lipids in the skin enabling transfer of liquids. The skin returns to its original state in the following 24 hours.

Loc8tor radio frequency emitting tags help you find commonly misplaced articles of daily use.

- The most popular and successful invention in the year 2005 was YouTube. The website which achieved the greatest consumer response is a video-hosting website that lets users share videos across the globe. The website invented by Jawed Karim, Steve Chen and Chad Hurley is currently one of the most famous websites in the world!

- Year 2006 was slightly slow-paced in the field of scientific inventions. Although a lot of prototypes and beta-testers were released, only a few actual products were seen in the markets. One of these products was the Loc8tor. Loc8tor attaches radio frequency emitting tags to all your small possessions that you forgetfully misplace the most. It points in the right direction, left and right, and up and down too, bringing you as close as an inch from the item. The tag does its part and beeps to pinpoint the exact location too.

- The Invention of the year 2007 was none other than Apple's famous iPhone. When first released, the iPhone was a breakthrough in mobile technology boasting unprecedented sensor technology, a brand new operating system, which actually fits the operations of a computer inside the attractive body of a phone. iPhone as we know today has restructured the entire world of Mobile gadgets and was Apple's ace in the world of technology.

- The scientific and medical miracle for the year 2008 was the personal retail DNA testing kit. Through a saliva test the DNA kit can estimate your genetic links to more than 90 hereditary traits ranging from baldness to chronic diseases. Although the kit was not invented in the year 2007, it was released publicly to the common consumers. Human genotyping has been available to every person rather than just the executive order thanks to the inventors 23andMe. Consider the possible benefits

2002 Tamil Tigers, an insurgent group in Sri Lanka, sign cease-fire agreement with the government.
- Hindu-Muslim riots in Gujarat, India.
- USA and Russia agree to reduce nuclear weapons by two-thirds over the next 10 years.
- Timor-Leste, formerly East Timor, gains independence from Indonesia.
- First solo balloon flight round the world.
- Terrorist attack on nightclub in Bali, Indonesia; over 200 die.

2000 onward WORLD

Teleportation is the next big thing attracting scientific interest all over the world. Though it is still in its testing phases.

and consequences of such an invention that can track your chances of being in a specific state, or medical condition based on your genes and not just social, environmental and purely technological factor. Genotyping through this DNA kit can identify the chances of genetically inheriting any traits out of 6 million different traits. Another notable invention of this year was the Bionic Lens. Babak Parviz from the University of Washington invented contact lenses that use tiny LEDs powered by solar cells and use radio frequency receiver to display images, maps and other data over the wearer's visual field.

- The Sixth Sense developed in the year 2009 by Pranav Mistry at the MIT media lab USA is a wearable gestural interface turning all actions into digital information capable of being processed in any technologically advanced device, such as a computer, mobile, etc. It has been the fundamental technology of digital effects in sci-fi movies for almost a whole decade. The Sixth Sense consists of a pocket size projector and a camera connected to a portable computing device. The camera identifies the hand gestures and movements of the user while the projector can use surfaces to display visual data and let them be used as computer interfaces. The device uses the video streaming from the camera and processes it with the software in synchronization with the visual tracking referencing sensors that the user wears at his fingertips.

- Teleportation is the next big thing attracting scientific interest all over the world. Although only in its testing phases, this technology makes traveling over a distance in

a blink of an eye possible. The stuff of the movies might finally come true in the near future. For now, scientists at Joint Quantum institute at the Maryland University, USA have been successfully able to 'teleport' information from one atom to another atom, placed in separate containers, one meter apart in distance!

Sixth Sense is a wearable gestural interface turning all actions into digital information.

2003–2004

- Chechen rebels hold 763 people in Moscow theater; rescued by troops, but 116 die.
- Hu Jintao succeeds Jiang Zemin as general secretary of the Communist Party in China.
- **2003** Ariel Sharon reelected in Israel.

- US space shuttle *Columbia* disintegrates in flight. All seven astronauts aboard killed.
- **2003** The USA and Britain launch war in Iraq, capture Baghdad and Saddam Hussein.
- Mahmoud Abbas becomes the first Palestinian prime minister; resigns in a few months.

Energy

With world energy consumption constantly rising, nuclear power, natural gas, geothermic energy, solar heating, and wind power complemented coal, oil, gas, and hydro power.

A geothermal power station.

STEPHEN HAWKING

This brilliant British astrophysicist (b. 1942) has tried to develop a "theory of everything." One of his great contributions has been to make science available to general readers through books such as *A Brief History of Time* (1988), *The Universe in a Nutshell* (2001), *A Briefer History of Time* (2005), and, along with his daughter, a children's book, *George's Secret Key to the Universe* (2007).

- Membership of Non-Aligned Movement rises to 116.
- Major earthquake in Algeria, North Africa; more than 2,000 killed, 9,000 injured.
- Libya agrees to pay compensation for bombing of plane over Lockerbie, Scotland.

- Shirin Ebadi of Iran wins Nobel Peace Prize for promoting rights of women and children.
- **2004** Terrorist attack on trains in Madrid, Spain; 200 killed, 1,400 wounded.
- Seven new countries from East Europe join NATO.
- Ten new states join the EU.

Tackling terrorism

A defining aspect of the 21st century is the "war on terror" that followed "9/11," when on September 11, 2001, hijackers flew two airplanes into the twin towers of the World Trade Center in New York, a third plane into the Pentagon, and crashed a fourth in a field in Pittsburgh. At least 3,000 people died, and it was believed that Osama bin Laden, leader of the Al Qaeda Islamist group, had directed the attacks from Afghanistan. A US-led coalition attacked Afghanistan in October 2001, and in 2003, US-led forces invaded Iraq to remove alleged weapons of mass destruction. The USA, Britain and several other nations are helping Iraq and Afghanistan to overcome radical philosophies and terrorism.

The attack on the twin towers of the World Trade Center (September 11, 2001).

Globalization

Political, economic, and social boundaries are being transcended, and the world is becoming more interdependent. Cities across the planet look similar, with high-rise buildings and "international" architecture. Through media connectivity and real-time television images, distances have been reduced. Hundreds of inter-governmental international organizations, and thousands of non-governmental ones have been created. Trade and cultural exchanges are ever increasing. Globally linked foreign exchange and capital markets operate 24 hours a day. More than one-fifth of goods and services produced each year are traded across the world. Some multinational companies control budgets larger than those of several sovereign countries. Despite the shrinking world, the relative gap between rich and poor nations, or the rich and poor within nations, is greater, as income disparities have increased.

2005–2007

- Floods in Bangladesh, Nepal, and north India; thousands killed, millions homeless.
- School children held hostage in Beslan, Russia, by Chechen rebels; several killed during rescue.
- Palestinian leader Yasser Arafat dies.
- Earthquake off the coast of Sumatra, followed by tsunami; over 200,000 killed across 11 countries bordering Indian Ocean.

2005 Mahmoud Abbas becomes the president of Palestinian Authority; first presidential election since 1996.
- Benedict XVI becomes pope after death of pope John Paul II.
- Bomb attacks in London.
- Baku-Tbilisi-Ceyhan oil pipeline opens, connecting Caspian Sea to the Mediterranean Sea.

Profusion of the Internet and electronics

Computers and the Internet have revolutionized the way the world functions.

Rapid technological progress has taken place in computing and the Internet. In 2014, an estimated 2 billion personal computers were in use. New softwares are constantly developed, and there is a growing use of Internet broadband, along with a host of new facilities: YouTube, a website for uploading videos; blogs, where anyone can write anything; Twitter and other micro-blogging platforms; social networking sites such as MySpace and Facebook. In 2017, Facebook alone had 2 billion active members, but trends change every year.

INFORMATION SOCIETY

This term defines the current age, due to the availability of information which can be used for economic, scientific, cultural, and political activity. The "knowledge economy" generates wealth through the use and manipulation of information, and is the economy of the future, replacing manufacturing and industry. The information revolution of the last few years is as significant as the Industrial Revolution.

Digital technology is applied in almost every kind of electronic products: Cameras, televisions, audio players (referred to as MP3/MP4), portable media players, and smart phones with music, video, camera, and Internet facilities. Data storage capability is a fundamental aspect of everyday life; devices range from tiny flash memory drives, to hard disk drives with huge capacity Cloud storage has become common for individuals and businesses. Satellites are being used to generate and transmit data: Global Positioning System technology is increasingly used for navigation and fixing location. Robotics is developing for medical and domestic use.

ADVANCES IN GENETIC RESEARCH

The Human Genome Project, founded in 1990 to sequence the three billion chemical letters in DNA, was completed in 2003. DNA can now be taken apart, recombined, or even moved from one organism and placed in another. The Project has identified more than 1,800 disease genes. In 2005, another major step was the development of the HapMap, a catalog of common genetic variations, or haplotypes, in the human genome. Cloning, stem cell research, the preservation of endangered species—and even the possible revival of extinct species—are all aspects of Genetic Science.

- Hurricane Katrina causes flooding in New Orleans, USA.
- **2006** Ehud Olmert becomes the prime minister of Israel.
- Muhammad Yunus of Bangladesh and his Grameen Bank win Nobel Peace Prize for creating "economic development from below."

- **2007** Romania and Bulgaria join the EU; expands to 27.
- Nicholas Sarkozy becomes the French president.
- **2007** Intergovernmental Panel on Climate Change confirms global warming, with rising temperatures and seas.
- Earthquake and tsunami hit Solomon Islands.

2000 onward WORLD

Ecology and natural resources

Economic growth is draining the limited natural resources of the world. Fossil fuels such as petroleum, natural gas, and coal remain the primary energy sources, accounting for about 81 percent of energy resources in 2014. There is a move towards nuclear, solar, and other renewable and non-polluting forms of energy, along with measures to improve fuel efficiency. Biofuel is getting attention, although growing it takes up land often

Due to warming temperatures, the Bering glacier in Alaska, America's largest, has retreated 7.5 miles since 1900. Other glaciers in Alaska are also steadily retreating. One side effect has been an increase in earthquakes.

needed for food crops. Soil erosion has affected fertility, while water resources are imperiled. Forests everywhere are being depleted, and wildlife is declining. The world population, 2.5 billion in 1950, is more than 6.8 billion now, and is estimated to stabilize at 9.3 billion in 2050. This will lead to a further strain on resources.

A stranded ship on Central Asia's Aral Sea, which shrunk to 10 percent of its size between 1960 and 2007.

2008–2009

2008 Fidel Castro resigns as the president of Cuba after 49 years.
- Kosi river changes course in north India, causing floods; hundreds die, over two million displaced.
- Conflict between Russia and Georgia.
- Maoist prime minister elected in Nepal.

- Iraq and the USA agree on timeframe for troop pullout.
- Eleven mountain climbers die on K2, the worst accident on this mountain since **1986**.
- Anti-government protests escalate in Thailand.

Climate change

Fossil fuels produce huge amounts of carbon dioxide, contributing to greenhouse gases and global warming. While the use of coal, the most polluting fuel, has declined in some countries such as the UK, it has increased in others. In 1973, it was discovered that chlorofluorocarbons (CFCs) used in refrigeration, air-conditioning, and other products were depleting the ozone in the Earth's atmosphere, and allowing excessive ultra-violet radiation to reach the Earth. The use of CFCs has been reduced, but climate change and global warming is increasingly becoming evident, and is a real threat to fundamental aspects of life on the planet. Despite international forums on these issues, disagreements between countries have hampered significant progress.

Right: An aerial view of the Amazon rainforest around the headwaters of the Xingu river in Brazil shows how much forest has been lost due to pressure from agriculture on its fringes.
Below: Entrance to a small coal mine in Shanxi, China. The Asian country is the largest producer of coal in the world.

- G8 nations pledge funds to fight disease in Africa; agree on the need to cut greenhouse gases in half by **2050**.
- US banking crisis leads to global recession.
- Terrorists kill 173 people in Mumbai, India.

2009 G20 leaders pledge $1.1 trillion to encourage world trade and stimulate economies of developing countries.
- Earthquake in Italy affects 26 towns.
- North Korea conducts second nuclear test.
- Barack Obama becomes the US president.

THE NEW MILLENNIUM AND THE FUTURE

Rights for all

An important modern concern is to ensure rights for individuals, communities, nations, and even animals. Fundamental human rights include non-discrimination based on race, religion, gender, physical or mental ability, and sexual orientation. Children have their own rights. Rights also pertain to intellectual property, education, and health care while civil liberties include freedom of speech and expression. Generally, these are granted most liberally in developed countries, and are severely restricted in others. The right of countries to govern themselves without interference from major powers remains unfulfilled, and many countries do not have democratically elected governments.

A monument to victims of the terrorist train bombings in Madrid, Spain, in 2004.

Fundamentalism and new sects

In some countries, fundamentalism is a growing trend. Fundamentalists are resistant to change, to freedom for women, to education, and generally, to any activities that could bring about a different way of thinking. They emphasize a strict observance of religious and social laws and customs, and attempt to impose these on others, sometimes through violent means. In the Western world, there are new Protestant churches and new religious sects, as well as a revival of "pagan" religions.

Identity politics

The growing emphasis on national, religious, and ethnic identities is perhaps a reaction to globalization, but religious and political movements that arouse mass emotions have led to genocide and warfare. Political observers and intellectuals now believe the concept should be replaced with more inclusive policies.

2010–2013

2010 Suicide bombers kill 40 in Moscow subway.
- The USA and Russia agree to reduce nuclear arsenals.
- European air traffic is grounded by ash from a volcano under the Eyjafjallajokull glacier, Iceland.
- Oil spill in Gulf of Mexico threatens wildlife and coastlines.

- Israeli forces storm flotilla carrying aid to Gaza; kill nine activists.
- Thai army disperses "Red Shirt" protestors.
- Tropical storms cause a huge sinkhole to open up in Guatamala City; swallows three-story building.

2011 A 6.3-magnitude earthquake hits Christchurch, New Zealand.

Science and technology

France's TGV train, currently in service, is one of the world's fastest, capable of reaching speeds in excess of 300 mph.

Humankind continues to explore the universe. Private spaceflights and space tourism have begun. Biological research suggests that a complete overview of the brain will be possible in the future. The search for the elusive particle known as the Higgs bosun, which endows others with mass, continues. Innovations in transportation include giant planes such as the Airbus 380 commercial airliner, introduced in 2007, which can carry up to 850 people. Driverless cars have been tested in real-life traffic in several countries.

VIRTUAL WORLDS

As life becomes increasingly complex and stressful, people have sought solace in computer-simulated worlds. Virtual worlds can include games, text-based chatrooms, and computer conferencing. A popular software is Second Life, in which users, known as residents, can create a make-believe life for themselves and interact with other residents through a fictional persona.

A virtual reality (VR) parachute trainer used by the US navy. The VR glasses create computer-generated scenarios, which help aircrew learn how to handle a parachute.

- Arab Spring begins in Tunisia.
- The Libyan ruler Colonel Gaddafi killed.
- Osama Bin Laden's death.
- A tsunami hits Japan.
- Curiosity rover launched from Cape Canaveral, Florida, USA.
2012 Curiosity rover lands on Mars.
- London hosts the Olympic Games.

- The Mayan calendar reaches the end of its current cycle.
- The Abraj Al-Bait Towers are completed in Mecca.
- 60th anniversary of Queen of UK.
2013 Work to repair the damage begins after the militants are routed from Timbuktu in early 2013.
- Barack Obama inaugurated for a second term as the president of the United States.

THE NEW MILLENNIUM AND THE FUTURE

Foray into Mars' atmosphere

The Mars Science Laboratory and its rover Curiosity is the most ambitious Mars mission by NASA to date. Its primary mission is to find out if Mars is, or was, suitable for life. It has another objective, that is, to learn more about the red planet's environment. The spacecraft was launched from Cape Canaveral, Florida, on November 26, 2011, and it landed on Mars on August 6, 2012, after a daring landing sequence.

For many years, Curiosity roamed the surface of the red planet, gathering information successfully, but an image of one of its six wheels shows that it developed breaks in its zigzag Curiosity is sadly showing its age.

As regards Curiosity's primary mission, that is, to determine whether Mars was capable of supporting life or not, it was fulfilled within the rover's first year. It found evidence that Mars once had water and the chemical ingredients needed for life. A long-lasting lake that provided stable environmental conditions was found by the rover during the first three-and-a-half years of its mission. The Curiosity rover has also found evidence of copious silica, which shows that ancient Mars had water for a long time.

The Curiosity rover is immensely popular. Almost five million people after watched the online stream or TV coverage of its landing in 2012, and more than 3.5 million follow Curiosity on Twitter.

The Curiosity rover.

2014–2017

- 85-year-old Pope Benedict XVI resigns.
- NASA reveals the much-anticipated results of analysis carried out by its rover Curiosity.
- **2014** Malaysia Airlines Flight 370 disappears.
- Scotland votes to remain part of the United Kingdom.
- Ebola strikes West Africa.

- ISIS declares an Islamic Caliphate.
- Russia annexes Crimea and threatens the rest of Ukraine.
- **2015** China builds islands in the South China Sea.
- Russia intervenes in Syria.
- The Trans-Pacific Partnership comes into shape.

Donald John Trump

The 45th president of the United States, Donald John Trump, was elected on January 20, 2017. Before entering politics, he was a businessman, real estate mogul, and television personality.

The US president Donald John Trump.

Donald John Trump was born in 1946 in Queens, New York. In 1971, he was instrumental in building large, profitable projects in Manhattan. In 1980, he opened the Grand Hyatt, the luxury five-star hotel. In 2004, Trump began starring in the hit NBC reality series *The Apprentice*. Soon after, Trump gave his attention to politics, and in 2015 he announced his candidacy for president of the United States on the Republican ticket. In 2017, Trump was elected after defeating Democratic candidate Hillary Clinton.

A FEW OF TRUMP'S POLICIES:

Health Care: Trump promised that the old healthcare legislation (Obamacare) would be replaced by new measures at the same time as it is repealed. However, as part of the before was suggested that the protections for patients with pre-existing conditions should remain, as well as the measure that allows parents to keep their children insured until age 26.

Illegal Border Crossings: The month after Donald Trump was elected, the number of undocumented immigrants caught crossing the border into the USA dropped significantly. He always maintained that there would not be a pathway to citizenship for undocumented immigrants currently in the United States. Trump stated his intention to deport the "criminal" immigrants.

NATO: One of Trump's policies was to request all members of NATO to make their full and proper financial contributions to the alliance, maintaining their support to the same. In addition, Trump was clear about the goals of NATO, as far as fighting terrorism is concerned.

Foreign Policy: Donald Trump said that Barack Obama's deal with Iran, which sought to prevent the Islamic Republic from attaining nuclear weapons, would be revamped. His decision to launch cruise missiles against Syria in the wake of a chemical attack was widely applauded for setting firm red lines, with minimal risk to US personnel or of being sucked into a Middle East conflict.

- Primitive stone tools, dating as far back as 3.3 million years, found embedded in the rocks by a dry riverbed near a lake in Kenya.
- **2016** In a referendum, the UK votes to leave the European Union.
- Colombia strikes a peace deal.
- Brazil and South Korea impeach their presidents.
- Rodrigo Duterte becomes the president of the Philippines.
- North Korea conducts missile and nuclear tests.
- **2017** Donald John Trump elected as the US president.
- Emmanuel Macron wins French presidential election..

259

INDEX

IMAGE CREDITS

The Publishers wish to thank the following for illustrations used in this book:

Bookbuilder: 43 Alexander, The empire of Alexander; 51 Buddha; 64 The Roman Empire; 74 Nalanda; 82 the Caliphate; 102 the Mongol Empire; 161 Guru Nanak, Taj Mahal; 182 Revolt Memorial; 193 Africa; 204 World War I; 225 Israel. BookBuilder/Prithvi Narayan Chaudhari 20 Brick structure. **Cyber Media Services:** 195 Simon Bolivar; 208 Second Soviet Congress; 227 Nelson Mandela; 229 Mikhail Gorbachev. **Dreamstime:** 8 handax © Diego Barucco; 12 cave © Edurivero; 41 Romulus © Rafael Laguillo; 29 Troy © Maxfx; 49 pyramids © Uros Ravbar; 65 Roman forum © Richard Mcguirk; 75 Nazca lines © Jarnogz; 92 Al-Azhar s M890-osque © Aleksandrov Valentin Mihaylovich; 103 Qutb Minar © Ajay Bhaskar; 115 Alhambra © Jan Vanmiddelem; 163 A Delft blue and white vase © Palabra; 174 Fasilides's palace © Dmitry Kuznetsov; 230 United Nations building © Svlumagraphica. **iStock:** 17 Jomon village © Sean Barley; 157 Sankore mosque © David Kerkhoff; 228 Berlin Wall © Henk Badenhorst; 251 typing on laptop © Dmitriy Shironosov. 194 Ghost Dance Library of Congress; 234 Harry Truman. lithuaniatourism.co.uk 235 Margaret Thatcher. Margaret Thatcher Foundation; 252 Bering Glacier NASA; 253 Amazon rain forest nobelprize.org 239 Boeing 747 Playne Photographic 17 anklet; 150 Christopher Columbus: Third Millennium Press/41 Olmec head BookBuilder; 119 Manco Capac; U.S. National Human Genome Research Institute; 239 James D. Watson

U.S. National Human Genome Research Institute; 255 parachute trainer U.S. Navy. **Wikimedia CC licensed under the Creative Commons Attribution-Share Alike license:** 6 ape caricature; 17 Catal Huyuk goddess; 18 Hammurabi's code; 27 Skara Brae, W. Knight; 27 Knossos, Olaf Tausch; 28 coin; 40 David; 32 Rig Veda; 32 Darius III in battle; 43 Parthenon; 44 Terracotta Army, Mauryan coin; 49 Julius Caesar; 50 Lyceum; 56 Ardashir I; 63 Han pottery soldier; 65 Roman home; 66 Hagia Sophia; 71 Bodhisattva, Vishnu; 75 Todaiji; 76 Charlemagne, casket; 77 *Lindisfarne* manuscript; 80 Our Lady of Limerick Catholic Church, Ian Poellet; 86 Rabia al-Adawiyya, Pudukkottai; 90 Longboat, Thor and Hymir; 91 Vladimir I; 92 Chaco pot; 93 Monte Alban; 94 Manuscript illustration of Roland, Bamburgh Castle; 95 Templar seal, Knights of Christ; 96 Kharagan; 97 samurai, Shah Namah; 98 seige of Antioch; 100 Kincaid site, Heironymous Rowe; 101 the church in Lalibela, Armin Hamm; 114 Magna Carta, Dante; 115 plague; 116 Easter Island; 117 longbow, Edward III; 118 Mansa Musa, lamp, Chimu mantle; 120 Akbarnama; 133 Suleimaniye mosque; 134 *Battle of Castillon*; 135 Joan of Arc; 136 Elizabeth I; 138 Martin Luther, Vasco da Gama, Kremlin; 141 Marriage of the Virgin; 144 Kepler, 142 Copernicus; 159 Great Zimbabwe; 151 Machu Picchu, Allard Schmidt; 257 Kangxi emperor; 163 Oliver Cromwell; 166 Ferdinand II; 167 Peter the Great; 168 Louis XVI, Bastille; 169 Mozart,

Rousseau, Frederick II; 170 Isaac Newton; 176 Boston Tea Party; 177 George Washington; 178 Napoleon; 178 The Battle of Austerlitz; 183 Dost Mohammad Khan; 186 Crystal Palace, Manchester, 187 Karl Marx; 189 Davy's safety lamp, Edison, Bell; 184 Chinese junks get destroyed by British warships; 185 Hokusai painting; 180 Bismarck; 203 A painting by Claude Monet, poster; 195 Canadian Pacific, White gerfalcons; 196 Contemporary cartoon, Bohr, Einstein, Freud; 199 Franz Ferdinand, 200 Roosevelt; 203 A portrait by Juan Gris; 204 A British trench; 207 Nijinsky; 210 Franklin Delano Roosevelt; 211 Hitler/Mussolini; 213 Bauhaus, Chrysler building; 216 Traction Avant car; 217 poster for Battleship Potemkin; 218 Poland, Yalta meeting; 219 shipping, Prisoners in Mauthausen labor camp, Nagasaki bomb; 220 Gandhi/Nehru, 225 Viet Cong camp; 226 Mugabe; 227 Apartheid signboard, F.W. de Klerk; 233 EU flag; 234 Marin Luther King Jr., war protesters; 237 Mumbai, Luxembourg; 250 9/11 attacks; 253 Aral Sea; 250 coal mine, Peter Van den Bossche; 254 Monument, emijrp; 255 TGV; **Worth Press/ Bookbuilder:** 27 Neolithic settlement; 20 Indus valley seal; 24 Osiris; 29 oracle bones; 28 Tutankhamun mask; 55 Confucius; 97 Chinese movable type; 102 Gengis Khan, Kublai Khan, Marco Polo; 185 Hong Xiuquan; 206 Sun Yat Sen. **Shutterstock:** 9 Increasing size of the skulls during different phases of human evolution; 34 chariot.

While every effort has been made to trace copyright holders and seek permission to use illustrative material, the Publishers wish to apologise for any inadvertent errors or omissions and would be glad to rectify these in future editions.